CONTENTS

Abbreviations and Terms		2
Author's notes		3
Acknowledgements		4
Introduction		5
1	Overview	6
2	From Colony to Constituent State	8
3	From Autonomy to Independence	19
4	The *Sergeantencoup*	32
5	The Chin A Sen Period	44
6	1982 – A Most Violent Year	54
Appendices		77
I	Surinamese Population in Suriname and the Netherlands and their Ethnicity	77
II	Attempted, Successful and Alleged Coups in Suriname up to 1982	78
III	Coup Plotters of the Sergeanten coup	79
IV	The Nationale Militaire Raad (NMR)	81
V	8 December 1982: The December Murders	83
Bibliography		84
Notes		85
About the Author		92

Helion & Company Limited
Unit 8 Amherst Business Centre
Budbrooke Road
Warwick
CV34 5WE
England
Tel. 01926 499 619
Email: info@helion.co.uk
Website: www.helion.co.uk
Twitter: @helionbooks
Visit our blog http://blog.helion.co.uk/

Published by Helion & Company 2023
Designed and typeset by Farr out Publications, Wokingham, Berkshire
Cover designed by Paul Hewitt, Battlefield Design (www.battlefield-design.co.uk)

Text © Sander Peeters 2023
Illustrations © as individually credited
Colour artwork © David Bocquelet, Luca Canossa, Anderson Subtil and Tom Cooper 2023
Maps drawn by George Anderson © Helion & Company, Sander Peeters and Tom Cooper © respectively 2023

Every reasonable effort has been made to trace copyright holders and to obtain their permission for the use of copyright material. The author and publisher apologise for any errors or omissions in this work, and would be grateful if notified of any corrections that should be incorporated in future reprints or editions of this book.

ISBN 978-1-913118-71-6

British Library Cataloguing-in-Publication Data
A catalogue record for this book is available from the British Library

All rights reserved. No part of this publication may be reproduced, stored in a retrieval system, or transmitted, in any form, or by any means, electronic, mechanical, photocopying, recording or otherwise, without the express written consent of Helion & Company Limited.

We always welcome receiving book proposals from prospective authors.

Dedication

This book is dedicated to my late father, René Peeters, who has been my biggest inspiration in life. He has taught me to work hard and to treat people from all walks of life equally and to never ask anything from anybody that you would not do yourself, a work ethic that I will always strive to maintain.

This book is also dedicated to my late uncle and godfather Jacques Maes (himself an avid reader of military history), who was enthusiastic about me embarking on this project before he passed away unexpectedly far too soon.

In addition, the book is also written for the people of Suriname, who underwent immeasurable hardship during the periods of conflict covered in this series of books. However, Surinamers are a resilient group of people and I sincerely hope that better times lie ahead for Switi Sranan.

ABBREVIATIONS AND TERMS

Alcoa	Aluminum Company of America
Amerindian	Surinamers that are a member or descendants of indigenous Amazon Indian tribes (such as Arawak or Carib).
ANP	*Algemeen Nederlands Persbureau* (General Dutch Press Agency)
AVVS	*Algemeen Verbond van Vakverenigingen in Suriname* (a.k.a. *Moederbond*): General Union of Trade Unions in Suriname. Allied with the NPS.
APC	Armoured Personnel Carrier
BBZ	*Bosbivak Zanderij* (Forest Bivouac Zanderij)
Bevel	Commander-in-Chief (also *bevelhebber*)
BN	Britten-Norman (British airplane manufacturer)
Bomika	*Bond Militair Kader* (Union of Military Staff)
BWKW	*Bureau Waterkracht Werken* (Bureau of Hydroworks)
C-47	*Centrale-47*: Federation of 47 trade unions. Allied with the Party of the Nationalist Republic (PNR).
CCK	*Committee van Christelijke Kerken* (Committee of Christian Churches)
Cie/Coy	*Compagnie*/Company
Creoles	Surinamese people that are descendants of African slaves that remained on plantations until the abolishment of slavery.
COTRIS	Commander of the *Troepenmacht* in Suriname
DAF	*Van Doorne's Automobiel Fabriek*: Dutch manufacturer of heavy trucks and military vehicles.
DEFAT	Defence Attaché: military attaché that serves with the diplomatic mission of the embassy.
DEFPOL	*Defensie Politie*: police unit that received military training and was used to guard the Tigri Area.
FAL	*Federatie van Arme Landbouwers* (Federation of Poor Agriculturists)
GAC	Guyana Airways Coorporation
GDF	Guyanese Defence Forces
GMC	General Motors Company – American manufacturer of cars and heavy vehicles
Hindustanis	Surinamese people that are descendants of contract workers that came from former British India
HMG	Heavy Machine Gun – typically 12.7mm or .50-calibre
Javanese	Surinamese people that are descendants of contract workers that came from the former Netherlands East Indies (mostly the island of Java)
KCT	*Korps Commando Troepen* (Dutch Commando Troops); part of the *Koninklijke Landmacht* (KL)
KL	*Koninklijke Landmacht* (Royal [Netherlands] Army)
KMA	*Koninklijke Militaire Academy* (Royal Military Academy) [for Officer Training] in Breda, the Netherlands
KMS	*Koninklijke Militaire School* (Royal Military School) [for NCO training] in Weert, the Netherlands
KNIL	*Koninklijk Nederlands Indisch Leger* (Royal Netherlands Indies Army)
korjaal	Wooden dugout canoe, usually equipped with a motor that is used for transporting people and goods over the rivers in Suriname that lead to the hinterland in the tropical rainforest
KTPI	*Kaum Tani Persatuan Indonesia* (Indonesian Workers Peasants Party): later renamed *Kerukunan Tulodo Pranatan Inggil* (Party for National Unity and Solidarity)
LMG	Light Machine Gun – typically 7.62mm or .30-calibre
LUMA	*LUchtMAcht* (Air Force): Surinamese Air Force
Mariniers	Members of the Netherlands Marine Corps (*Korps Mariniers*), the elite infantry component of the Royal Netherlands Navy
Maroons	Surinamese people that are descendants of African slaves that escaped the plantations and settled in the rainforests.
MBK	*Memre Boekoe Kazerne* (Boekoe Memorial Barracks: main barracks in Paramaribo with training facilities and equipment yard
mofokoranti	Sranantongo for 'mouth newspaper' – gossip circuit
MP	Military Police
NATO	North Atlantic Treaty Organization
NBR	*Nationale Bevrijdings Raad* (National Liberation Council)
NCO	Non-Commissioned Officer

NDVN	*Nederlands Detachement Verenigde Naties* (Netherlands Detachment UN)	RVP	*Revolutionaire Volkspartij* (Revolutionary People's Party)
NEI	Netherlands East Indies: present day Indonesia	Sfl	*Surinaamse Florijn* (Surinamese guilder)
Nfl	*Nederlandse Florijn* (Dutch guilder)	SBM	*Surinaamse Bauxiet Maatschappij* (Surinamese Bauxite Company), later Suralco
NL	*Nationaal Leger* (the name for the Surinamese army after August 1980)	SKM	*Surinaamse Krijgsmacht* (Surinamese Armed Forces): the name of the Surinamese army following independence in 1975
NMR	*Nationale Militaire Raad* (National Military Council)		
NPK	*Nationale Partij Kombinatie* (National Party Combination)	SLM	*Surinaamse Luchtvaart Maatschappij* (Surinam Airways)
NPS	*Nationale Partij Suriname* (National Party of Suriname)	SNA	*Surinaamse Nieuws Agentschap* (Surinamese News Agency)
OCOSD	*Opleidingscentrum officieren van speciale diensten*: training of officers done at the KMA, meant to train NCOs and reservists in a concise specialised course.	SRS	*Stichting Radio-omroep Suriname*: State owned radio network
		STVS	*Surinaamse Televisie Stichting*: State owned television network
		Suralco	Suriname Aluminium Company
PALU	*Progressieve Arbeiders – en Landbouwersunie* (Progressive Workers' and Farmers' Union)	TRIS	*TRoepenmacht In Suriname* (Dutch armed forces in Suriname): responsible for territorial defence
PNR	*Partij Nationalistische Republiek* (Party of the Nationalist Republic)	UN	United Nations
Radio ABC	Ampie's Broadcasting Corporation – radio network owned by André Kamperveen.	Uzi	Israeli produced 9mm machine pistol, the standard weapon of the TRIS and SKM
Radio Radika	Radio Dihaat Ki Awaaz – privately owned radio network.	VHP	*Verenigde Hindoestaanse Partij* (United Hindustani Party): renamed *Vooruitstrevende Hervormings Partij* (Progressive Reform Party) in 1973.
Rapar	Radio Paramaribo – privately owned radio network.		
RUMINT	RUMour INTelligence – information gained via rumours, see *mofokoranti*	WIC	*Geoctroyeerde Westindische Compagnie* (West India Company)
		YP	DAF designation for military armoured vehicle – in Suriname it refers to the YP408

AUTHOR'S NOTES

Dutch vs English

The main language of Suriname is Dutch, as it used to be a colony of the Netherlands between 1667 and 1975. As such, the names of people and places used in this book will use the Dutch spelling found in the sources. To pronounce the names correctly, the main differences in pronunciation of consonants and vowels between Dutch and English have been listed as shown in Table 1. This should be taken as a rough guide.

The various ethnic groups of Suriname

The author would like to note that Surinamese society is a mixture of people from a wide variety of cultures and nationalities. Descendants of African slaves (Creoles & Maroons), people descending

Table 1: Dutch Pronunciation of consonants and vowels different from English

Letter	Sounds like	Example
a	'o' as in 'block' 'ah' as in 'bra' (at the end of a syllable)	Bak-huis Ge-berg-te Sa-ra-mac-ca
aa	'ah' as in 'bra'	Kor-jaal
au	'ow' as in 'cow'	Au-ka-ners
ch	'ch' as in 'loch'	Lucht-macht
e	'a' as in 'at' 'uh' (at the end of a syllable) 'a' as in 'cake' (at the end of an emphasised syllable)	Els-tak Cop-pe-na-me Nic-ke-rie
ee	'a' as in 'cake'	Beek-hui-zen
eeuw	'aywuh' (as one syllable), where the 'ay' is pronounced like 'way' and the 'u' in 'wuh' is pronounced like in 'mutt'	Zeeuw
ei	'ey' as in 'whey'	Ka-pi-tein
eu	'ö' in the German word 'Öl'	beul
i	'i' as in 'fish' 'ee' as in 'sheep'	Wa-ge-nin-gen Go-ni-ni
ie	'ee' as in 'sheep'	Com-pag-nie
ieuw	'ew' as in 'new'	Nieuw Am-ster-dam
ij	'ey' as in 'whey'	Ma-ro-wij-ne
j	'y' as in 'yam'	Jen-ny

Table 1: Dutch Pronunciation of consonants and vowels different from English (*continued*)		
Letter	Sounds like	Example
oe	'oo' as in boot	M**oe**n-go
ou	'ow' as in 'cow'	B**ou**-ter-se
o	'o' as in 'loch' 'oa' as in 'boat' (at the end of a syllable)	C**o**p-pe-na-me Gr**o**-nin-gen
oo	'oa' as in 'boat'	Graan-**Oo**gst
sch	's' and 'ch' fast after each other	**sch**ut-te-rij
u	'u' as in 'nut' 'ew' in 'stew' but with rounded lips (at the end of a syllable)	Br**u**ns-wijk R**u**-ben
ui	The 'euí' in the French word 'fauteuil'	Beek-h**ui**-zen
uu	'ew' in 'stew' but with rounded lips	Sta-t**uu**t
y	'ee' as in 'beet' (at the end of a word)	Le-l**y**-dorp

Table 2: Military Ranks in Dutch and English[1]			
Name	Dutch Abbreviation	English Equivalent	English Abbreviation
Enlisted Personnel/Non-Commissioned Officers			
Soldaat	*Sld*	Private	P
Soldaat 1e klasse	*Sld1*	Private First Class	PFC
Korporaal	*Kpl*	Corporal	Cpl
Korporaal 1e klasse	*Kpl1*	Corporal First Class	CFC
Sergeant	*Sgt*	Sergeant	Sgt
Sergeant 1e klasse	*Sgt1*	Sergeant First Class	Sgt1
Sergeant Majoor	*Sgt Maj*	Sergeant Major	Sgt Maj
Adjudant	*Adj*	Warrant Officer	WO
Officers			
Vaandrig	*Vdg*	Officer Cadet	OC
2e Lieutenant	*2e Lt*	Second Lieutenant	2nd Lt
(1e) Lieutenant	*Lt*	(First) Lieutenant	Lt
Kapitein	*Kapt*	Captain	Capt
Majoor	*Maj*	Major	Maj
Lieutenant Kolonel	*Lt Kol*	Lieutenant Colonel	Lt Col
Kolonel	*Kol*	Colonel	Col
Brigade Generaal*	*Brig Gen*	Brigadier General	Brig Gen
Generaal Majoor**	*Gen Maj*	Major General	Maj Gen

* Rank was only introduced in February 2014 when Colonel Ronni Benschop was promoted and became the commanding officer of the *Nationaal Leger*.

** Rank was only introduced in June 2020, when outgoing President Bouterse promoted Brig Gen Benschop to this rank as gratitude for services rendered. Benschop was serving as the Minister of Defence at the time.

from Indian (Hindustanis), Indonesian (Javanese), Chinese and European immigrants and indigenous Amazon Indians (Amerindians) all form a unique nation. It is important to explain the two groups formed by the descendants of slaves.

Under Dutch rule, thousands of slaves were brought from Africa to Suriname to work on plantations. Due to the poor working conditions and ill-treatment by slave owners, a sizeable group of slaves (some studies cite 10 percent) escaped into the jungle to form their own settlements. These people are called Maroons and are often referred to as *bosnegers* (bush negroes) by the Surinamese themselves. In contrast, the slaves that stayed on the plantations and in the cities are referred to as Creoles and again, the Surinamese themselves sometimes refer to these people as *stadsnegers* (city negroes). In this age of political correctness, these groups will be referred to by the terms Maroons and Creoles respectively, unless the title of an article refers to, or the name of a unit, specifically uses one of the names that are now considered to be politically incorrect.

Dutch and Surinamese military ranks

A comparison of Dutch, Surinamese and English ranks is shown in Table 2. The abbreviations (both Dutch and English) will be used throughout the text.

ACKNOWLEDGEMENTS

The author would like to thank the many people that helped him in putting the volumes in this series of books together so far. I would like to thank Surinamese military veterans Anthony del Prado, Waldo Jameson, Azemalie Panchu and Jules Vasilda for their time and patience with giving information on the Surinamese Armed Forces during the 1980s and 1990s. In addition, I would like to thank civilian pilots Dan Rogers of the Mission Aviation Fellowship and Gerard Brunings of Gonini Air Services for sharing their experiences during the *Binnenlandse Oorlog* of 1986–92.

The following authors and editors were kind enough to discuss their work with me and were helpful in bouncing off ideas for my work and in sourcing additional references: Ken Conboy, Dave Francois, Rende van der Kamp, Eric Kastelein, Ellen Klinkers,

Anthony Rogers, Vann Spencer, Neil Thomas, Jonathan Ursum, Richard van der Velde, Klaas Voss and Ellen de Vries.

A book such as this one is not much without pictures. For that my gratitude goes out to the following people who allowed me to use their pictures for illustrating this series: Agnes Apintoe, Han van Amersfoort, Dick Bloemendaal, Lieutenant Colonel Robert K. Brown (Editor of Soldiers of Fortune Magazine), Patrick Chauvel, Jessica Dikmoet, Dave Edhard, Lucien Chien a Foeng, Steven Jakaoemo, Arjen Kamphuis, Thomas Kautzor, the Kowid family, Marc Lohnstein (of the Bronbeek Museum), Frank McMeiken, Rachel Seerden, Ozires Maraes, Nardi Soerodimedjo, Wim Sonneveld, Winnie Versol, Huib de Vries and William Watson.

In addition, I must thank the following people for their support in various manners: Karel Bagijn, Alan Boydell, Alessandro Huber, Dan Hagehorn, Darren Hazes, Mario Overall, Peter Sanchez and Peter Witt. I am also grateful for Henk Goos, webmaster of the DAF YP408 website for supplying me with some excellent information, feedback on profiles and additional pictures on Surinamese APCs.

Robby Parabirsing's book on the *Binnenlandse Oorlog* has been a big inspiration for this series. In addition, he was of invaluable help in getting me access to Surinamese documents, which were otherwise inaccessible to me and he has always been helpful in giving context to some information. Dankjewel Rappa!

Ad van Wingerden, the chairman of the TRIS museum and TRIS Army Cars, was so kind to give me a tour of the maintenance facilities of the museum in Zwijndrecht when I visited in August of 2019. A visit to this museum is highly recommended for anyone with an interest in Suriname and the Dutch military presence there during the second half of the last century. In addition, I would like to thank all the TRIS veterans at the museum and on Facebook forums for their kindness, time and patience in answering the many questions I had about serving in Suriname.

In addition, I must thank my friend, ACIG and Helion editor Tom Cooper for his patience, time and eye for detail when trying to put this work together. This also applies to Andy Miles and Carla Rosenthal who went through my manuscript with a fine-tooth comb, profile artists George Anderson, David Bocquelet, Luca Canossa and Anderson Subtil – who put up with all my pickiness – and Duncan Rogers, whom I have to thank for giving me this opportunity to write something I am very passionate about. Besides helping me with proofreading, fellow author Sanjay Badri-Maharaj was kind enough to share some of his information on Suriname and offered me plenty of words of encouragement. Having visited his native Trinidad and Tobago in 1989, we had plenty to talk about besides Suriname.

Special thanks to the various members of my extended family in the Netherlands and Belgium for their support, including my mother, sister and in particular Piet Peeters. Last but certainly not least, I thank my beautiful wife and my children for all their love, patience and support. This undertaking would not have been possible without you!

INTRODUCTION

It was the fall of 1986 in Stramproy, the Netherlands when I was about to go to bed. Instead of the regular goodnight greetings, my father came into my room for a talk. 'Sander', he said, 'I have a new job and we are moving to Suriname next year'.

We were not strangers to living abroad. However, I had never heard of Suriname before. That was about to change as in the next few months, Suriname seemed to be all over the news. There was trouble in that country.

As my father left for Suriname in January 1987, the news did not get any better. Power lines seemed to be blown up every week, troops from Bouterse were fighting the Jungle Commandos led by Brunswijk and so on. As we were packing up our house for the move to Suriname, my mother prepared our belongings making sure to stock up on plenty of non-perishables and other food items we heard were in short supply over there.

When our family left the Netherlands in June to join my father, we noticed that there was something different about this country. Besides the oppressive jungle heat and humidity that struck us as soon as the door of the Surinam Airways (SLM) DC-8 *Stanvaste* opened, we noticed the presence of military personnel everywhere. That left quite an impression on my sister and me.

On our way from the airport to Paramaribo, we were stopped at a checkpoint manned by government soldiers and our luggage was searched. During our stop, my sister turned to my mother and asked, 'Are these men with Brunswijk or Bouterse?' My parents nervously shushed my sister but luckily for us, the soldiers that were

The author's family in Suriname, 1989. (Author's collection)

searching through our stuff just chuckled and went on rummaging through our personal effects.

We lived in Suriname from 1987 to 1991 and I have experienced no country like it. People from so many races and cultures living together peacefully. It is probably the only country where I have seen a mosque, synagogue, church and Hindu temple in one street, basically next to each other. Despite the harmony in Paramaribo, a civil war was being waged in the eastern part of the country between various Maroon groups, the Amerindians and the military. Paramaribo did not escape the turmoil as on one occasion, the Jungle Commandos seized the Afobaka dam and shut off the power to Paramaribo. But in general, the war in the jungle seemed far away to the inhabitants of the nation's capital.

Our family experienced a nation overjoyed when swimmer Anthony Nesty won the country their first – and thus so far, only – gold medal at the 1988 Seoul Olympics. On the other hand, we also shared in the national grief of the SLM disaster, where nearly 200 people were killed in an air crash. In a country of 350,000, nearly everyone had lost a friend or family member or knew someone who did. We left Suriname in 1991 to return to our native Netherlands when my father switched jobs.

Fast forward 30 years …

With the internet giving access to a wealth of information to everyone, I have been surprised that the turbulent history of Suriname has barely been discussed on the web and in literature, save for some books and articles that are often printed only in Dutch and usually serve a political agenda or only talk about politics. After discussing our family's experience in Suriname at the dinner table one day with my parents, my wife remarked that I should write a book about my time there.

This is the first one of those books…

Sander Peeters, Alberta, Canada

1
OVERVIEW

Suriname is located on the north-eastern coast of the South American continent.[1] The country is bordered by French Guiana in the east, Brazil in the south and Guyana in the west. In the north, the muddy coast of the Atlantic Ocean is formed by the fertile silt carried westwards by oceanic currents from the Amazon River basin, giving all rivers in Suriname their brown, muddy colour.

Painting by Joes Wanders of the battle of Fort Willoughby in 1667 when a fleet from Zeeland, under Abraham Crijnssen, defeated the English and renamed it Fort Zeelandia. (NIMH Collection)

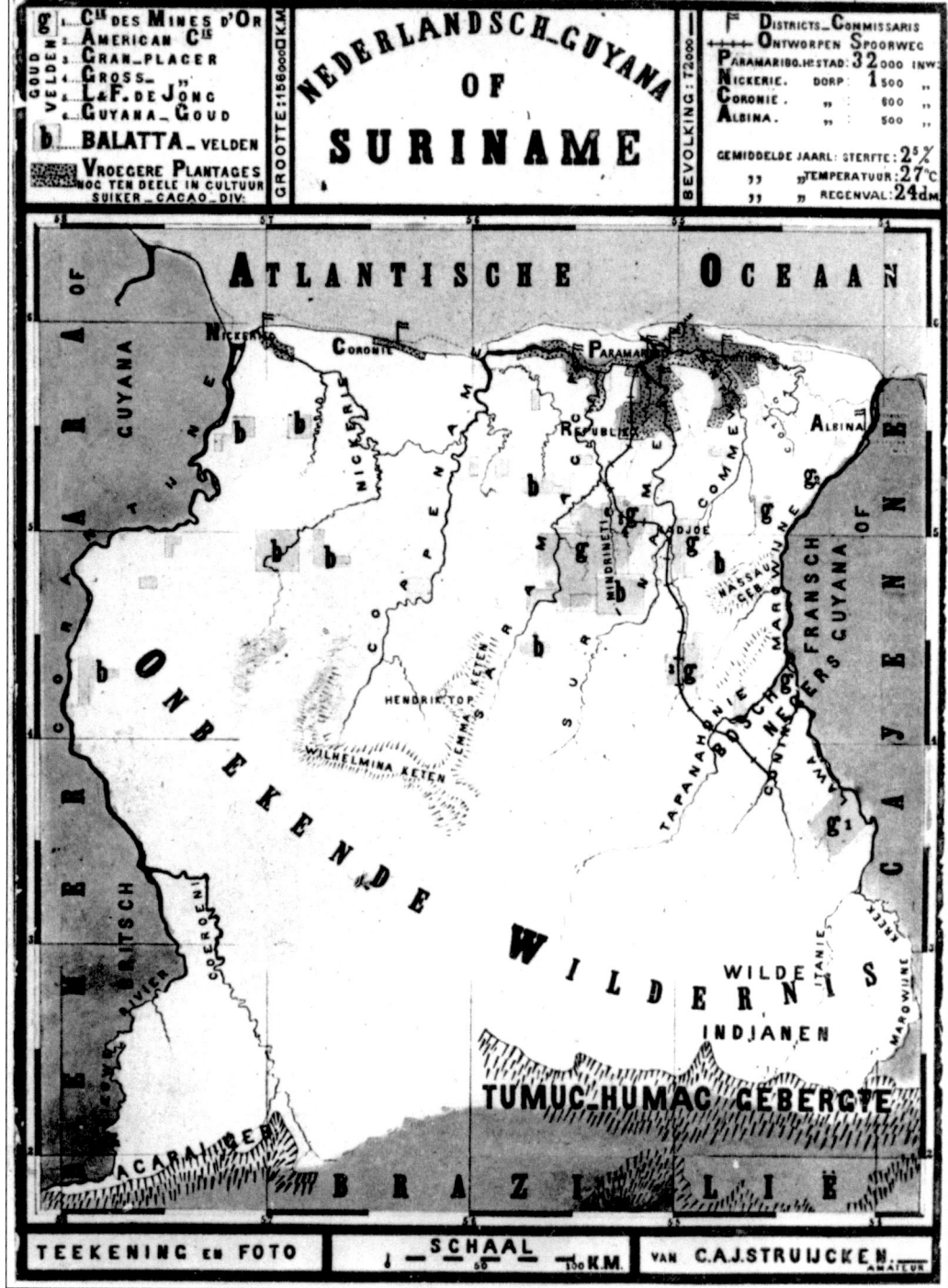

Map of Suriname, dated 1940, clearly illustrating the lack of details in the unchartered vast rainforest further away from the coastline. (Collection of the Netherlands Institute for Military History, NIMH)

Suriname is the smallest independent nation in South America.[2] The official language of Suriname is Dutch, with English being widely spoken by most of the population. In addition to Dutch, other languages spoken in Suriname are Sranantongo, Hindustani, Chinese, Javanese, Maroon languages (as each tribe has its own language) and Amerindian languages of the various tribes, such as the Carib and Arawak.

Being located slightly north of the equator, Suriname has a tropical climate with an average temperature of 29 to 34°C and average humidity of 80 to 100 percent. In addition, Suriname sees a lot of rain with two rainy and two 'dry' seasons.[3]

Geographically, Suriname consists of two areas. The northern part consists of lowlands that contain nearly all the cultivated land and house most of the population. The southern part of the country is a sparsely populated area that is mostly made up of dense tropical rainforests and savannah. It also contains several mountain ranges including the Van Asch van Wijck and the Bakhuis mountains. The highest peak in Suriname is the Julianatop at 1,280 metres above sea level.

Suriname has several large rivers that flow from south to north. These include the Suriname River that flows through the capital of Paramaribo, the Marowijne River that forms the northern part of the border with French Guiana and the Corantijn River, which forms most of the border with Guyana. These and other rivers form the main access routes from the towns on the coast to the villages and settlements in the hinterland.[4]

Early History

The first people who are known to have settled in Suriname are Amerindians known as Arawaks. Based on prehistoric findings, the first Arawaks reached Suriname in 7000–8000 B.C. in the southern part of the country. The first permanent settlements were formed in 500 A.D. In 1100 A.D., another Amerindian tribe, the Caribs, invaded Suriname from the west and drove the Arawaks from settlements, resulting in war between the two tribes. This war was still being waged when the first European settlers reached the western hemisphere.[5]

After Christopher Columbus made his first expedition and discovered the Bahamas and Cuba in 1492, European explorers went on further expeditions to map out the New World. Spanish explorer Alonso de Ojeda has been credited with discovery of the Guianas and called it the 'wild coast'.[6] Although originally suspected to be of little value, tales of cities of gold led to European expeditions to the area between the Orinoco and the Amazon Rivers.

In 1613, a trading post was founded by Dutch merchants in what is now Paramaribo. In addition, multiple trading posts were established on the 'wild coast', where tools, mirrors and guns were traded for gold, resins and wood, among others. Except for crops grown for their own consumption, one could not speak of plantations nor the colonisation of Suriname.[7]

The trade posts in the Guianas were controlled by the Dutch province of Zeeland. The most important ones were Essequibo and Berbice (both in current day Guyana). However, in 1651 the British were the first Europeans to form an actual colony in Suriname under Sir Francis Willoughby when he sailed a ship with about 100 colonists and a number of slaves from Barbados up the Suriname River. This skilled group of people formed a settlement that flourished. The capital was called Thorarica, located 75 kilometres upstream.

During the Second Anglo-Dutch war, a fleet of seven ships under Abraham Crijnssen (from the Dutch province of Zeeland) made a surprise attack on the colony in 1667. This was a reprisal for the English attacks on Zeeuw settlements of Essequibo and Berbice during the First Anglo-Dutch war (1652–1654). The Dutch conquered the settlements in Suriname. Afterwards, Fort Willoughby in Paramaribo was renamed Fort Zeelandia and Paramaribo itself was renamed New Middelburgh (although the name did not stick).

On 31 July 1667, England and the Dutch Republic signed the Treaty of Breda which determined that both countries could keep their latest conquests. The Dutch therefore gained Suriname, whereas the British kept the former Dutch colony of New Holland and renamed it New York.[8] Although both the expedition led by Crijnssen and the defence of the colony were paid for by the Staten-Generaal (the parliament of the seven provinces of the Netherlands), the province of Zeeland would administer the colony.

2
FROM COLONY TO CONSTITUENT STATE

At first, things did not work out well for the Dutch in Suriname. Disease and emigration of British planters to Jamaica threatened to collapse the plantation economy of Suriname. In addition, attacks by Amerindians and English troops, who had not heard of the treaty yet as news travelled slowly to these parts of the world, caused several years of strife. It took the fortification of Paramaribo and long years of negotiation with both the Caribs and Arawaks to end hostilities.

In order to improve the productivity of the colony, the *Geoctroyeerde Sociëteit van Suriname* (Chartered Society of Suriname) was founded in 1683 in which the province of Zeeland sold Suriname to the WIC. This private enterprise was set up with the intention to make a profit running the colony. The *Sociëteit* had the responsibility to administer and defend the colony, while concurrently having the monopoly on the supply of slaves, colonists and planters. The *Sociëteit* was owned by the city of Amsterdam, the *Geoctroyeerde Westindische Compagnie* (see box) and the family Van Aerssen Van Sommelsdijck – one of the richest Dutch families during the Dutch Golden Age – each of whom had an equal share in the new venture.

The Dutch sought to compensate for the lack of labour and expertise by campaigning to attract new planters to the colony under favourable conditions, such as religious freedom. This attracted Hugonots, Jews and Catholics. As peace treaties with the Amerindians agreed that they were not to be enslaved, the labour to run the plantations would come from Africa, supplied by the WIC. It would take some time for the supply in slaves to meet demand.[1]

Since the late seventeenth century, Europe was in a continuous state of war. As the major colonial powers fought out battles, their colonies were involved in some of the fighting. Suriname was not to be spared. A French raid by 10 warships under Admiral Jean du Casse, conducted a bombardment on Fort Zeelandia in May 1689. The defenders held on and after a week the raiding force left.[2]

In 1712, a French military force of 38 vessels with 336 cannons led by privateer Admiral Jacques Cassard was no match for the small garrisons at Fort Zeelandia and Fort Sommelsdijk.[3] The French bombarded Fort Zeelandia and sailed up the Suriname River, pillaging and plundering Paramaribo. After three weeks, the colony surrendered and had to pay a ransom of a year's income (paid mostly in sugar, slaves, valuables and foodstuffs) under threat of total plunder.[4]

A 1790 drawing of an armed and alert Maroon in Suriname. Once wars with European powers had ended, the Dutch had made peace with most of the escaped slaves, except for the Maroons under Boni. The Dutch would conduct several campaigns to drive the Boni Maroons out of Suriname. (Public Domain – John Stedman)

In order to withstand future attacks, a new fort was built at the confluence of the Suriname and Commewijne Rivers. Fort Nieuw Amsterdam was completed in 1747 and included guns manned by a separate 50-man strong *korps artillerie* (artillery corps) and replaced Fort Zeelandia as the main defensive work.[5]

By then, the United Provinces (as the Netherlands was known at this time) had lost their position as a major European power. As the Dutch were keeping themselves more distant from international politics, the threat of foreign invasion subsided. The largest threats to peace came not from the sea but from the tropical rainforest.

The West India Company

In 1621, the *Geoctroyeerde Westindische Compagnie* (West India Company or WIC) was formed by the Republic of the Seven United Provinces (of which Holland was the most influential). The WIC was assigned the monopoly of the trans-atlantic trade, mostly as an instrument of war against the Spanish by denying them the resources to finance their war against the Dutch. The WIC was initially focused on the lucrative business of privateering (with the capture of the Spanish silver fleet in 1628 by Piet Hein as the high-water mark) but after capturing the area of Pernambucu in northeastern Brazil in 1629, the WIC invested in the production of sugar.

The plantation economy in the colony flourished and the resulting shortage of labour drove the WIC to control the slave trade in the area. For that purpose, the WIC captured the Portuguese slave depot of Sao Jorge da Mina on the African coast in 1637. The WIC founded other trading posts and depots in Curaçao, Gold Coast, Jamaica and Tobago (among others) and was mostly engaged in the trade of salt, sugar, tobacco, gold, copper and slaves.

The WIC did not invest in defence of the new colonies however and by 1654, the Dutch colonies in Brazil were recaptured by the Portuguese. The loss of revenue and mounting debt led to the WIC being declared bankrupt and it was dissolved in 1674.

In 1679, a second WIC was founded and would focus on the slave trade between the African coast and the colonies in the New World. WIC ships would typically bring slaves from Africa to America and sugar and other products back to Europe, before going back to Africa. It was this trade that the WIC would become involved with in Suriname.

Painting by Petrus Johannes Schotel of the capture of the Spanish Silverfleet by Piet Hein in 1628. (NIMH Collection)

Maroons

As the plantation economy grew and became more profitable, the workforce of slaves grew proportionally. Working long hours and being treated poorly by their owners, many slaves chose to flee the plantations that were mostly located along the rivers and ran off into the jungle. These escaped slaves, or Maroons, formed settlements from which they often raided plantations in search of food, tools and women (as most escaped slaves were men).

The plantation owners countered these raids by patrolling the jungle in search of Maroons. Militias were formed by calling free men to arms but it was soon apparent that these were not enough. Colonial troops were also put to the task of eliminating the Maroon threat but this conflict turned into an exhausting guerrilla-style conflict that was costly to both sides.[6] By 1767 the colonial administration had made peace with the Maroon tribes. These would be left in peace and in exchange, escaped slaves were to be handed over to the authorities. However, operations against Maroons led by the legendary guerrilla leader Boni, were increased.

The Boni Maroons had been raiding plantations from the Cottica area.[7] After being driven from their villages, this group built a fortress in the coastal area of the Commewijne River. Fort Boekoe was located in a deep swamp and was hard to reach being only reachable by a path hidden underwater.[8]

Conducted by colonial troops together with the *Corps Vrije Mulatten en Neegers* (consisting of people of mixed blood and free slaves), the first raid failed. After a siege of several months, the colonial troops withdrew. Surviving members of the Corps fought until they fell in battle and their green caps were captured by the Maroons.

In 1772, a second raid was conducted with the *Neeger Vrijkorps*. This corps, also known as the *Korps Zwarte Jagers* (Black Hunter Corps) or *redimoesoes*, consisted of 300 purchased slaves that would assist the additional 1,600 troops sent from the Netherlands.[9] This raid was successful and had a demoralising effect on the Bonis. Although not beaten, the Bonis would be chased down continuously and were eventually driven off into French Guiana.

The Abolition of Slavery

When slavery was abolished in 1863, approximately 34,000 slaves became free men and women. However, many of them were forced to work as paid labour on the plantations of their former owners for another 10 years. Afterwards, most Creoles would leave the plantations they worked on to become small scale farmers on land that they rented from planters or the government. Over time, agricultural areas were set-up in the districts away from the capital where newly cultivated land along rivers (such as the Nickerie and Saramacca Rivers) produced crops such as cacao. In other places, such as Coroni and Para, plantations were set-up to successfully grow crops and wood.[10]

However, as the Surinamese economy was still mostly running on plantations, the emancipation of slaves threatened to cause a shortage of manpower. As recruitment efforts for African contract workers to Suriname did not yield good results, the Dutch turned to Asia as the future source for the manpower shortage.

From 1865, about 2,000 Chinese contractors were brought to Suriname from Hong Kong and Macao. The British and Portuguese later closed the trade of these ports to foreign markets due to their own manpower shortages. The majority of these people were Hakka Chinese originating from the province of Guangdong.[11]

From 1873 to 1916, approximately 34,000 contract workers from British India arrived in Suriname to work on the plantations as indentured servants. Most of these eventually settled in Suriname, forming one of the largest population groups, known as the Hindustanis. About one-third of the contract workers elected to return to India upon completion of their contract.[12]

British interference and high costs drove the Dutch to find an alternative source of contract workers. This was found in Java, which at the time was part of the Netherlands East Indies. By the end of

Dutch Armed Forces in Suriname 1815–1975 [16]

The defence of Suriname was never the main priority of the government in The Hague. After the country was liberated from French occupation, specific units of the KL and the KNIL were tasked with the defence of the only Dutch colony left in South America.

1814: After the Netherlands were liberated from France, new regiments were formed for the new KL (Royal Dutch Army). A regiment of *West-Indische Jagers* was founded in the Netherlands for service in the Caribbean colonies.

1815: The 10th and 11th Battalion of the regiment participated in the Battle of Waterloo, before transferring to the Caribbean in 1816. The two battalions of Jägers (light infantry) were reinforced by an artillery battalion.

1819: The 10th and 11th Jäger Battalion, together consisting of 12 companies, were renamed 27th and 28th Battalion respectively.

1821: Both battalions were amalgamated into the 27th Battalion, with 7 companies remaining in Suriname. The artillery battalion was transformed into the 1st Field Artillery Battalion, with one company remaining in Suriname.

1832: The 27th Battalion was reduced to three companies in Suriname.

1846: The 27th Battalion was entirely transferred to Suriname, with four companies consisting of 34 officers and 668 enlisted personnel.

1868: The defence of Suriname was transferred from the Dutch Army to the Ministry of Colonies and renamed the *West-Indische Landmacht*. The armed forces in Suriname consist of two infantry and one artillery company of 18 officers and 618 enlisted men.

1873: The artillery company is reduced to a detachment of 40 men.

1902: The artillery company is disbanded. The total troop strength is 15 officers and 370 enlisted men.

1907: The number of troops is reduced to one company with seven officers and 292 enlisted men.

1908: Starting 8 May the defence of Suriname is transferred to the KNIL. This falls under the Ministry of Colonial Affairs vs the Ministry of War.

Drawing of Flank Company Sergeant (right) and 'Jäger' of the Corps Jägers in the Dutch West-Indies, 1823. (Public Domain – Dirk Sluyter)

the nineteenth century, the first Javanese contract workers arrived in Suriname. These people were brought to Suriname under the same agreements as the Hindustanis. Javanese immigration continued up until 1939 and by that time, about 33,000 contract workers had come to Suriname with about a quarter of them choosing to go back to Java at the end of their work contract.[13]

As the administration sought to control the different elements of the population, the Dutch invested in the civil service of the country. Children's education was made compulsory and at schools, the Dutch language, western European values and often Christianity, were taught.

By the beginning of the Second World War, this had resulted in a plural society containing people from different ethnic races, each with a different religion, background and language. Most Surinamers were capable of speaking Dutch and this would be the main language of the colony. It would be these groups of people that would form the nation of Suriname in the late twentieth century.

Military Developments

By the end of the eighteenth century, Suriname was affected by the turmoil that was started by the French Revolution in 1789. As the Dutch Republic fell in 1795 to Napoleon's army (resulting in the vassal state of the Republic of Batavia), the governor handed formal control over to the British in 1799 when one of their fleets arrived in Suriname.[14]

With the defeat of Napoleon at Waterloo and the end of the war with the French, Suriname was handed back to the newly formed Kingdom of the Netherlands in 1815. Other Dutch possessions that were protected by the British were kept (such as Ceylon and the Cape Colonies). Demerara, Essequibo and Berbice were kept under British control as well and would assimilate into British Guiana in 1831.

Once back in control, the Dutch built up their troop strength to control the Maroons that were mounting the occasional raid. In 1816, the Dutch sent about 800 troops to Suriname, which formed an autonomous unit, the *West-Indische Jagers,* together with the other forces based in the Dutch West-Indies.[15]

However, there was no guerrilla-type war on the scale as it had been in the eighteenth century. The British had introduced abolition laws during their rule of Suriname. As the abolition of slavery was coming closer and treatment of slaves was getting better, the need for a strong military force was reduced as the civil unrest caused

---

1915: The number of troops is reduced to one company with seven officers and 234 enlisted men.

1931: The number of troops is reduced to one company with five officers and 200 enlisted men.

1939: *Surinaamse Schutterij* (Surinamese Home Guard) is formed, mobilised and trained.

1940: On 10 May 1940, when Germany invaded the Netherlands, 215 KNIL personnel were present in Suriname. These were reinforced with 50 *Mariniers* (Dutch Marines) from Curaçao.

1941: Detachments of the Prinses Irene Brigade reinforced the KNIL and *Schutterij* units present in Suriname.

1943: Prinses Irene Brigade units transferred to the UK to participate in the liberation of Western Europe. Fifty men of the brigade remained in Suriname as staff.

1946: *Schutterij* disbanded and the armed forces reorganised into the *Landmacht Suriname.*

1950: KNIL disbanded, majority of Surinamese veterans (including those returning from Indonesia) discharged from armed forces.

1950: The Royal Dutch Marine Corps were assigned the responsibility to protect Suriname. Starting in December 1950, *Mariniers* were stationed in Suriname and operated alongside the units of the *Landmacht Suriname* until these were fully disbanded. The last *Mariniers* stationed in Suriname left in July 1953.

1952: In August, the decision was made to reassign the defence of Suriname back to the army. An infantry battalion, consisting of four companies made up of conscripts that volunteered to go overseas, would take on these duties. The 103 Commando Compagnie of the KL arrived in Suriname in September and stayed for six months until the newly formed companies arrived in the country, thus reforming the *Landmacht Suriname.*

1957: *Landmacht Suriname* is renamed *Troepenmacht in Suriname* (TRIS).

1975: TRIS disbanded upon Surinamese independence. All equipment, installations and Surinamese personnel were transferred to the newly founded Surinamese Armed Forces (SKM).

The emblem of the KNIL responsible for the defence of Suriname from 1908 to 1950. (Wikimedia by user Orange2000)

The emblem of the TRIS (1957 to 1975) as used by the conscripts serving in Suriname. (TRIS Online)

by marronage slowly ceased to exist. In addition, the decline of the economy reduced the investments in the military.

Due to the policy of neutrality, the colonial administration focused on the formation of a police force for peacekeeping duties; the military was only used in cases when the police could not maintain order. An example was when contract workers rose to protest working conditions at the Mariënburg plantation in 1902.[17]

In 1908, the Dutch government had decided that the defence of Suriname was the task of the *Koninklijk Nederlands Indisch Leger* (Royal Dutch Indies Army or KNIL). The colonies in the west were unprofitable and thus priority was given to the Netherlands East Indies (NEI). The number of troops based in Suriname stayed relatively low and gradually decreased over time until the outbreak of the Second World War in 1939. As the Netherlands stayed neutral during the First World War, the colonies were isolated from the fighting and thus, were not affected as much as the colonies of other nations.[18]

As the threat of another world war loomed on the horizon, Governor J.C. Kielstra sought to strengthen the defence of the country against foreign invasion. With only 200 KNIL soldiers, armed with infantry weapons (carbines) and a few anti-aircraft guns, the military force in Suriname was woefully under-equipped to deal with a foreign threat. His pleas for more troops and weapons fell on deaf ears in Dutch government capital of The Hague and he was only allowed to purchase a small number of weapons. When the Second World War broke out on 1 September 1939, these had not yet arrived.[19]

Economic Developments

Until the early twentieth century, all major products that were exported from Suriname were agricultural ones, such as coffee, sugar, cacao, rice and balata (an insulator used in telegraph cables). Although the discovery of gold in the Lawa-Tapahoni area led to investments that grew exports and peaked in 1908, the main source of income for Suriname would turn out to be an aluminium-rich mineral called bauxite.[20]

Bauxite was originally discovered at the Rac à Rac plantation on the Suriname River by a German geologist working for the Surinamese Goldmining Company. Its discovery went unnoticed until 1914, when a British mining engineer found a 'new' discovery in Saramacca. His publications peaked US interest as the western hemisphere was cut off from bauxite due to the outbreak of the First World War.[21]

The US company Alcoa started investing in Suriname in 1916 when the *Surinaamse Bauxiet Maatschappij* (Surinamese Bauxite Company or SBM) was founded. The first exports of bauxite left Suriname in 1922. With worldwide demand for aluminium rising, by the end of the 1920s bauxite had become the most valuable export product of Suriname. By the late 30s, Alcoa started expanding their bauxite-related activities with the construction of an ore processing plant in Moengo that would be completed by 1941. With BHP Billiton (a subsidiary of the British-Dutch Company Shell) opening more mines in the Lelydorp area, bauxite production increased significantly in the early 1940s. Surinamese bauxite would be used in 65 percent of the aircraft built during the Second World War. It is therefore unsurprising that the United States kept a close eye on developments in Suriname.

Suriname in the Second World War

With the outbreak of war, the *Surinaamse Schutterij* (Surinamese Homeguard) was mobilised and trained. These 80 men, together with the 215 soldiers of the KNIL, a detachment of 50 to 80 *Mariniers* and a ship of the Royal Dutch Navy based in Curaçao, formed the entire defence of the country when German forces invaded the Netherlands on 10 May 1940. Except for the dramatic attempt of the crew of the German ship *Goslar* to block the port of Paramaribo, no sabotage or actions were taken by Germans living in Suriname.[22] All were swiftly rounded up by the police and military and interned.[23]

In June 1940, Governor Kielstra had discussed the threat of war from Brazil with his colleagues from neighbouring British and French Guiana as there was a concern that the large number of German expatriates would probably try to persuade the Brazilian authorities to invade the Guianas. They reached a consensus on how to handle the situation in case hostilities broke out. A month later however, the French governor sided with the Vichy government of General Pétain (which collaborated with the Germans). This raised the concern of invasion as the strategically important bauxite

Bauxite from Suriname was used in about 65 percent of all aluminium used in Allied aircraft. Pictured is the B-25 production line in Wichita, Kansas, USA in October 1942. (Public Domain – US Office of War Information)

The Aluminium Industry in Suriname

Bauxite, a mineral abundant on the Guiana Shield, is a red powder that is the main source of aluminium. Suriname was one of the largest suppliers of bauxite and alumina in the world, holding 11 percent and six percent of the world market in 1972 respectively. By 1965, Suriname was the only country in Latin America that had a complete aluminium industry, capable of exporting bauxite, alumina and aluminium mined and produced locally.

In brief, the process of mining bauxite and turning it into aluminium consists of the following steps:
1. Bauxite is strip-mined from open pits at the mines.
2. Ore is processed by grinding and filtering it from non-ore materials in a processing plant.
3. The fine ore is mixed with caustic soda and lime after which it is heated, calcified, precipitated and dried into alumina (Al_2O_3) at a refinery.
4. Alumina is molten and electrolysed to remove oxygen at a smelter and cast into aluminium ingots, sheets or pieces.

By independence in 1975, the aluminium industry in Suriname consisted of the following facilities:
- Bauxite mines in Moengo, Para and Lelydorp that were owned by the companies BHP Billiton and Suralco (the former SBM).
- Ore processing plant at Moengo run by Suralco since 1941.
- An aluminium refinery and smelter at Paranam run by Suralco since 1964.
- The hydroelectric plant at Afobaka run by Suralco that supplied power to the refinery at Paranam as well as the city of Paramaribo since 1965.

Bauxite, alumina and aluminium would be Suriname's main export products up until the beginning of the twenty-first century, when the majority of mines in eastern Suriname were exhausted. With reserves in western Suriname being far away from existing plants and the surplus of cheap, subsidised aluminium from other countries available on the world market, production became unprofitable.

The smelter was closed in 1999 and BHP Billiton sold its mining operations to Suralco in 2009. When Alcoa closed the mines and remaining facilities in 2015, the aluminium industry in Suriname shut down and the Afobaka hydroelectric plant was handed over to the Surinamese government. Attempts to resume profitable production of aluminium products by private and government enterprises have so far been unsuccessful at the time of writing.

The Moengo bauxite ore processing plant in the 1940s. (Suralco Magazine)

mines in Moengo and the shipping lanes to export the ore, were very close to the border with French Guiana. The airport of Zanderij, a regional transportation hub, was also within the potential bombing range of Dakar in Senegal.[24]

Kielstra requested additional troops and aircraft from the Dutch government-in-exile but the only reinforcements that were considered were naval guns to guard the navigation channel of the Suriname River. Dutch indecisiveness did not result in the strengthening of the military defences despite US pressure. Again, the defence of the NEI was a larger priority and the military strength of the Netherlands was limited. Before these additional troops arrived in South America, President Franklin D. Roosevelt of the United States had decided to act.

Roosevelt, being concerned about the possibility of Axis attacks, had run out of patience. On 1 September 1941, he sent a telegram to Queen Wilhelmina of the Netherlands stating that the disruption of bauxite would endanger the output of the aircraft industry. To safeguard Suriname's bauxite supply, he formally asked for approval for the US to base troops in Suriname. For the Dutch government-in-exile, this was a blow to prestige.

A year before, in the summer of 1940, the Dutch had allowed British forces to occupy the islands of Aruba and Curaçao in the Dutch Antilles. The refineries on these islands processed Venezuelan

Members of the Prinses Irene Brigade in the UK before shipping off to South America. A contingent of this unit was sent to Suriname in 1941 to beef up local forces. 15 Surinamers would later join this unit to participate in the campaign to liberate Northwest Europe from German occupation. (Collection Nationaal Archief/Anefo)

oil and provided the British with most of the high octane fuel for their armed forces.[25] As Britain was an ally, the Dutch saved face by claiming that the force had arrived by invitation.

Now however, the Dutch had to swallow their pride and accept the help of a neutral nation to protect their colony. Within a week, the Dutch responded to the telegram with several conditions, one of them being that troops would leave as soon as the threat of war to Suriname had subsided.[26]

Being in a rush to reinforce Dutch forces in Suriname before the Americans arrived, the Prinses Irene Brigade, a Free-Dutch unit formed in Great Britain from Dutch expats, was ordered to send volunteers to Suriname. Happy to trade the cold British weather for the tropics, plenty of volunteers were found. The first detachment of 156 soldiers would arrive in Paramaribo on 26 September, followed by a second detachment of 92 men on 20 November.[27] By the end of 1941, Dutch troops in Suriname would number about 600, including about 250 soldiers of the Prinses Irene Brigade.

On 24 November 1941, the first of 2,000 American troops arrived in Suriname. These troops fortified the naval and air defences of the country by placing guns at the forts of Nieuw Amsterdam and Purmerend at the mouths of the Suriname and Saramacca rivers respectively, as well as all strategically important bauxite mines and processing plants. In addition, the US patrolled the Surinamese coasts against German submarines and surface raiders, using vessels and aircraft flying from Zanderij Airport (see box).[28]

American troops standing at attention in Paramaribo. Starting in November 1941, the US sent several thousand soldiers to Suriname to protect the valuable bauxite industry in case of a foreign attack. These troops were under KNIL command. (Collection Nationaal Archief/Anefo)

Zanderij Airport

Fokker F.XVIII 'Snip' and the four-man crew that made the first transatlantic flight from the Netherlands to Suriname in 1934. (NIMH Collection)

Zanderij Airport, located 50km southwest of Paramaribo started out as a small, unpaved airport that was first used as a stopover point for Pan American World Airways in 1928, when it was used for mail flights between Miami and Paramaribo. Up until the Second World War, the airstrip mostly received flights passing through the area. Royal Dutch Airlines (KLM), starting with the first transatlantic crossing of Fokker F.XVIII 'Snip' in December 1934, established services in the area and by 1938 a regular shuttle between Paramaribo and Willemstad (Curaçao) was in operation.

After the arrival of American forces in November 1941, the US Air Force based a composite squadron of fighters and patrol bombers at Zanderij. Due to the primitive set-up, the base was expanded by the US Corps of Engineers to become a transport base for sending Lend-Lease supplies across the Atlantic Ocean. As part of improvements for the road network of Suriname, they also built the road from Onverwacht to Zanderij, connecting the capital to its main airport.

During the war, Zanderij was used by the Air Transport Command on the South Atlantic route ferrying supplies and material to Freetown in Sierra Leone. In addition, fighters and patrol bombers would launch from the airfield to search and hunt U-boats operating off the coast and in the Caribbean Sea. On 2 October 1942, a B-18A Bolo from the 99 Bomb Squadron managed to sink submarine U-512 off Cayenne, French Guiana by depth charge.[30] By the end of the war, military operations were scaled down with the airport being handed back to the Dutch authorities in 1947.

From 1947, Zanderij Airport was transformed into the main civilian airport for international flights with a 3,500m hardened runway being built in 1959 to support large jet aircraft. As such, the US Air Force's Military Air Command used the base as a stopover point for transatlantic flights in the 1960s. In addition, Zanderij hosted the first 747 Jumbo Jet in South America when a KLM aircraft landed in April 1972.[31]

Despite the airport being renamed Johan Adolf Pengel International Airport on the 15th anniversary of independence in 1990, the airport is still popularly called 'Zanderij' by the Surinamese people.

Zanderij Airfield pictured in March 1945. The base was expanded by the US Corps of Engineers for the Air Transport Command. (Via Mr. Ozires Moraes/http://www.sixtant.net – World War Two in the South Atlantic)

Table 3: US Army Air Force Units Operating From Zanderij Field, Suriname 1941–1943[29]

Unit	Date	Aircraft	Notes
99 Bomber Squadron (9 Bomber Group)	27 November 41 – 31 October 42	A-20/DB-7 Havoc, B-18A Bolo & P-40C Warhawk	Composite Squadron for air patrols and anti-submarine duties.
22 Fighter Squadron (36 Fighter Group)	16 September 42 – 16 February 43	P-39 Airacobra, later P-47 Thunderbolt	Operated detachments in Trinidad, Aruba and Curaçao.
35 Bomber Squadron Medium (25 Bomber Group)	October 42 – October 43	B-18A Bolo, later B-25 Mitchell	Operated detachments in British Guyana and Trinidad. Took over equipment from the 99 Bomber Squadron.
23 Antisub Squadron Heavy, 25 Antisub Wing	15 August 43 – December 43	A-29 Hudson	Part of the Trinidad detachment of the Antilles Air Command. Attached to the 35 Bomber Squadron.

The entry of Japan into the war had grave consequences for the Dutch. Two weeks after the arrival of US troops in Suriname, the Japanese armed forces attacked Pearl Harbor and commenced their campaign to conquer the possessions of the Western colonial powers in Asia, such as the Philippines, the Malayan Peninsula, the NEI and others. When the KNIL capitulated to the victorious Japanese in March 1942, 38,000 Dutch troops were sent off to spend the rest of the war in captivity. For Surinamers, the loss of the NEI hit home as Surinamese soldiers also fought and died with the KNIL. This meant that Suriname and the Netherlands Antilles were the last unoccupied territories of the Kingdom of the Netherlands.

After the Japanese attack, the Dutch transferred 146 enemies of the state from the NEI to Suriname. These people, most of them supporters of the Dutch fascist party NSB, arrived in Suriname on 1 March 1942. After being held in former slave houses in Fort New Amsterdam for half a year, the men were transferred to a concentration camp in August of that year. This camp was located in the jungle on the Suriname River in the Jodensavanne and was called the 'green hell' by the prisoners. The men were treated poorly, with the low point being the execution of several escaped prisoners by *Mariniers* in Fort Zeelandia. After the war was over, the remaining 136 prisoners were released and shipped to the Netherlands.[32]

The Dutch continued to build-up their defensive forces in Suriname, as war materiel arrived from the US. These included searchlights for coastal batteries, anti-aircraft artillery and radar for defensive purposes, and also small arms, mortars, artillery, anti-tank weapons and tanks. The latter group of weapons was meant to be used to build up an offensive KNIL force in Suriname that would be sent overseas to liberate the NEI. The build-up of this force took longer than expected.

The Atlantic Charter
Even before American troops set foot on Surinamese soil, British Prime Minister Winston Churchill and President Roosevelt met in Newfoundland in August 1941. They declared in a joint statement called the Atlantic Charter, that they supported the sovereignty of all nations: people all over the world had the right to choose their own government free of oppression and tyranny. Roosevelt also questioned the right of colonialism.

In response to this, Queen Wilhelmina indicated in a series of radio speeches that she was willing to grant more autonomy to the different territories of the Kingdom. In addition, she also spoke about equality between the various countries, most prominently on 6 December 1942. This encouraged the Surinamese elite (mostly Creole) to form political parties to challenge colonial authorities in a bid for more independence.

When war first broke out in 1940, most of the Suriname population supported the Dutch royal family and loyalty towards the Netherlands was strengthened. About 500 Surinamese volunteered to serve with the armed forces and funds were set-up to raise money for the Red Cross, various aid groups to support Dutch families overseas and to buy a Spitfire fighter plane dubbed *Suriname*.

In the meantime, the presence of US forces also had its effects on society. The Americans influenced the Surinamese population with US products and movies. Local workers were paid well by US forces to support their logistical infrastructure. Due to the increased production of bauxite, the economy flourished as never before. But as the standards of living increased, wages remained the same and were not growing with costs of living. Dissent amongst the population rose.

A Zanderij-based B-18A of the 99 Bomb Squadron on patrol during early 1942 (note the pre-war style roundels on the aircraft). An aircraft from this unit sank the German submarine U-512 in October of that year. (Public Domain – US Air Corps via Dan Hagedorn)

As the governor declared a state of emergency and took more security measures, people became more critical of the local government. Realising that Suriname was doing well without support from the Netherlands, the desire for more autonomy increased as a national identity was being formed. Protests and strikes were held and increased over time. This in turn led to more police actions, censorship and incarcerations. The local governing body (*de Staten van Suriname*) continued to voice their disapproval of actions taken and blocked legislation that made would it permissible for Surinamese conscripts to be sent overseas.[33]

Even when conscription was introduced in 1942, many were exempted from serving overseas because they were employed in the bauxite industry. Surinamers were not allowed to join the Prinses Irene Brigade, due to objections from Dutchmen who had joined from South Africa.[34] Instead they were assigned to the KNIL, which was to form a unit to liberate the NEI. Instead of the desired 3,500, only 500 Surinamers were found to be willing to fight for the Dutch with the KNIL by the time the Second World War ended.

It must be noted however, that several thousand Surinamese men and women served in the *Schutterij* (home guard) in addition to Surinamese men that served, fought and died in Europe, the NEI and onboard convoys serving as gunners.[35] In addition, some Surinamers fought with the Dutch underground resistance in German-occupied Netherlands, most famous of whom was Anton de Kom.[36] All in all, 160 Surinamers are known to have been killed during occupation and fighting in the Second World War.[37]

As the battle for the Atlantic raged on and German submarines were wreaking havoc on Allied transport ships, enthusiasm to serve waned in combination with the social factors mentioned previously. By mid-1943, the Battle of the Atlantic was won, North Africa was securely in Allied hands and Brazil and French Guiana had joined the allied cause. The threat of war in Suriname was over and by the end of the year the Prinses Irene Brigade was sent to the UK to participate in the upcoming campaign to liberate Europe.

In September 1943 the first troops from Puerto Rico arrived to replace the first group of 'white' US troops. Governor Kielstra protested as he believed the arrival of 'coloured' US troops with their high salaries, would cause unrest amongst the local population. The resulting political tensions, combined with his unpopularity, eventually resulted in the dismissal of governor Kielstra as he was sent to serve in the dead-end post as the Dutch Ambassador to Mexico in 1944. The final withdrawal of all US troops started from Suriname in July 1944. It would not be until 1947 that the last American troops, stationed at Zanderij Airport, left the country.

Surinamese Soldiers in Indonesia and Korea

After the liberation of the Netherlands in May 1945, the Dutch armed forces focused on the liberation of the NEI. By 1943 the first KNIL troops from Suriname had arrived in Australia followed by 400 soldiers who were shipped to Australia for training the following year. After joining up with approximately 1,000 KNIL troops that had escaped the Japanese, these men were sent into combat in the campaign to liberate New Guinea and later Borneo, until the capitulation of Japanese forces on 15 August 1945.

The KNIL was dispatched to the NEI to restore Dutch authority but before any soldiers arrived, President Sukarno had claimed independence on 17 August forming the state of Indonesia. The Dutch government attempted to form a union with Indonesia and the other colonies (with the Dutch queen as head of state) but after several years of campaigns and guerrilla warfare, the Netherlands accepted the inevitable. The KNIL was disbanded in 1950 and Dutch military forces returned home. During these years, Surinamese soldiers fought until they were replaced by Dutch conscripts. The last soldiers did not return until the early 1950s.

Most of the former KNIL soldiers who returned to Suriname were not able to join the army units back home as

The first detachment of Surinamese volunteers receiving weapons training in Camp Casino, New South Wales, Australia in 1944. The men are armed with Johnson M1941 rifles. (Collection Nationaal Archief/Anefo)

Surinamese volunteers during their training in Roosendaal, the Netherlands, before deployment to the Korean peninsula in 1952. (Collection Nationaal Archief/Anefo)

funds were limited. In addition, many of the Javanese soldiers (135 in total) were not allowed to return to armed service as the governor was concerned that these men would be inspired by recent events in Indonesia to seek independence.[38] Back in Suriname, many KNIL veterans were denied grants and allowances and had trouble finding jobs in the civilian sector, thus causing dissent amongst the veterans.

On 25 June 1950, North Korean troops invaded South Korea, starting the Korean War. The newly formed United Nations condemned the attack and led by the US, various UN member states sent troops to the embattled peninsula to counter the invasion from the north. Although invited to join, the Dutch government was not keen to participate in this conflict as the country was still recovering from the Second World War and the campaigns in Indonesia. After

Korea Monument in Paramaribo. This monument was built in 2008 by the South Korean government to honour the Surinamese veterans who served during the Korean War. (Thomas Kautzor)

Simon Sanches (left in white shirt and tie) during his trial in 1948. Sanches was found guilty of attempting to overthrow the government and sentenced to seven months in jail but was released after a short time in prison and sent to the Netherlands. (Public Domain – Wikimedia)

US pressure, an infantry battalion was sent to Korea as part of the NDVN (Netherlands Detachment of the UN forces).

This battalion was formed from Dutch volunteers, most of whom were veterans of the KNIL. Most volunteers were recruited from the Netherlands but Surinamese volunteers were given the green light to join as Governor Klaasenz was of the opinion that it would increase solidarity within the Kingdom of the Netherlands. Although the call for arms first came in January 1951, the first Surinamese soldiers did not get to Korea until August 1951, relieving the 1st Dutch Battalion. The NDVN served in various campaigns in the conflict, most notably in the Iron Triangle between Chorwon, Pyonggang and Kumhwa. By the time the armistice was signed in Panmunjeon in July 1953, a total of 102 Surinamers had served in Korea of whom two had died during hostilities.[39] The NDVN mission ended at the beginning of 1954, which was followed by the repatriation of all soldiers.[40]

The Road to Self-governance

Since the Queen's speech in December 1942, the Surinamese were still yet to receive greater autonomy. Part of the reason this process was delayed was a lot of political effort went into the attempted formation of a union and the conflict in Indonesia. Not all Surinamers were willing to wait.

In late 1947 former naval Sergeant Simon Sanches, a Surinamer of Creole descent, returned to Paramaribo. After his service and education in the Netherlands, he was convinced that Dutch colonial rule in his native country must end. Together with a group of about 80 people (among them a large number of disgruntled Suriname war veterans that returned from the NEI), Sanches organised a coup.[41]

The conspirators intended to first occupy the barracks and police headquarters in Paramaribo, followed by occupation of the governor's residence, the radio station, Fort Zeelandia and the telephone and telegraph offices. Dutch soldiers would be captured and disarmed and Dutch civilians would be interned. As several members of the group were soldiers that were still in active service, the group was well informed about the strength and presence of the military. The plan was never carried out however, as it was leaked to the police.[42]

The local authorities apprehended and jailed all the conspirators before the coup was carried out. Sanches was put on trial, which gathered a lot of attention locally and made him somewhat of a hero. He was found guilty but was released after a short incarceration and shipped off to the Netherlands in order to relieve the tense atmosphere in Suriname.

After the coup attempt of 1947, tensions remained high in Suriname. The Second World War had drawn lots of Hindustanis and Javanese to the city. The Surinamese elite, who consisted mostly of Creoles, felt threatened by the former two groups as they were becoming more politically active and formed their own parties. The three largest parties in Suriname at the time were the NPS (Creoles), VHP (Hindustanis) and KTPI (Javanese).[43]

Despite these tensions, the first general elections held in Suriname went quietly. It was the first time the public could vote for their parliament (called the *Staten van Suriname*). The elections were won by the NPS who gained 13 of the 21 available seats. Dutch troops were standing by to act in case riots broke out but military action was not necessary as the situation remained calm.

The Surinamese political elite had not forgotten the Queen's promises and the *Staten van Suriname* kept on insisting to turn the promise of autonomy into a reality. After talks between the *Staten of*

Dutch Marines on patrol in 1951. The *Mariniers* formed the main defence of Suriname between 1950 and 1953, while the Dutch struggled with the question of which branch of the armed services would defend Suriname. In the end, it was decided to form a specific unit of the army dedicated to the defence of Suriname: the *Troepenmacht in Suriname* (TRIS). (NIMH Collection)

Suriname and the Netherlands Antilles and the Dutch government in Den Haag (The Hague), an initial agreement was reached in 1950 that the former colonies would receive self-governance in local affairs including the local police force. Matters of defence and foreign affairs would be arranged in agreement between the members of the Kingdom. Tough conferences would continue to be held until the agreements would be galvanised into the charter of 1954. In the meantime, the military forces in Suriname were reorganised.

Landmacht Suriname[44]

After the Second World War had ended, about 100 to 150 KNIL personnel remained in country. The *Schutterij* was demobilised in 1946 and the armed forces were reorganised as the *Landmacht Suriname* (Army Suriname). The task of the military in Suriname was to defend the nation's borders and to support the local police in case of political unrest – tasks that were estimated to require about 500 troops.

As many Surinamese troops had been sent to the NEI, the governor requested that more troops were sent to Suriname from the Netherlands. Several Dutch detachments of conscripts, originally earmarked for deployment to the NEI, were sent to Suriname in 1946 and 1947. As the cost of the conflict in the NEI was a big burden to the Dutch economy, force reductions were planned. Political developments, however, caused planned reductions to be scrapped.

As the group of conspirators of 1947 involved a high percentage of Surinamese veterans and military personnel, the governor was convinced that local soldiers could not be trusted to stay loyal to the Crown. Therefore, the ratio of Dutch to Surinamese personnel in the military was to be maintained and preferably increased. It was decided that Dutch conscripts would be sent to increase the numbers as the cost of sending professional soldiers was deemed to be too high.

Once KNIL was disbanded, Dutch military personnel were transferred to the KL (Royal Dutch Army) in the Netherlands. As the core of personnel of the *Landmacht Suriname* was locally based, additional professional troops would have to be brought over from the Netherlands. Sending conscripts overseas was no longer allowed after the conflict in Indonesia ended. As most of the Dutch armed forces were committed to serving NATO, sending expensive professional soldiers from the small cadre of officers available within the Dutch armed forces to Suriname, was seen as a diversion from the main task.

Initially, the solution was found in sending *Mariniers* to Suriname as these were an all-volunteer force meant to serve overseas. The first detachment of *Mariniers* arrived in December 1950. However, the integration of locally based army troops into the Dutch Marine Corps was deemed too difficult as both organisations were fundamentally different in their purpose. In the end, it was decided that conscripts who volunteered for duty in Suriname would be the best solution in the long term as Surinamese society had been accustomed to the *Landmacht*. Dutch conscripts, serving their country overseas, were seen as ambassadors of the Dutch Kingdom to the Surinamese people. The last detachment of *Mariniers* left Suriname in 1953 but small units would regularly visit Suriname to conduct training in jungle warfare.

On December 15 in 1954, Queen Juliana signed the *Statuut voor het Koninkrijk der Nederland* (Charter of the Kingdom of the Netherlands), turning Suriname into a constituent state. The *Staten van Suriname*, led by the prime minister, would govern Suriname while the governor would represent the Kingdom of the Netherlands and act as commander-in-chief of the Dutch military forces in country.

3
FROM AUTONOMY TO INDEPENDENCE

After gaining autonomy, Suriname set its own course to determine its future. With support from the Netherlands, a lot of projects were started that improved the living standard for many Surinamers. However, ethnic tensions remained in the country as the Creoles were competing more and more with the other groups, especially the Hindustanis.

As most political parties were formed along ethnic lines, no party in Suriname held the absolute majority in parliament. To form a cabinet, coalitions had to be formed between ethnic groups. This was especially true when the Creole NPS split into multiple parties.

Starting in 1958, the leaders of the NPS and VHP (Johan Pengel and Jaggarnath Lachmon respectively) started recognising that cooperation between Creoles and Hindustanis was necessary to ensure a bright future for Suriname. This started a period of *verbroederingspolitiek* (fraternisation politics) in which both parties

Jaggernath Lachmon (VHP) left and Prime Minister Johan Adolf Pengel (NPS) centre, at a press conference in 1963. Both men saw cooperation between the various ethnic groups as the only way to build a good future for Suriname. The Creoles and Hindustanis would govern Suriname together until 1973 when the NPK won the elections. (Collection Nationaal Archief/Anefo, Jac de Nijs)

would form the government. Although the Creoles held most seats, Hindustanis and Javanese also held important cabinet posts.[1]

The 1950s and 1960s were years of calm and prosperity for Suriname. Before the Second World War broke out, it was recognised that the economy of Suriname needed to diversify as it was mostly dependent on the export of bauxite. Starting in 1947, Suriname received a significant amount of development aid in a so-called *Tien Jaren Plan* (Ten Year Plan) that was meant to improve infrastructure, housing, healthcare and economic development of forestry, agriculture and mining. During this time several large projects were started to improve the economy.[2]

The Wageningen project improved agriculture in the Nickerie district, forming mechanised rice cultivation companies that significantly contributed to the Surinamese rice production. The interior of the country was mapped and surveyed during Operation Grasshopper which located natural resources such as wood and bauxite.

Despite that fact that the gross national products (GNP) of Suriname grew from 112 in 1955 to 741 million Sfl in 1975, most of this was the result of foreign investment and development aid.[3] Unfortunately, most of these investments were more to the advantage of foreign companies than the local economy. The Dutch company, Bruynzeel, dominated the export of lumber, the American companies SAIL and United Fruit Continental, dominated the shrimp and plantain exports respectively.

The largest project by far was the Brokopondo Project. An agreement was signed between the Surinamese government and Alcoa in 1957. Alcoa would build a dam and hydroelectric power plant on the Suriname River at Afobaka, which would supply electricity to a newly built aluminium smelter and alumina factory. This was done in exchange for mining concessions and economic benefits. The facilities would be run by Suralco.

The new facilities were opened in 1965. Water rising behind the dam would displace 4,000 to 6,000 Maroons of the Saramacca tribe. These would be relocated to camps at the government's expense. The water rose until 1971 as the Brokopondo reservoir (officially called the Van Blommenstein Lake) was created.

By 1975, the Surinamese economy was based on the export of bauxite and aluminium products (approximately 80 percent), agricultural products (such as rich and fish – 14 percent) and lumber (three percent). Unfortunately, almost all of these were in foreign hands and only employed a relatively small part of the population. The largest employer in Suriname remained the government with 32 percent of the working population being employed as civil servants.[4]

Troepenmacht in Suriname

By the time the Brokopondo Project was finished, the build-up of Dutch troops in Suriname had been completed. This force of colonial troops had grown from 400 men in 1952 to

Table 4: The Organisation of the TRIS in 1968 [10]		
Name	English Translation	Description
TRIS *Troepenmacht in Suriname* – Administrative Parent Unit Infantry Regiment Oranje Gelderland		
Personnel: Approx 1,000		
COTRIS: Colonel D.C. Vooren		
Staf-Cie	Command Coy	Military staff Military police (*Koninklijke Marechaussee*) Military band (*Militaire Kapel*) Medical platoon Training section
Verz-Cie	Medical Coy	Military hospital
A-Cie	Alpha (Infantry) Coy	1 Staff section 3 Infantry platoons 1 Support platoon
B-Cie	Bravo (Infantry) Coy	1 Staff section 3 Infantry platoons 1 Support platoon
C-Cie	Charlie (Infantry) Coy	1 Staff section 3 Infantry platoons 1 Support platoon
Vzg-Cie	Support Coy	1 Signals platoon 1 Supply platoon 1 Engineering platoon 1 Transport platoon 1 Intelligence unit

During the early 1960s, the largest industrial project in Suriname was the Afobakadam. It included 180MW of power generation capacity which was designed to supply power to the aluminium refinery and smelter. A quarter of the power generation would be supplied to Paramaribo. (Collection Nationaal Archief/Rijksvoorlichtingsdienst)

the border into Suriname as both countries had a roughly similar ethnic composition.

Other tasks were to support the population living in the rainforest with medical care, evacuation in times of disaster and by supporting infrastructure projects such as building or repairing bridges. Another task of the TRIS was to be prepared to evacuate Dutch nationals in case of an emergency. Plans were drawn up which could be called upon in case of emergency, one of which *Operatie Zwarte Tulp* (Operation Black Tulip) was later the subject of controversy.

The TRIS was an independent infantry battalion within the KL with support elements consisting of a staff company, three infantry companies with three platoons each, and a support company with three platoons. At the head of the TRIS was a colonel, dubbed COTRIS, who commanded the entire force. The TRIS was supported by 16 members of the *Koninklijke Marechaussee* (military police).[9] Although the organisational structure changed over time, the main structure of the TRIS would be maintained until it was disestablished following independence in 1975.

nearly 1,000 in 1966.[5] In 1957, the Ministry of Colonial Affairs was abolished and as a result, the *Landmacht Suriname* was reassigned to the KL. The force became a part of the *Oranje Gelderland* Infantry Brigade and was renamed *Troepenmacht in Suriname* (TRIS). Most of these soldiers were Dutch conscripts who volunteered for serving 12 months in Suriname. However, starting in 1963, Surinamese of conscript age could join the TRIS and follow the same training as the conscripts.[6]

The main tasks of the TRIS were to protect the borders of the country.[7] Even though Suriname was surrounded by friendly nations, the effects of the Cuban revolution on Latin America caused concern for communist uprisings in the area. The intelligence service of the TRIS closely monitored society for subversive elements and kept an eye on the activities of the Surinamese left-aligned parties such as the PNR.[8] Most of all, the TRIS was to fly the Dutch flag throughout Suriname, from the small Maroon villages in the jungle, to the capital city.

Secondary tasks were to support the local police in case of civil unrest and when instructed to do so by the governor. However, most of this support was done by supplying the police with training and equipment as the Dutch did not want to be actively participating in police operations. With racial tensions and violence in neighbouring British Guiana, there was a real fear of this violence spreading across

The soldiers of the TRIS were initially equipped with small arms and support weapons supplied from the Netherlands. Standard weapons included the Lee Enfield Nr.4 .303 (7.7mm) rifle and Thompson M1 0.45 (11.4mm) machine gun from stocks supplied during the Second World War.

Starting in 1963, these were replaced by the Garand M1 .30 (7.62mm) rifle and Uzi 9mm machine pistol. After 1968, the M1 .30 (7.62mm) Carbine was often used in place of the Garand M1, due to the heavier weight of the latter – especially on jungle patrols.[11] Other weapons supplied to the TRIS were Bren .303 (7.7mm) LMGs (light machine guns), Browning FN 9mm sidearms and Ordnance SBML two-inch mortars, also known as knee mortars.

The support platoons operated heavy weapons including the PIAT anti-tank weapon (up to the early 60s), Browning M1917 and M1919 .30 (7.62mm) and Browning M2HB .50 (12.7mm) HMGs (heavy machine guns), 57mm M18 and 75mm M20 recoilless rifles and M1 81mm mortars.[12]

The TRIS was supported by a variety of vehicles including jeeps and trucks. These included DAF YA-126 one-ton trucks, DAF YA-314 three-ton trucks, one BA-616 six-ton recovery vehicle, NEKAF M38A1 Jeeps (Willys Jeep copies), VW Beetle cars, VW buses and motorcycles. Several US-built vehicles were also used in the early 50s and 60s before newer vehicles were shipped from the Netherlands.[13]

Dutch conscripts doing a live fire exercise with an 81mm M1 mortar at BBZ during the 1950s. These weapons were still in use in the 1980s. (NIMH Collection)

A Marmon-Herrington CTMS-1TB1 in the early 1950s during an exercise. Serving with the KNIL and *Landmacht Suriname*, these light tanks briefly saw service with the TRIS in 1957 and were withdrawn from service shortly after. (NIMH Collection)

A GMC Otter armoured car at the Nieuw Amsterdam open air museum. The TRIS received seven or eight of these machines in 1960 and were lightly armed with a Bren LMG in the turret. They were taken out of service when the YP408 arrived in 1972. (Thomas Kautzor)

Soldier Seerden in 1971 of the 4e Platoon – Company B – 1971/1 was a conscript with the TRIS. He is seen here armed with a Bren LMG and carrying his jungle bag that included a hammock and other items for jungle survival. TRIS soldiers would regularly patrol the jungles during exercises but they would also be deployed to the various villages in the rainforest to give medical aid or to support construction projects. (Rachel Seerden)

Three 25-pounder 88mm field guns set up for testing in November 2022. The TRIS had at least five, most likely six, of these pieces in service that were mostly used for ceremonial purposes, often being showcased in parades. After these were taken out of service in 1996, three of these guns were restored and used to fire a 21 gun salute during Independence Day on the morning of 25 November 2022. (Surinamese Government)

For combat vehicles, the TRIS was originally equipped with leftover Marmon-Herrington CTLS, CTMS and MTLS light tanks from the Second World War. The last of these were taken out of service in 1957. In 1960, the TRIS was equipped with seven to eight GMC Otter armoured cars that were used until they were replaced by five YP408 APC in 1972.[14] The TRIS also had about four M45 .50 Quadmount AA guns and five or six QF 25-pounder towable artillery guns in its inventory, being most often used for displays in parades.[15] The latter was only fired during ceremonies and three of them are still in use at the time of writing.

For transporting troops over water, the TRIS had two CL-boats (named *Maurits* and *Frederik Hendrik*) that could each transport a platoon of troops to the posts at Albina and Nieuw Nickerie. Additionally, the TRIS also had numerous wooden dugout canoes in its inventory. Equipped with outboard motors, these are locally known as *korjalen* (pirogues).

The TRIS operated several facilities in Suriname. The main barracks was in Paramaribo with smaller camps in Albina, Nieuw Nickerie, Zanderij and Brownsweg. The smaller camps would be used to conduct platoon-sized patrols into the jungle. The O.P. Savanne and Bosbivak near Zanderij (BBZ) airport functioned as the main training centre as well as the weapons practice range.

Tensions With Guyana[16]

In the 1960s, Suriname went into its most prosperous time since the introduction of universal suffrage. However, during 1963, ethnic violence broke out in British Guiana between Creoles and Indo-Guyanese (as Guyanese descendants of Indian contract workers are known, similar to Hindustanis in Suriname). This started a period of tension with Suriname's western neighbour.

Just like Suriname, British Guiana was a colony of a European power. After the Second World War, political parties were formed and Guyanese could vote for their own parliament. In 1964, a strike in the sugar industry saw tensions between mostly Indo-Guyanese sugar workers and Creole strike breakers. The tensions led to riots all over the country with both ethnic groups attacking each other in various locations. In the end, the British Army had to come in to restore order. The riots left nearly 200 people dead, 1,000 wounded and many more people displaced. In the ensuing political upheaval, Creole Forbes Burnham was voted into office and would lead the country into independence from the British Empire in 1966, forming the dominion of Guyana before declaring full independence in 1970.

The border with Suriname is formed by the Corantijn River. This river runs into the Atlantic Ocean and is fed by two rivers about 400km upstream – the New River in the west and the Coeroenie River in the east (which is fed by the Koetari River).[17] The area between these two rivers and the Brazilian border is known as the Tigri Area.[18] This area was claimed by both the British and the Dutch.

The British claim is based on historical agreements between the Netherlands and the UK, dating back to 1843. However, when it was discovered in 1873 that three-quarters of the water of the Corantijne was coming from the New River, the Dutch sought to claim the area as part of Surinamese territory. As the area consisted of a thick jungle, it was not the main focus of both governments and formal agreements were never signed.[19]

Thus, the issue of the Tigri Area remained dormant until May 1965, when the Surinamese government decided to claim the area by unilaterally announcing the name change of the New River to Upper-Corantijn. Despite protests from Guyana and several talks with Suriname directly and between the Netherlands and the UK, ownership of the disputed area was not settled before Guyana became independent. One of the reasons why the Surinamese wanted to claim an area covered in dense forests was the West Suriname Plan.

During Operation Grasshopper (which took place in 1963), large deposits of minerals, particularly bauxite, were discovered in western Suriname. The West Suriname Plan was drawn up to exploit these resources by building new industrial complexes and supporting infrastructure in the largely uninhabited part of the country. Part

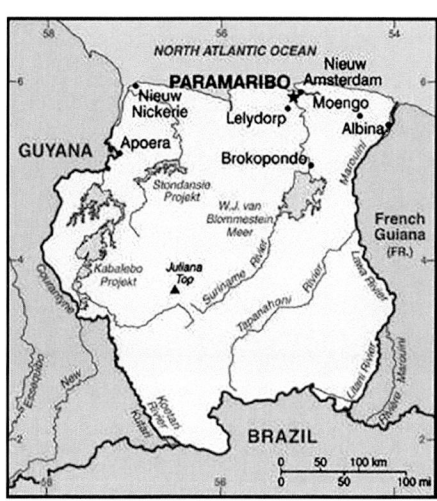

Map of Suriname, showing the reservoirs that would be created by building hydroelectric dams under the West Suriname Plan: the Kabalebo and Stondansie projects. (CIA website – https//www.cia.gov/the-world-factbook/countries/suriname/map)

of the plan foresaw a future requirement for hydroelectric power supplied by dams built on rivers in the area.

Surveys of the area bordering British Guiana started two years later and hydrologists of the Bureau of Hydroelectric Works (BWKW) were sent into the Tigri Area to determine rainfall and river currents. A camp was built near the Orinoque falls from which the workers would operate. Guyanese aircraft patrolling the area had noticed the presence of foreign workers. Despite Guyanese protests, Pengel refused to recall the labourers. When the Surinamese prime minister visited Caracas in 1967, the Burnham government felt threatened from two sides as there were latent hostilities between Guyana and Venezuela as well.[20] As a result, Guyana swiftly responded to the Surinamese workers in the Tigri Area.[21]

On 10 December 1967, a Guyanese Defence Forces (GDF) patrol ran into a group of BWKW surveyors on the eastern bank of the Upper-Corantijn and sent them away after confiscating their only shotgun.[22] On the 12 of December, the GDF launched Operation Kingfisher and sent a Guyana Airways Corporation (GAC) Grumman G-21 Goose amphibian with seven police officers to the BWKW camp at the Orinoque falls where they confiscated the surveyors' shotguns and expelled them as illegal immigrants.[23] As the workers were scheduled to leave the area for Christmas holidays on 15 December, the camp was evacuated as planned and occupied by GDF soldiers afterwards.[24]

The expulsion of the BWKW workers caused an outrage in Suriname. Pengel sent a message to the Dutch minister of foreign affairs requesting support to retake the occupied territory of Suriname and military support for the workers in the area. The Netherlands, not wanting to escalate the tense situation, agreed on 10 January 1968 that the workers could return to the area under police supervision but under no circumstances were the TRIS troops allowed to enter the area or get involved in the conflict 'unless all other means had failed and the situation should require action'. In order to support the police force, the TRIS stationed a small detachment of troops at the Coeroeni airport that bordered – but was not located in – the Tigri Area on 17 January.[25]

At the same time, the Netherlands protested the police actions to Guyana and requested that the GDF withdrew from the area while concurrently offering to mediate between both countries. The Guyanese government was under the impression that the Netherlands did not fully support Suriname in this matter. Except for several letters of protest, the Dutch did not take a stand against

Guyana, as there was no political will to get involved in what they saw was a Surinamese internal affair.

Pengel, on the other hand, spoke firm words against Guyana and threatened (military) action. He ordered the expulsion of about 100 Guyanese seasonal workers from Suriname, although this act was more symbolic than policy. Surinamese society, always critical of Pengel, would be united in this cause celebre behind their prime minister for now.[26]

DEFPOL

Pengel named retired KNIL officer Major Sjoerd Lapré as the commander of the Police Corps that was sent to patrol the area. This corps, called DEFPOL (DEFence POLice), would consist of up to 200 volunteers. Made up of mostly policemen and ex-TRIS soldiers, these men were armed with Uzi machine pistols, M1 carbines and second-hand khaki uniforms, all supplied by the TRIS.[27]

After receiving military training from the TRIS at the BBZ, the DEFPOL policemen were flown to the Coeroeni airstrip by SLM Dakotas. From there they would move into the contested area by korjaal and on foot to patrol the area.

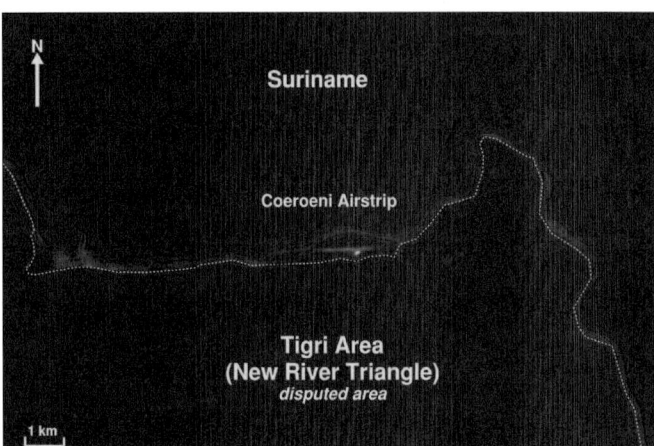

Coeroeni airstrip was located on an island of the Coeroeni River. It was located in the middle of the jungle, bordering the Tigri Area. (Google Maps)

Lapré, who was a veteran in jungle warfare, taught his men survival skills while setting up four camps in the Tigri Area. The camps were Camp Zulu, located across the river from the Coeroeni airfield, the former BWKW camp between the Oronoque and Upper-Corantijn, Camp Gonini by the Goodall Waterfalls and Camp Tigri in a hard to reach island between the rapids in the Corantijn River.[28]

DEFPOL was also reinforced by a secret delivery of weapons from a 'friendly nation' after the Dutch refused to send more weapons.[29] Although the TRIS conducted flag patrols along the Corantijn River, the TRIS did not venture into the Tigri Area. DEFPOL patrols did encounter settlers, whom they sent back to Guyanese territory.[30]

Tensions flared up in April when DEFPOL members captured a GDF patrol consisting of nine soldiers near one of their camps.[31] The soldiers transported their prisoners to Coeroeni and handed them over to the TRIS unit where they were questioned by the military intelligence personnel on site. The COTRIS was notified of the situation and consulted with Governor Ferrier who in turn, informed The Hague.

A few days later – and much to their surprise – the TRIS post at Coeroeni received the order to release the Guyanese prisoners with their weapons and equipment and bring them back to their point of capture. The members of DEFPOL were not amused and saw this as a betrayal by the Dutch government as the TRIS was supposed to protect the borders of Suriname.[32]

Due to the incident, the governor asked The Hague for reinforcements. Although more Uzis and materials were delivered, heavy equipment such as Bren LMGs and helicopters were refused. Except for the occasional Guyanese reconnaissance flight, all remained quiet in the area and as the tensions eased, most policemen left the area. Over time, three of the four camps were closed due to lack of funding from the government with Camp Tigri being left as the remaining camp. Military training for DEFPOL ended in November 1968 after 90 members had been given a course at the *Bosbivak Zanderij*.[33]

Distractions

As tensions between the neighbouring countries subsided, discontent of the population with Pengel increased. Government expenditures had risen and Pengel was accused of corruption, wasting government funds and lining his own pockets. In the beginning of 1969, teachers went on strike to demand higher wages as had been promised during the 1966 election campaign. Soon, other unions joined in the strikes, which resulted in tough confrontations between the protesters and the police. The resulting political crisis led to the fall of the government when Pengel resigned in February.

Meanwhile in the Dutch colony of Curaçao (the largest island of the Netherlands Antilles), several trade unions started a series of strikes demanding better wages for

The TRIS outpost at the Coeroeni. It was built in the late 1960s in order to support DEFPOL and to monitor Guyanese activity in the area. (NIMH Collection/W.M.M. Calting-Houwing)

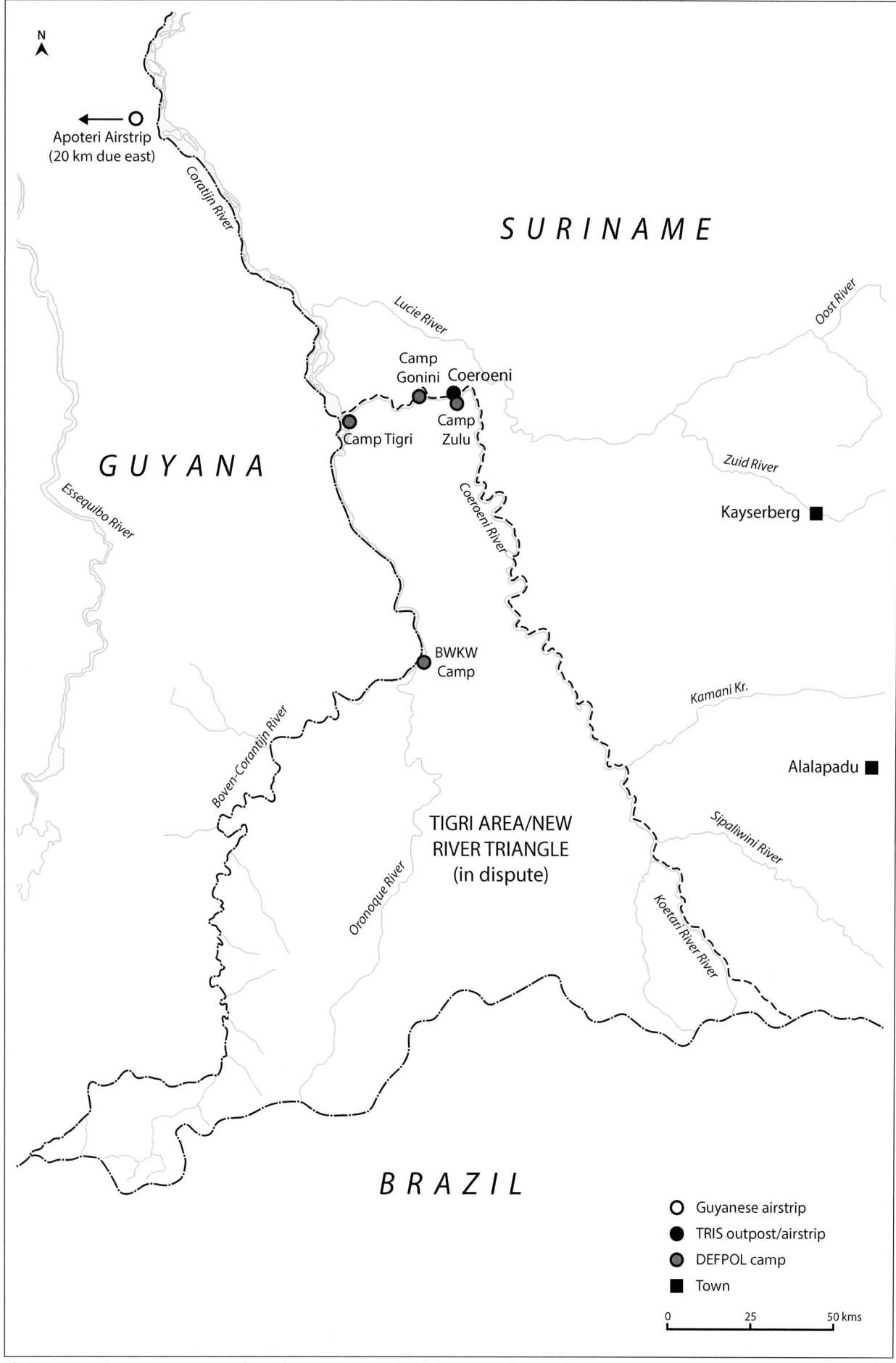

The Tigri Area (or New River Triangle as the Guyanese call it) is located in the southwest corner of Suriname and lies between the New River/Boven-Corantijn River, the Kuruni River and the Brazilian border. This map shows the four DEFPOL camps, the TRIS outpost at Coeroeni and the Guyanese airstrip at Apoteri, from which Operation Climax was launched. (Map by George Anderson)

30 May 1969 – *Mariniers* enter a burning neighbourhood of Willemstad during the 1969 uprising on Curaçao. The political fallout from the military intervention contributed to the decolonisation process speeding up significantly as the Dutch government did not want to get involved in colonial conflicts. (NIMH Collection)

their members. On 30 May 1969, the strikes turned violent calling for an uprising against the government. Arson and looting occurred in the capital Willemstad. The police attempted to halt the protests but failed. The Antilles' government requested the assistance of *Mariniers* to restore order. Within a few days, the situation had calmed down but the deployment was viewed as an example of colonial intervention against the population – especially by the media – and the Dutch government was embarrassed.

These riots and the subsequent intervention of Dutch forces started a discussion in the Netherlands about the charter of 1954. It effectively marked the beginning of the decolonisation process of the Kingdom of the Netherlands. The Dutch government did not want to become involved in local conflicts, especially if the local government requested military aid, as they were bound to supply military forces as stipulated in the charter. Instead, the Netherlands would try to convince their colonies to seek independence.

Back in Suriname, a caretaker cabinet was formed under Prime Minister Arthur May. The newly assigned Minister of Justice and Police, Ramsewak Shankar called Lapré back from the Tigri Area and thanked him for his service. This resulted in the latter resigning. Civil unrest remained in Suriname and the government was concerned that the situation might escalate with elections in October coming closer. With the lessons of Curaçao in mind, where the police got overwhelmed by the protesters, Shankar sought to integrate DEFPOL into the Police Corps. He requested training and material aid from the TRIS without getting them directly involved in any crowd control operations, as the *Mariniers* did in Curaçao.[34]

With the Dutch making it clear that the TRIS would only defend the recognised borders of Suriname and the Surinamese focused on the up-and-coming election, Guyana saw an opportunity to capture the police post at Tigri and to claim the contested area for themselves.[35]

Operation Climax

At the beginning of August 1969, a newspaper supported by Burnham's political opponent, published a story on Surinamese forces present in the New River Triangle which it considered Guyanese territory. Feeling obliged to comply, the prime minister ordered the GDF to remove the Surinamese from the Tigri Area.

Having gained recent experience with the Rupununi uprising,[36] the GDF called upon the GAC to conduct an airborne assault on Camp Tigri. Aerial reconnaissance had seen that the facilities at the camp were expanded with bunkers. The perimeter of the camp was lined with watch towers and the Surinamese were in the process of building a runway with a bulldozer. Up until that point, 1,200ft of runway was completed and blocked off with oil drums, while an extension of 600ft was under construction.[37]

A plan was hatched whereby two DHC-6 Twin Otters (with registrations 8R-GCP and 8R-GDC) would land and deploy 44 soldiers. If any aerial attack were to be successful, the element of surprise was needed and thus the airplanes would land at the crack of dawn and soldiers would storm the camp after landing.[38]

The pilots of the GAC conducted trials with the Twin Otter airplanes over several weeks and showed that these airplanes, when flown properly, would be able to land within 300 ft of airstrip and take off within 300 to 500 feet. Both airplanes' interiors were stripped and the doors were removed. In addition, 8R-GDC (a series 200 Twin Otter with a long nose) had its nose cone removed and holes cut into the bulkhead to allow the seating of a gunner with a machine gun.[39]

On August 18, the assault group moved to Apoteri airfield about 145km to the west of Camp Tigri to position itself before the attack. The next morning, a Helio H-295 Supercourier (registration 8R-GCU) of the GDF performed a pre-dawn, short weather reconnaissance flight to Tigri. After he returned to Aporteri, GAC Capt Jardim jumped into one of two Twin Otters and both set off to the Surinamese camp to arrive from the east as the sun started to rise.

The first aircraft touched down, stopped and unloaded its soldiers who attacked the camp with a two-inch mortar and their Sterling machine guns, while the nose gunner laid down suppressive fire. After the first aircraft taxied to the end of the runway and took off, the second aircraft landed and did the same. Both aircraft unloaded their troops within five minutes and were headed back to Apoteri to get reinforcements.[40]

The Surinamese in the camp, numbering 24 DEFPOL policemen and about 50 construction workers, were awoken by the sound of mortar and gunfire. The GDF forces shot towards the camp forcing the Surinamese to take cover. One worker and a TRIS radio operator, who was on site in civilian clothes to check the DEFPOL radio, had a close escape when the GDF forces threw a hand grenade into the supply tent they were hiding in. The explosion resulted in both getting covered with canned food but otherwise they were unhurt.[41]

After token resistance, all present in the camp fled by boat as soon as they could towards Surinamese territory. Luckily, no one on either side got killed. One DEFPOL policeman, Gerrit van Dams, got captured by GDF forces and was brought to Georgetown. He was released and flown to Zanderij a month later, where he was dropped off unceremoniously.[42]

By the end of the day, about 200 GDF soldiers were flown into Tigri, consolidating their recent gains. The GDF troops found that the camp was well prepared for military purposes with bunkers, a large refrigerator and well-stocked kitchen. Equipment left behind were a bulldozer, a jeep, an electric powerplant, a mechanical water pump and power tools. Tigri was renamed Jaguar by Guyana.[43]

In Suriname, people were outraged at the operation and small demonstrations were held calling for military action. DEFPOL was unable to act against the GDF due to lack of military force. The TRIS would not perform any military operations but maintained its presence at Coeroeni to ensure that the GDF would not cross into undisputed Surinamese territory.

After the election of October 1969, Prime Minister Sedney did not allow DEFPOL to return to the area and sought to de-escalate the situation by exercising restraint. After mediation from Trinidad and Tobago by Prime Minister Williams, both the Prime Ministers – Sedney and Burnham – signed a treaty at Crow's Nest in Chaguaramas in April 1970 that would require demilitarisation of the contested area but did not settle the dispute.

After 1969, incidents between Suriname and Guyana were limited to two brief incidents in November 1981. On 3 November a Guyanese aircraft carrying six soldiers landed at Zanderij without prior authorisation. The following day, GDF forces were claimed to have fired tracers at night in the direction of Suriname forces at the Coeroeni border post. Dutch newspapers claimed that on the Surinamese side, one soldier was killed and two were injured.[44]

The Suriname government denied there were any casualties whilst the Guyanese remained silent on the matter. After student demonstrations at the Guyanese embassy in Paramaribo on 7 and 8 November, Minister Naarendorp spoke with Guyanese diplomats and accused them of arrogant indifference. The situation subsided and there have since been no more incidents.

Guyanese forces have not withdrawn and have remained in the area ever since, with the government in Georgetown claiming any people there are settlers. Thus, Guyana still maintains control of this area at the time of writing, with no intention of relinquishing ownership to Suriname.[45]

Towards Independence

Conscription was reintroduced into Surinamese society in 1970. Up until then, Surinamese volunteers had joined the TRIS. Since most of the volunteers were Creoles, Prime Minister Sedney wanted to balance the ethnic composition of the armed forces so that the composition of the army reflected Surinamese society. The Dutch government supported this initiative as it was foreseen that Suriname would eventually become independent. Therefore, from

Surinamese conscripts participating in a live fire exercise with M1 carbines at BBZ in 1973. The M1 carbine replaced the heavier M1 Garand and was the standard rifle of the Surinamese army until the early 1980s. (NIMH Collection)

1970 onwards, approximately 200 Surinamers joined the ranks of the TRIS every year.

Unfortunately, the draft was not a solution to achieve the desired ethnic ratios. As the Dutch standards of physical fitness were maintained for the draft selection (such as minimum weight and height), many Javanese and Hindustanis were declared unfit for military service resulting in a continued relatively high ratio of Creoles in the army. This would be a cause for concern as independence neared midway through the decade.[46]

The fall of the Pengel government and the elections of October 1969 did not end the civil unrest in Suriname. Although there had been no large outbreaks of riots, public discontent about the high unemployment rate and the growing power of the trade unions, resulted in more protests and strikes. Within parliament, opposition against the government grew as well.

In the beginning of 1973, the situation escalated and when demonstrations and protests led to the destruction of civil property, the police responded harshly resulting in the arrests of journalists, demonstrators, union leaders and the death of a protester by police bullets. The TRIS did not have to be deployed to quell the unrest but did supply the police force with teargas grenades.[47]

After Johan Pengel passed away in 1970, Henck Arron became the new leader of the NPS and declared that he would seek independence from the Netherlands within five years. Together with the pro-independence PNR, the NPS won the 1973 elections in a political alliance (the NPK) with other parties (such as the Javanese Pendawa Lima) which for the first time, excluded the Hindustanis from the government. Soon after forming a cabinet, Arron declared in February 1974 that the country would be independent before the end of 1975, much to the dismay of the opposition who were shocked at the declaration as it was not part of the NPK election programme.[48]

On the other side of the Atlantic, the Dutch elections of 1973 resulted in the formation of a left-wing government under the leadership of Prime Minister Joop den Uyl. During the election campaign, the governing parties had already announced they would support Surinamese independence and thus Arron's declaration was happily received in The Hague The first rounds of talks between the governments started in May of 1974.[49]

Due to civilian unrest in Paramaribo in 1973 and the threat of more riots in the 1974 and 1975, the TRIS practised crowd control tactics at BBZ on a regular basis with the support of YP408s. YP408 KN 75-28 can be seen at the top of this picture. (NIMH Collection)

The main reason the Netherlands supported independence was that after the Curaçao unrest and Guyana border dispute of 1969, the Netherlands was afraid that it would be forced to get involved in local conflicts and be seen as a colonial aggressor. At the time, Portugal was involved in several wars in Africa (including Angola and Mozambique) and the Netherlands did not want to run the risk of getting involved in a similar conflict.[50]

In addition, immigration of Surinamers to the Netherlands had been steadily on the rise as the newcomers sought to find employment.[51] The Netherlands saw the influx of Surinamers in the late 1960s and early '70s as a drain on their economy, as more people (especially the ones that had a lower education and trouble finding employment) received unemployment benefits during the economic crisis that hit Europe in the early 1970s. Since Surinamers were equally entitled to benefits under the

A platoon of soldiers, armed with bayonet-equipped M1 carbines, undergo a crowd control exercise at Zanderij. They are supported by two barrier-equipped YP408s. (Dick Bloemendaal)

Dutch welfare state, Surinamese independence was also seen as an opportunity to limit Surinamese immigration.[52]

Negotiations

The two governments conducted a series of negotiations on several issues including the constitution, citizens' rights, development aid and defence. It was eventually agreed that Suriname would receive independence from the Netherlands on 25 November 1975 if the parliaments of both countries approved.

Negotiations for Dutch aid would continue until June 1975 when it was agreed that upon independence, Suriname would receive a three-and-half billion Dutch guilders development aid package (nearly five billion euros in 2022 currency) that was to be issued in the next 10 to 15 years. This package was intended to support the local economy and the allocation of funds would be decided by a joint Surinamese-Dutch commission. In addition, it was agreed that Surinamers living in the Netherlands would be able to receive Dutch citizenship if they chose to. Surinamers could freely migrate to the Netherlands until 1980, after which they would have to apply for visas for permanent residence.

Seeing what happened in neighbouring Guyana in the previous decade, many people feared that independence would bring ethnic violence between the Creoles and the Hindustanis. As a result, many Surinamers left the country to emigrate to the Netherlands. Immigration went up and in 1975 alone 40,000 Surinamers left the country.[53] In addition, demonstrations were held against independence resulting in several cases of arson, destruction of property and small riots between Hindustanis and Creoles. Emotions ran high as a lot of Surinamers felt the country was not ready for independence and that the time to prepare for full independence was too short.

The Surinamese parliament voted to accept the new constitution on 19 November, six days before planned independence from the Netherlands. The NPK barely won the vote by 20 to 19, with one of the VHP opposition members voting in favour as he was worried a civil war might break out. After the vote, VHP leader Lachmon conceded defeat and accepted that Suriname independence was now inevitable.[54]

From TRIS to *Surinaamse Krijgsmacht*

During negotiations with the Dutch government, Arron made it clear that he wanted the new Republic of Suriname to have its own army. This suited the Dutch government very well as it would end the need for the TRIS to remain in Suriname, clearing the Dutch government of any requirement to get involved in any conflicts that could arise in the new state.[55]

In September 1974, the final decision was made that the Dutch soldiers of the TRIS would leave Suriname on Independence Day and hand over all equipment and facilities to the SKM. With only 15 months left to go until 25 November 1975, more Surinamese conscripts were to be trained in preparation for transitioning them to the new army. Called the *Surinaamse Krijgsmacht* (SKM), the

A sign hanging in front of the Ministry of Domestic Affairs reminds Surinamers how many days until independence. (Collection Nationaal Archief/Anefo, Bert Verhoeff)

Opposition Leader Lachmon and Prime Minister Arron presenting the new Surinamese flag on 24 November 1975. Lachmon had been opposed to Surinamese independence up until the very end but conceded defeat when a new Surinamese constitution was accepted by parliament. (Collection Nationaal Archief/Anefo, Bert Verhoeff)

The DAF YP408 With The SKM[58]

Designed in the late 1950s, the YP408 was an eight-wheeled armoured personnel carrier that was the standard wheeled APC of mechanised infantry battalions of the KL until 1989. Built and designed by the DAF vehicle manufacturer in Eindhoven, the vehicle was powered by a diesel engine that drove six of the eight wheels (the second set of driving wheels was not powered) and could carry 10 soldiers, along with a driver and a gunner. The latter sat out of a hatch on top of the vehicle and manned a machine gun.

In early 1972, the KL shipped five YP408s to the TRIS to replace the ageing Otter scout cars. As far as can be determined, four of these were the standard PWI-S GR version and the fifth being the PWI-S PC version.[59] The latter is the platoon commander's variant, which was equipped with an additional radio and a periscope/observation device. Night fighting equipment and equipment for recoilless rifles and anti-tank missiles (standard on vehicles based in the Netherlands) were removed.

Table 6: YP408 Specifications	
Engine:	DAF DS-575 6-cylinder 165HP Diesel Engine
Length:	6.23m
Width:	2.40m
Height:	2.35m (including HMG support)
Road Range:	500km
Weight:	10,000kg (empty), 13,000kg (max loaded)
Speed:	82km/hr road speed
Armament (in TRIS/SKM Service):	1x .303 (7.7mm) Bren Gun or .50 (12.7mm) Browning M2HB HMG with 100 rounds per belt 6x smoke canisters

YP408 KN 75-32 equipped with a barbed wire barrier for crowd control. (Han van Amersfoort via DAF YP408 website)

TRIS YP408s were sometimes equipped with a 7.7mm Bren LMG, probably taken from the GMC Otters. This YP408 is also taking part in a crowd control exercise. (Han van Amersfoort via DAF YP408 website)

Surinamese army would be reorganised to form four companies with three platoons each. In addition, the structure of the armed forced would accommodate a naval section and an air component.[56]

Table 5: The organisation of the SKM as planned in 1975

Name	English translation	Units
Surinaamse Krijgsmacht		
Personnel: Approximately 877 (including civilians)		
Commander: Colonel Y.D.F. Elstak		
Commando & diensten	Command & Services	Personnel Service, incl. Military Band Military Police Training Centre Maintenance Centre Medical Centre (incl. Military hospital)
SSV-Cie	Command & Medical Coy	Battalion staff Medical platoon Support platoon Company staff
A-Cie	Alpha (Infantry) Coy	1 Staff section 3 Infantry platoons
B-Cie	Bravo (Infantry) Coy	1 Staff section 3 Infantry platoons
C-Cie	Charlie (Infantry) Coy	1 Staff section 3 Infantry platoons
D-Cie	Delta (Infantry) Coy	1 Staff section 3 Infantry platoons
Boot eenheid	Boat Unit	Transport and patrol boats
Helikopter eenheid	Helicopter Unit	Planned helicopter unit

As most facilities were in poor shape, renovations were made to the military facilities at Paramaribo, Albina, Nieuw Nickerie and Zanderij. The facilities at Brownsweg on the other hand would be closed. In addition, all vehicles would be repaired and serviced to allow a minimum availability rate of 80 percent.[57]

Most of the equipment that was given to the SKM was not state-of-the-art and was relatively old. An exception being the five YP408 APCs that were sent to the TRIS as a replacement for the ageing GMC Otter scout cars.

In addition to the TRIS materiel, the Surinamese government requested that the Netherlands would also pay for and supply the SKM with patrol boats and helicopters. In the end, 10 patrol boats were ordered for use by the SKM and paid for by the Netherlands with deliveries to be completed after independence.

On top of the withdrawal of men and transfer of equipment and infrastructure, the Dutch ministry of foreign affairs also set-up a military mission for four years. Its goal was to assist in technical matters and advise the SKM on its formation and growth. The mission consisted of five Dutch officers and NCOs and two local support staff members, led by Colonel Hans Valk. Valk was a veteran of the TRIS and an Infantry officer and would also serve on the Dutch embassy staff as the military attaché (DEFAT).[60]

As 500 conscripts were drafted into the SKM in 1975, it was realised there would be a serious shortage of staff personnel for SKM. The SKM was planned to consist of 29 officers, 136 NCOs, 520

Surinamese and Dutch conscripts stand at attention in April 1975. In the last year before independence, the TRIS trained Surinamese conscripts so that they could fill the ranks of the new Surinamese Armed Forces (SKM). (Collection Nationaal Archief/Anefo, Bert Verhoeff)

enlisted men and 194 civilian support staff, about 250 less personnel than the TRIS.[61]

On one hand, the TRIS would help to decrease the shortage in professional staff by training Surinamese soldiers that were considered qualified for the position of NCO. On the other hand, the Netherlands would continue to train NCOs and officers in Dutch military institutions such as the KMA, KMS and OCOSD after independence for another 10 years,[62] thus ensuring the SKM would have a steady influx of professional military personnel.

In order to alleviate the manpower deficiency on short notice, Surinamese officers and NCOs in service with the Dutch military, were offered a transfer to Suriname to build-up the armed service of the new nation. The offer included a monthly pay supplementation that would ensure the personnel would not lose any salary when going into SKM service. About 40 Surinamers would make use of this arrangement, including sports instructor Desiré Delano Bouterse and *marinier* Arty Gorré. These men were mostly driven by idealism and the outlook of continued career growth.[63]

Even though conscription brought in young Surinamese men from all backgrounds, the Surinamese platoons within the TRIS still consisted mainly of soldiers of Creole descent (about half). Only a quarter of the draftees were Hindustanis. This ethic ratio was the same for the NCOs – an example being the March 1975 group that underwent NCO training consisted of 14 Creoles, five Hindustanis and two Javanese. Thus, the new SKM was considered a largely Creole force by Independence Day.[64]

During the transition to the SKM, the TRIS was split into Dutch and Surinamese sections, the latter being led by Lieutenant Colonel Y.D.F. Elstak. After joining the military in 1946, Elstak was the most senior Surinamese officer with experience in personnel administration. This made him the most likely candidate to become the new commander-in-chief of the fledgling Surinamese Armed Forces. Elstak was assigned to be the head of conversions and was promoted to colonel in early 1975.[65]

However, the cooperation between the COTRIS and Elstak was not smooth, mostly being for the latter's demands for future funding of his potential army and the differences in approach to leadership (as will be described later). After a long period of uncertainty, Elstak decided that on Independence Day, he would accept the post of commander of the SKM despite being absent during the state banquet the previous evening as he was packing up his belongings. Thus, Suriname had its first own commander-in-chief, although his relationship with the men serving him would always be very strained.

As Independence Day came closer, the TRIS conducted plenty of anti-riot training in the last months before independence. Armed with rattan shields, visors and sticks, platoons practised crowd control tactics under the support of the YP408s that had barbed wire screens installed on them. Despite being well prepared for any civil unrests, the TRIS did not have to respond.

When the clock struck 12.00 at midnight on 25 November 1975, Suriname became independent ending 300 years of Dutch colonial rule. Governor Ferrier became the first president of the new nation replacing Queen Juliana as head of state. The last Dutch-manned TRIS company flew out the same day from Zanderij Airport, leaving the SKM to protect and to serve the new Republic of Suriname. However, in the following years, Suriname would be more dependent on the Netherlands than ever before.

Independence Day in Suriname, high-ranking officials watch the Dutch flag being lowered and the new Suriname flag being raised. From left to right: Prime Minister Henck Arron, Crown Princess Beatrix of the Netherlands and a saluting Johan Ferrier, the last governor and the first president of Suriname. (Collection Nationaal Archief/Anefo, Bert Verhoeff)

4

THE *SERGEANTENCOUP*

The elation of 'Suriname *fri* (free)' after independence soon gave way to a feeling of mistrust of the government and depression. The government had promised new elections within eight months of independence but these were delayed until October of 1977. By then, the NPK was tainted with several corruption scandals that involved ministers taking bribes for land distribution and overtime.[1]

After the NPK (with the NPS, KTPI and two other parties) won the election by a small margin, it seemed that Arron would continue to press on with policies without interference from his main political rivals of the VHP. However, by then, the *Parlement van Republiek Suriname* (as the *Staten van Suriname* was renamed after independence) was deadlocked as two members of the KTPI had left to go over to the opposition and one member of the NPS died in office in May 1979.[2]

As the opposition hindered the approval of a replacement for the deceased member of parliament, the seats were divided 19 v 19 between the government and the opposition, making it impossible for the NPK government to implement measures and changes. This led to many heated, chaotic debates in which neither side was willing to give an inch. Combined with the corruption and nepotism in the government, it led to the parliament being regularly called *circus stupido* amongst many Surinamers, especially since it was an ineffective institution.[3] As it was impossible to govern with

The new coat of arms of the Republic of Suriname. Two Amerindians flank a shield which has a trade ship, a palm tree, a diamond and a five pointed star – referring to the colonial past and current trade, the rainforest and agriculture, the mining industry and the five ethnic groups respectively. (Public Domain)

The Surinamese parliament on 1 April 1975. During the first years of independence, the Surinamese population lost faith in their parliament as it was tainted by scandals and deadlocked in making any decisions, leading it to be nicknamed *Circus Stupido*. (Collection Nationaal Archief, Anefo, Bert Verhoeff)

a deadlock in parliament, Arron announced new elections. These were to be held in March 1980.

Even though Suriname did receive a significant amount of money from aid and bauxite levies, many lower and middle-class Surinamers did not profit from the financial influx leaving them with a feeling of despair. As a result, Surinamers immigrated to the Netherlands en masse in search of a better future. Immigration peaked especially in 1979 and 1980, just before the five-year term ended whereby Surinamers could freely immigrate to the Netherlands. From 1976 to 1980, approximately 55,000 Surinamers left, resulting in the population of Suriname shrinking from about 380,000 in 1975 to 355,000 in 1980.[4] By then about 200,000 Surinamers were living in the Netherlands, which was 30 percent of the Surinamese population worldwide.

Development Aid[5]

Immediately after independence, the distribution of development aid promised by the Netherlands did not go as smoothly as hoped. The Dutch members of the commission who oversaw the distribution of develop aid, disagreed with the plans proposed by the Surinamese government. Part of the issue was that the aid package came with several political strings attached.

All aid received from the Netherlands was to be approved by the Dutch government. It had been agreed the money would be spent on improvements in production (50 percent), infrastructure (25 percent) and social-educational projects (25 percent). The Surinamese government wanted to invest a larger portion into improving productivity, in part because they were financially involved with the local industry that benefitted this aid.

The agreement also stipulated that Suriname would commit itself to spending the aid money on Dutch products and services. These were often more expensive than products that could be purchased in markets in the region. As a result, about 80 percent of the aid received by Suriname went back to Dutch businesses, tax-free. To make matters worse, the value of the package was set in a fixed monetary value which meant that it was not corrected for inflation.

By 1979 it had lost about 20 percent of its monetary value.

When the Dutch cabinet fell under Den Uyl in 1977, it was replaced by one under Prime Minister Van Agt which was not as emotionally involved in the deal and was more business-like when conducting negotiations. Up to that point, projects requested by the Surinamese government had been approved (in part) due to the fear of being accused of maintaining 'colonial policies'. Tough negotiations between both countries followed with a low point being when the Surinamese delegation walked out of a commission meeting. The Dutch Minister of Development did offer in 1979, to add 700 million Nfl to the aid package to compensate for inflation but only if the rules of the agreement were strictly followed. Negotiations had already halted when the events of February 1980 took place.

Up to that point, Suriname had received 580 million Sfl (1,190 million euros in 2022) of development aid. About 60 percent of this was spent on large industrial projects – most prominently the earlier mentioned West Suriname Plan which sought to achieve the mining and processing of aluminium ore in the underdeveloped western side of the country. The construction of a new port and expansion of the city of Apoera was started whilst a railway was built from Apoera to the Bakhuis Mountains. The previously planned aluminium mines and processing plant were never buiLieutenant This was due to dropping aluminium prices so the entire undertaking was found unfeasible and thus the mining company that was assigned the mineral rights, backed out.

By the beginning of 1980 Suriname had spent about 170 million Sfl (350 million euros in 2022) in development aid on a 'railroad that started at nothing and led to nowhere', a half-built port and a construction of a suburb that turned into a ghost town. Most of this money ended up with foreign companies (often Dutch) and companies run by friends of the political elite. In contrast, small scale economic projects did not develop as it was very difficult for businesses to start up due to bureaucratic inefficiency and corruption. The West Suriname Plan was eventually shelved in 1981 by which time it was clear it would not be profitable considering the prices of bauxite and oil at the time.

People who were well-connected tried to get employment with the growing civil service. By 1979, the number of civil servants had grown from 32,700 at independence, to 39,600. This meant that nearly 40 percent of the Surinamese workforce was employed by the government.[6] Thus, most of the state income from taxes and levies was used to pay employees of the civil service.

The mass immigration of Surinamers to the Netherlands also led to a chronic shortage of well-trained workers for the labour market since many people who were in the financial position to do so, purchased their family a one-way ticket to Amsterdam and left Suriname – many of them permanently. Although Suriname had one of the highest GNP per capita in the region, one-third of the Surinamers lived in poverty.[7]

Military Developments

In the weeks following independence, Colonel Elstak decided to rename the former TRIS barracks in Suriname. The barracks in Paramaribo were renamed the *Memre Boekoe Kazerne* (Boekoe Memorial Barracks – see Chapter 2), the installation in Albina was renamed the *Akontoe Valenti kampement* and the barracks at Nieuw Nickerie received the name *Dr. R. Ali kampement*.

During 1975, the SKM started to receive patrol boats previously ordered in the Netherlands. By the end of 1978, all were delivered, making the naval branch of the SKM the most modernly equipped (see box). As all these

As part of the ambitious West Suriname Plan, a railway was built between the Bakhuys Mountains and the town of Apoera and paid for by Dutch development aid. As the port and mines on both ends were never completed, the railway turned out to be a track from 'nothing to nowhere'. It was seen as the most glaring example of the misspending of the Arron governments. (Suralco Magazine)

vessels were unarmed, the Surinamese government purchased seven 40mm guns from the Swedish armaments firm Bofors which were to be installed on the S-class patrol boats before the end of 1979. Five members of the SKM received their training abroad on how to operate the weapons and handle the ammunition.[8] The Bofors cannons would be a significant weapon in the coming years.

In the meantime, *Kolonel* Elstak sought to develop 'his' SKM into a development army where the army would maintain order, patrol the coast and assist in civil construction projects. This unfortunately clashed with what Arron had requested from the Dutch – an army solely focused on defence.

After independence, the SKM was largely ignored by the government. Seen as a money drain, the SKM was not funded sufficiently to expand according to Elstak's plans and the defence budget was cut from 25 million Sfl before independence, to 12 million Sfl. Although the naval arm received new equipment, no helicopters or aircraft were ordered for the planned air arm. Most of the SKM had to soldier-on with the materiel passed on from the TRIS. In addition, there was no clear mission statement written for the military and the organisation was not fully staffed.

Elstak also clashed with the government on several occasions. At the conclusion of a cabinet meeting in 1976, Elstak was asked by Arron if he had something to add. His response, 'Yes. I was just looking at my watch, wondering if I shall seize power either this afternoon or the coming Monday'. Met with silence, it was clear that his sense of humour was not appreciated, alienating him further from the government.[14]

Elstak's archaic approach to discipline rubbed a lot of Surinamese soldiers the wrong way, especially the ones who had seen service with the KL in the Netherlands. In a time when the Dutch military personnel was known as the 'hippy army' amongst NATO members (with the typical long hair associated with the 1970s fashion and relaxed military discipline), Elstak instilled strict military dress code, obligatory salutation duties, drills and hair grooming discipline amongst the Surinamese platoons in the TRIS. He sought to make

Kolonel Yngwe Elstak, seen holding the SKM standard on Independence Day, was the first commander of the Surinamese Armed Forces. He proved to be unpopular with his men and would not accept the formation of a trade union for the NCOs. (Collection Nationaal Archief/Anefo, Bert Verhoeff)

the SKM an army along the lines of local armies and those of former British colonies. Elstak developed into an authoritarian commander, who expected to be asked 'how high' when he said 'jump'.[15]

Frustration arose over the sad state and lack of operational equipment, seemingly useless deployments to isolated posts in the jungle and the lack of clear purpose. In addition, the ex-KL personnel who had returned from Europe were also disappointed to find that many of them were passed over for promotion in favour

Surinamese Patrol Boats[9]

During the first few years of independence, Suriname received new patrol boats to be used for river, coastal and high seas patrols (tasks normally done by the TRIS and Royal Dutch Navy). All were built in the Netherlands and were unarmed upon completion.

Port Patrol Boat
A small wooden harbour patrol boat (10 tons displacement, 10m long, 14kts max speed) was delivered by the Schottel Shipyard in Warmond in 1975.

River Patrol Boats
These small boats (named RP201 *Bahadoer*, RP202 *Fajablow* and RP203 *Karangon*) were used for patrolling the various waterways in Suriname. Built by the Schottel Shipyards in Warmond, these small craft could accommodate a crew of four. All were delivered in 1975.

High Seas Patrol Boats
Built by De Vlijt Shipyards in Alsmeer, these boats (named S401, S402 and S403) were built from steel with an aluminium superstructure. These boats were equipped to accommodate a crew of 15 and were also delivered with a Decca 110 radar installed. In 1978, these vessels were armed with two SAK-40/L-70-315 40mm cannons often referred to as 'Bofors'.[11] Their main task was to patrol and enforce a 200-mile exclusion zone against illegal fishery. These boats were delivered to Suriname in 1976 and 1977. Each boat cost 8.2 million Nfl (12.1 million euros in 2022) without armament (as it was up to the Surinamese government to arm these boats) but was paid for with development aid money.[12]

S403 was the last of the high seas patrol boats paid for the Dutch government and was delivered to Suriname in 1977. It was equipped with two 40mm Bofors guns which were among the most powerful weapons in the Surinamese Armed Forces. (Surinamese Government)

River patrol boat RP203. Three of these boats were built in the Netherlands and delivered in 1975. (Surinamese Government)

Coastal Patrol Boats
The Coast Patrol boats (named C301, C302 and C303) built by the Schottel Shipyards in Warmond, were a bit larger and were meant to patrol the Surinamese coast. These were equipped with a Decca 110 maritime radar, echo sounder and air conditioning. These were delivered in 1976 and cost 1.8 million Nfl (2.65 million euros in 2022) each.[10]

Table 7: Surinamese Patrol Boat Specifications			
	RP-class	C-class	S-class
Displacement	15 tons	65 tons	127 tons
Length	12.6m	22.45m	32.0m
Width	3.8m	4.7m	6.5m
Draft	1.1m	N/A	1.7m
Max Speed	14kts	13.5kts	20kts
Engine(s)	1x 280HP Dorman 8JT diesel	2x 280HP Dorman 8JT diesel	2x 1,020HP Paxman 12YHCM diesel
Range	350km @ 10kts	650km @ 13.5kts	1,200km @ 13,5kts
Crew	4	8	15
Weapons	1x .50 HMG	1x .50 HMG 2x .303 LMG	2x 40mm Bofors cannons 2x .303 LMG

Coastal patrol boat C301, the first of three boats that were built in the Netherlands and delivered in 1976. They would be used for coastal patrols to prevent illegal fishing within coastal waters. (Surinamese Government)

In addition to these 10 patrol boats, the SKM also inherited the two old CL troop transports, the TRIS commander's yacht and about 40 *korjalen* from the TRIS.[13]

S401 during trails in the Netherlands. The Dutch government donated these boats to Suriname but without any weapons. It was up to the Surinamese government to arm these boats themselves. (Huib de Vries)

of Surinamers who were trained locally and were sent off to follow training courses in the Netherlands.[16]

As per experience in the KL, several members of the SKM formed a trade union to represent the interest of the military cadre. Called the *Bond Militair Kader* (Union of Military Staff – abbreviated Bomika), the council attempted to discuss their concerns with their commander-in-chief but their concerns were not taken seriously. Elstak, after being invited to meet the NCOs in their mess hall to hear their concerns, showed up at the meeting, held a speech and to the surprise of the troops made a handstand on the table. While standing upside-down, the colonel said in an archetypical Dutch accent: 'If you guys didn't have me …'.[17] Besides being out of touch with his men, Elstrak did not get along also with the members of the Dutch Military Mission.

The Dutch Military Mission in Suriname (NMMS) had arrived in the country before independence. Originally planned to consist of about 20 men, it was downsized to a team of seven. Besides *Kolonel* Valk, other leading officers were captains Briaire and Clements who were technical and administrative officers respectively, available to assist the SKM with its development. Former TRIS officer, Piet van Dijk, was assigned to train up members of the Surinamese military police. Some Dutch officers were assigned to support the SKM as well but were not part of the NMMS, one example being *Kolonel* Rochus de Jong who was working directly for the technical service of the SKM.

Hans Valk was not Suriname's first choice for leading the NMMS. Instead, the Surinamese Minister of Army and Police had preferred other former TRIS officers such as Maarseveen (who would come to Suriname in 1980) or De Jong. As the Dutch has assigned Valk as head of the NMMS and would not consider assigning the position to someone else, the relationship between the NMMS and SKM was strained. As Valk and Elstak did not get along as well,[18] the military mission was not able to start work until half a year after independence because it was not accredited by the Suriname government until then.[19]

If Elstak drove his troops away from him, they found a listening ear with the Dutch military mission. Most of the mission members had served with the TRIS previously and were accustomed to the way things were run in Suriname. The cadre members of the SKM could find sympathy and understanding with the NMMS. On top of this, Valk never hid his contempt for Elstak and even spoke out in public against him. The role of the NMMS would be the source of many accusations following the events of February 1980.[20]

Tense Times

As time went by, the discontent within the ranks grew. In January 1979, about 90 members of Bomika arranged a sit-in under the Mamabon in front of the parliament building demanding that the government fulfilled its promise to enlist the 55 volunteers serving at the Beekbergen naval base.[21] In addition, they demanded recognition of Bomika as a trade union. The members of the public took notice of the demonstrations. In order to defuse the situation, the government established a commission to investigate the problems within the SKM.

The Abendanon Report (named after the chairman of the commission) was completed by September 1979 and submitted to the government. Much to the frustration of the members of Bomika, Arron had the report shelved and refused to make its contents public. Not even the commanding officers of the SKM were allowed to read the report. Calls to publish the report were swept aside under the pretence that the problems had nothing to do with the formation of a trade union.[22] The Arron government thus refused to recognise Bomika. On 15 January 1980, members of Bomika occupied the NCO mess hall of the barracks and went on strike.

On January 25, the council of Bomika sent out a telegram to the prime minister stating that the military cadre had lost all trust in Commander-in-Chief Colonel Elstak and Battalion Commander Lieutenant Colonel Essed, accusing them of instigating actions against the government on the eve of the elections and demanded their dismissal. Arron responded by sending the council members an individual reply (thereby confirming that he did not recognise the union) and demanded that they produce evidence for the accusations before 28 January. When the council members refused to reply (as they had been addressed individually), Arron consulted with his secretary of defence and the military attorney general and acted swiftly.

On 30 January, the *Memre Boekoe Kazerne* (MBK) were closed off and the NCO mess was barricaded, denying entry to all military personnel on the premise that they were not dressed according to regulations. Despite this, the 150 military personnel on strike managed to break through and enter the barracks' mess. When SKM officers were ordered to use armed force against the NCOs should the situation arise, the commander of Alpha Company, Lieutenant. Michel Van Rey ripped the stars off his epaulettes and threw them onto the floor of the officers' mess. Disgusted with the order to fire on his brothers-in-arms, Van Rey left and joined the NCOs on strike, the only SKM officer to support the Bomika members openly.[23]

The same afternoon, the prime minister held a press conference in which he declared that the Bomika council members had not responded to the telegram in a timely fashion and that they were relieved of their duties. In addition, Arron also announced that the government would not recognise a trade union for the military, in the traditional sense.

Right after the press conference, Bomika chairman Sital and Vice-Chairman Neede were arrested by the military police. The police and military police locked down the barracks and summoned the soldiers to leave, being ordered to open fire if the men refused. Seeing no alternative, the troops left the barracks and assembled across the gate on the other side of the road, singing the national anthem.

A stand-off ensued during which the police ordered the soldiers to leave. The soldiers refused to do so, demanding that Neede and Sital should first be released. The police were about to open fire upon

In January of 1979, about 90 NCOs of Bomika had a sit-in protest in front of the Surinamese parliament building. The protest received widespread public support. (Revokrant)

the unarmed soldiers when politicians Herrenberg and Kamperveen stood in the middle of the road between the two groups.

After a tense few minutes, the two men managed to convince the soldiers to leave and gather at the Steeply sports stadium (run by Kamperveen) to spend the night there. Chief of Police Jimmy Walker arrived on the scene and scolded his men for not opening fire on the soldiers – something they took note of and which later proved to be a major source of resentment. When MP (and Bomika council member) Abrahams arrived at the gate to hand in his service weapon, he was also apprehended by the police. The other Bomika council members – Braaf, De Rhamdhanie, Horb and Mijnals – managed to evade the police and went into hiding.[24]

The NCOs on strike left the *Memre Boekoe Kazerne* for the stadium before settling in the ABO building in the city. There, the 200 soldiers spent most of the month of February exercising, marching and washing their cars, unsure of what was going to happen next. The building, dubbed Fort Bomika, received visits from trade unions leaders (including those from the police), politicians and ordinary citizens expressing their support and bringing food and drinks. In the meantime, the Bomika members waited for the day of the trial of Sital, Neede and Abrahams to arrive.

Coup Plotting[25]

The situation in Paramaribo was very tense. There had been plenty of demonstrations in the city with people complaining about the poor and intermittent supply of clean water, the rise of crime, poorly maintained roads and the inadequate sanitation services with rubbish piling up on the streets. With a government seemingly unwilling to take any affirmative action until after elections were held in March, several groups of NCOs and officers started putting a plan together to change the situation.

One group within the SKM that planned to dispose of the government was formed at the BBZ training detachment at Zanderij. Lieutenant Surendre Rambocus and three other officers were sympathetic to the plight of Bomika.[26] Together with their current class of recruits, they planned to take over the army and government on the 1st of July 1980. As the group was lacking NCOs, Rambocus approached the lead NCO in charge, Master Sergeant Desi Bouterse, in order to join them. Bouterse, however, was part of a different group of conspirators as well.

A second conspiracy consisted of (ex-) Bomika council members and included sergeants Mijnals, Sital, Neede, Horb and Bouterse. Several of these sergeants were aligned with the communist

Lieutenant Rambocus was the head of the training facilities at the BBZ. He was at the head of one of the groups within the SKM that were planning to stage a coup. (STVS)

Volkspartij (Peoples Party) led by politician Ruben Lie Pau Sam who was informed of their plan but did not support a military takeover, as he was convinced his party would win the up-and-coming elections in March. Thus, the group planned to come into action if the results of the election were not in their favour and the timing depending on who would win.[27]

Although there were several discussions between the Zanderij and the Bomika group of conspirators, no cooperation between both groups came to fruition. As a matter-of-fact, Bouterse even persuaded Rambocus not to act when the latter tried to expedite his plan before a third group could execute their coup d'état.[28] By February, three of the five members were in jail and the remainder in hiding and thus the plans of this group were not executed.

Bouterse was also a member of a third group. This group, consisting of 16 NCOs, had planned to take over the munitions depot, MBK and the naval base, thus taking control of the country. Later, it was claimed that the plan was to originally take place in late 1979, having been postponed several times due to various reasons. However, by now, the NCOs were ready to put the plan into motion soon. This 'Group of Sixteen' (see Appendix III) would be the one executed in what was later to be known as the *Sergeantencoup*. Chas Mijnals would later claim that Bouterse had taken his plan and executed it, without any plan on how to govern the country after the coup.[29] As Bouterse and Horb did not get any political support of plans beforehand, they decided to take care of that issue once the coup d'état was a fait accompli.

On February 20, the court-martial of the three jailed Bomika council members was held in the district courtroom. The situation was tense as the police were facing off with the Bomika members, both standing in lines across of each other with the backs of the police facing the courtroom building. At the nearby *Onafhankelijkheidsplein* (Square of Independence), 1,000 civil servants had gathered in support of the soldiers.

Abrahams, Neede and Sital were all charged with insubordination. After a trial which lasted several hours, the three accused men heard the attorney general demand a sentence of 10 months against them, followed by discharge from the SKM. The sentencing would take place on the morning of February 26.[30] The 'Group of Sixteen', recognising the urgency of the situation and fed by rumours that Bomika members would be dismissed by the government after the court-martial was over, decided to act on the night of February 22.[31]

Failed Attempt

After meeting at Sergeant Mahadew's house, the group swore allegiance to each other and Sergeant Gorré read a passage from the Bible regarding David and Goliath. Armed with only six shotguns and air rifles, the men set off to capture the ammunition bunker at the Doekhiweg, located near the local airport of Zorg en Hoop.[32]

Eight of the NCOs parked their cars close to the munitions bunker and proceeded to approach the facility on foot, cutting through the wire fence and crawling through the high grass.[33] Unfortunately, watchdogs detected the men and alerted the guards. Three of the men were spotted and Sergeant Hardjoprajitno was recognised. Calling the operation off, the would-be coup plotters snuck away undetected.[34]

Amazingly, despite the tense situation in Paramaribo and the aborted assault on the bunker, no general alarm was raised. Lieutenant Rob Behr, the officer in charge of the munitions bunker, had reported the incident to his superiors remarking that it could be part of a coup d'état. He was not taken seriously – at least not to his face.[35]

Despite what Lieutenant Behr was told, the conspirators received an intercepted message from Battalion Commander Essed, that the security at the bunker was to be increased from two to 10 guards and searchlights were to be set-up at both the bunker and the Memre Boekoe Kazerne. Thus, it would be impossible for the poorly armed men to capture the bunker.[36]

The government and military remained relatively relaxed. Sergeant Hardjoprajitno went into hiding at his brother's house in Lelydorp and was arrested on February 24. He was locked up in the MP stockade in Fort Zeelandia. Despite continued house searches for the Bomika council members, none of the other conspirators were arrested in the coming days.[37]

As Hardjoprajitno knew the full extent of the plot, the NCOs decided to execute their plan as soon as possible after making a few revisions. As the bunker was now fully guarded, the group would capture the naval base first, followed by the MBK, the munitions bunker and police headquarters. The naval base would be attacked by the entire group, after which seven men would go and silently capture the barracks. The navy patrol boats would be used to provide cover fire, whereas YPs from the barracks would be used to attack the munitions bunker and the police headquarters.

25 February 1980

Late in the evening of 24 February 1980, the 15 NCOs gathered their weapons and again swore allegiance. In addition, they also promised to take care of each other's families in case one of them fell in action.

The 15 men set off in cars to Beekbergen, arriving near midnight and parking close to the base. They entered the complex from the rear as the front was barricaded and guarded. Crawling slowly through the grass and under the wire fence, the men managed to get close. Having learnt from their previous experience, they distracted the guard dogs with large chunks of meat.[38] Surprising the guard, Bouterse (in his own words) put a gun to his face and took his helmet. The other members of the group sprang into action and overpowered the six men on duty. By 0200 hours the base was captured.

After the guards were locked away, Horb and Zeeuw left to go to Fort Bomika to pick up selected servicemen that would help with arming the boats and guarding the base. In the meantime, the group captured pistols, carbines and a .50 machine gun. As per plan, the seven men loaded a pickup truck and left to capture the MBK.

As the men from Bomika arrived, boats were prepared for action and their guns were mounted. After finding some of the boats to be out of order, S402 was mounted with Bofors cannons. Group members Brondenstein, Gefferie and Tolud, together with seven other soldiers, got aboard, cast off lines and set course for the waterfront of Paramaribo where the police headquarters were located.

Memre Boekoe[39]

The seven men charged with attacking the barracks were able to cut their way through the wire fence and force their way into the compound. This time, there were no dogs to alert the guards. The officer on duty, Lieutenant Van Aalst, was spotted sitting in the guard house.

The high seas patrol boats moored at the naval base at Beekbergen. During the *Sergeantencoup*, the conspirators sailed off with S402 to the police headquarters on the waterfront of Paramaribo. (Lucien Chien a Foeng)

The team decided to approach the guardhouse from two directions and in two groups. The team that approached Van Aalst from the front, was spotted. The lieutenant did not hesitate and pulled his sidearm, firing several rounds in quick succession. Bhagwandas, who had approached the watch commander from behind, saw Van Aalst take his comrades under fire and shot him, killing the lieutenant. He was the first deadly casualty that morning. Sadly, more were to follow.

The gunfight alerted the other guards, who panicked. The NCOs were able to subdue these men but the noise caused local residents to call the police who promptly sent patrol cars to the MBK. An MP approached the main gate and was fired upon which caused the officer to abandon his car and flee on foot. The .50 machine gun was set up across the main gate in case reinforcements came. They did not have to wait long before they were approached by another vehicle.

A Volkswagen police bus, driven by police officers Freddy de Mees, Mohamed Ramdjan Soeltan and Roy Jones, was dispatched to investigate reported shootings at the MBK. Upon arriving at the gate, the NCOs opened fire on the bus, instantly killing Officer Soeltan.[40] De Mees called in that they were being fired upon, both him and Jones having to lie flat in their vehicle to avoid the incoming fire. Both men survived the ordeal.[41]

With the MBK secured, the men in Kamp Bomika were sent over by Horb to sweep the barracks to round up all the men present. Entry was gained to the weapons lockers but ammunition was still in short supply. Across the road at MBK Zuid, several YPs that had been sitting idle for a long time were being readied and armed with .50 machine guns.[42] In the meantime, Bouterse and Horb set-up an HQ.[43]

At 0400, parts of Paramaribo were awoken when the rear Bofors cannon of S402 fired two shells on the police headquarters, hitting the roof.[44] This allowed people to leave the building. Zeeuw and Nelom drove to the waterfront and signalled with their headlights to inform Tolud that the MBK was in their hands and that the firing could continue.[45] However, a small crisis took place on the patrol boat.

The Bofors gunner, a corporal that was captured at the naval base, was initially reluctant to open fire as he feared that his brother, a police officer, was inside the police building. After being convinced to fire on the roof, he was shocked when he saw the effects of the first shells that he fired. After having a nervous breakdown, he was locked up in a room in the boat. This meant that the remaining crew members had to learn how to operate the gun on the job.[46]

Meanwhile, Bomika soldiers had managed to get the first YP armed and up and running, Sergeant Rozendaal drove off with a group of men to capture the munitions bunker at the Doekhiweg. The bunker had already been contacted on the orders of Bouterse. The military personnel present in the bunker had been informed that the facility would be taken over by the revolting soldiers and were ordered not to resist. After Rozendaal fired over the roof of the building, the soldiers came out with their hands raised. Unfortunately, Sergeant Major Comvalius lost his life during the takeover.[47]

At the Presidential Palace at Independence Square, several SKM officers had gathered to protect President Ferrier in case the coup plotters decided to attack. They were ready to do the utmost to defend him.[48] The Group of Sixteen now had control of all the major military installations in the city. The rebelling soldiers could now settle some scores.

The guard house at the Memre Boekoe Kazerne, where Lieutenant Van Aalst was the acting watch commander in the early morning of 25 February. (Lucien Chien a Foeng)

Police Headquarters

Although the police HQ had been hit by 40mm shells, the building was still standing. The three Bomika council members had been transferred from Santo Boma prison to the police headquarters. In the meantime, Prime Minister Arron, Attorney General Kruisland and Police Chief Walker had arrived at the HQ around 0430, while the police officers inside the building were arming themselves with carbines.[49]

At 0700, the S402 opened fire on the police station again. A YP and 20 soldiers were sent to support the attack. While driving to the headquarters, the YP opened fire while turning into the Knuffelsgracht-Heiligeweg behind the police station, injuring three people and killing two.[50] The police officers holed up in the station fired back, resulting in a gun battle between the police and the soldiers outside. The YP's gunner opened fire on the police station at vehicle height.[51]

The headquarters of police at the Waterkant in 1947. The building had not changed by the time it was destroyed in 1980. (Collection Nationaal Archief, Willem van der Poll)

Revolting soldiers in a YP take the police headquarters under fire from Knuffelsgracht, due south west of the building, using its .50 HMG. (Copyright inheritors of Jul M. Dubois)

The police station ablaze after being hit by a shell from S402's rear Bofors gun. By the time the fire was under control, the police station was burnt to the ground. The revolting sergeants had intentionally destroyed the building, even after the police had surrendered to the conspirators. (Lucien Chien a Foeng)

When a police inspector left the building and informed the revolting soldiers that the 70 policemen inside were willing to surrender, he was given eight minutes to collect his men. These were rounded up and sent to the Memre Boekoe Kazerne. Police Chief Walker was captured but the prime minister and attorney general had left the police headquarters before the shooting began.

Not long after the police had surrendered, the police building was hit again by a high explosive incendiary shell.[54] This started a fire that burnt the building to the ground.[55] The destruction of the police station was witnessed by hundreds of people gathered at Independence Square about 300 metres away. It was nine o'clock in the morning.

In the meantime, the military police had fled their headquarters at Fort Zeelandia, leaving Hardjoprajitno and two other prisoners behind in their cells. He managed to break out of his cell using a crowbar. Just as the S402 was about to fire upon the fort as per plan, Hardjoprajitno signalled the boat with a mirror,[56] Tolud saw the signals and received word from Bouterse to cease fire.[57]

Some of the revolting members of the military performed some reprisals. Immediately after the destruction of the police station, the newspaper office of the *De West* was attacked when a military bus arrived and a soldier placed an explosive inside the building and set it off. This was followed by a hand grenade thrown onto the roof of the building. Luckily no one was injured as the soldiers had warned the people inside to take cover. This was the first show of force of the military against the press as *De West* had been the only newspaper in Suriname not supportive of and even critical of, the Bomika strikes before the coup. In addition to the attack on *De West*, several other soldiers had driven by the prime minister's residence and fired several bullets into the house.[58]

The gunfire on the police station resulted in a panic among the policemen. The Bomika council members were pulled from their prison cells by Police Chief Walker. Neede was given a phone and instructed to call the MBK. By that time, Bouterse had already given Tolud the order to fire and burn the police station to the ground.[52]

When Neede was able to reach Bouterse, he was surprised to hear that the three were held captive at the police station. Bouterse told Neede to get out of there as it would be impossible to rescind the order to shell the police station. The three men convinced the police chief that they would be able to stop the attack and were allowed to leave, exiting the building around 0815 and making their way to the MBK.[53]

As reporters got in touch with the conspirators, messages were sent out that schools would be closed for the rest of the day and people were recommended to return home. In addition, it was announced that plunderers would be shot on sight. Throughout the city, cars were stopped and keys confiscated, shutting down traffic

S402 on the Suriname River. The boat was positioned off the waterfront and used its stern cannon to hit the police station with high explosive incendiary shells. (Revokrant)

and public life. With many police officers arrested, looters saw their chance. In the city centre, stores were plundered after windows were smashed in. Only when the military showed up and a YP408 fired its .50 machine gun into the air, the looters ran off and order returned to the centre. The damage caused by the plunderers ran into the hundreds of thousands of guilders.[59]

The *Nationale Militaire Raad*

In the morning, the Bomika council members, two members of the Group of Sixteen and Lieutenant Van Rey, formed the *National Militaire Raad* (National Military Council – abbreviated NMR) that would assume military, political and administrative leadership of the country.[60]

By noon, Bulletin No.1 of the NMR was announced on the radio. Surinamers were requested to make themselves available for 'the social-economic, societal and moral reorientation of the Republic of Suriname'. In addition, the NMR would respect all democratic principles of the state of Suriname and put the welfare of the Surinamese people first.

Shortly after this, a curfew was announced starting at seven o'clock in the evening. The NMR also applied censorship to the media, shutting down several radio stations and only allowing pre-approved news bulletins to be read. Military personnel were also stationed at the TV and radio stations.[61]

In the following days, SKM officers and military personnel that did not participate in the Bomika strikes and policemen were ordered to report to the NMR. Many of the officers were imprisoned and sent to the Santo Boma prison with some being physically abused. Attorney General Kruisland, Vice-Prime Minister Van Genderen and Police Chief Walker are among those that were arrested and jailed.[62]

In the evening of 26 February, Van Genderen announced that the government ceded power to the NMR, making the council the official ruler of the country. This was followed by a statement from Vice-Chairman Neede that the NMR would form a civilian council with the support of lawyer Bruma and Bomika Legal Councillor Leefland of the *Volkspartij* (a party that was supported by several Bomika members).[63]

President Arron, after hiding out with friends for several days, reported to the MBK on 28 February. He was jailed until his cabinet and himself formally transferred power to the new government on 5 March. Arron was placed under house arrest for almost a year.[64]

On 3 March, the NMR met with President Ferrier. They agreed that the president would remain in power and that the NMR would operate within the rules of the constitution. Furthermore, elections were to be officially postponed and a new government formed. Therefore, the NMR did not get its way to form a civilian council (something that Bruma had strived for).[65]

The fact that President Ferrier was left untouched and the NMR had respected the constitution without dismissing the *Staten of Suriname*, made it acceptable for the Netherlands to recognise the new government despite refusing to deal with the NMR directly. Ferrier was well respected and seen as a moderator within Dutch circles. Yet, the Netherlands can be partly blamed for the coup. First of all, by openly blaming Arron for misspending and questioning his policies, thus strengthening the anti-Arron sentiment in Suriname. Secondly, for leaving Colonel Hans Valk of the military mission, to go unchecked.[66]

The sergeants of the 'Group of Sixteen' in a staged, group photograph after the 1980 coup. More details of the group members can be found in Appendix III. (Lucien Chien a Foeng)

Paramaribo at night. Following the *Sergeantencoup*, the NMR put out a curfew which was enforced by the military. In the coming years, Suriname would see multiple curfews. (Lucien Chien a Foeng)

On 3 March 1980, several members of the NMR met President Ferrier at the presidential palace and agreed that they would adhere to the constitution. From left to right: Sergeant Horb, Sergeant Neede, Lieutenant Van Rey, President Ferrier, Sergeant Major Bouterse and Sergeant Major Sital. (Surinamese Government)

The Colonel and the Coup[67]

Not long after the coup d'état of February 25 took place, rumours started to surface that the Dutch military mission had actively supported NCOs in their coup. At Valk's farewell party in June 1980, Bouterse was said to have openly declared, 'the coup would never have taken part without him', much to the astonishment and embarrassment of some of the dignitaries present. As noted before, it was no secret that Valk thought poorly of the SKM command and that he listened to the complaints of the NCOs – but evidence for direct involvement was circumstantial.

Valk was accused of having approached several SKM officers directly to ask them if they were willing to participate in a coup d'état. Lieutenant Roy Bottse, who fled Suriname after the coup, explained in an interview in 1983 that he was approached by Valk in the officers' mess and told that he was 'the most suitable person to take power', and warned him that 'if he didn't do it, the NCOs would'. Valk was also alleged to have discussed how to act 'if one were to conduct a takeover', when meeting Surinamese NCOs and officers during social gatherings at the bar.

The colonel was also accused to have supplied Bouterse and his fellow conspirators, a blueprint on how to conduct a coup (Operation *Zwarte Tulp*) and was said to have spent a lot of time with the sergeant major just after to coup to advise on how to run the country after it was taken over.[68] Valk was not the only person within the mission accused of helping the NCOs. Captains Briaire and Clements had allegedly supported the NCOs by helping them

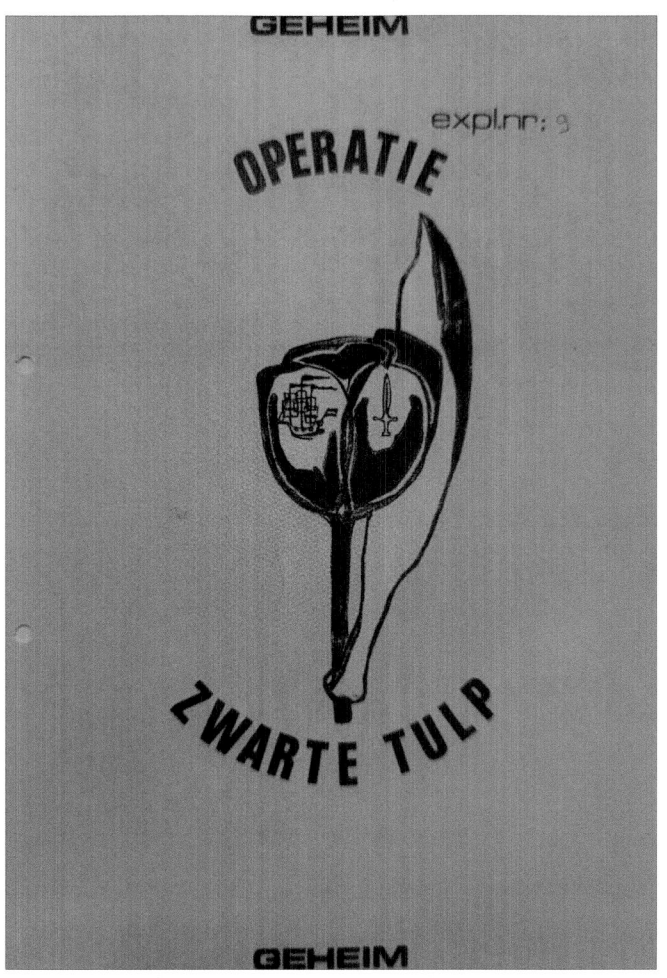

The cover of Operation Black Tulip, the plan that was alleged by journalists Verhey and Westerloo to be the blueprint for a coup. *Kolonel* Valk had supposedly supplied this plan to members of the Groep of Sixteen. (NIMH Collection)

ready the YP408s which had not run for a long period (among other issues).

Starting in 1981, three secret reports were written on the behaviour of the military mission in Paramaribo during the 25 February coup. These reports were kept top secret, allegedly in order to prevent a breakup of the fragile bilateral relations between the two countries. A series of articles and a book published in 1983 by *Vrij Nederland* journalists, Elma Verhey and Gerard van Westerloo, led to further investigations under the Pronk commission.

When the report was expanded and finished in 1985, it was sealed-off to protect the information of individuals until 2010, only for this to be extended until 2060 by the Dutch parliament. Author, Ellen de Vries, gained access to Westerloo's archive and found a copy of the classified reports. These were published as appendices in her book about Hans Valk in 2021. Since then, Dutch members of parliament have called for these documents to be officially declassified now that they have been published.

The conclusions of the report were that the Surinamese servicemen were unhappy with their situation in the army and sought support and advice from two sides: left-wing political parties and the Dutch military mission. The mission tried to temper their moods but showed too much solidarity and failed to distance themselves during the conflict between Bomika and the SKM leadership.

Although the members knew something was going on, they had no idea when or how. In general, the conclusion was that Valk was out of line by offering the Surinamese NCOs a listening ear when they voiced their discontent within the SKM but was not directly involved with the events in February. Additionally, in his role of defence attaché, Valk should have informed the Dutch Ambassador about the discontent within the SKM and kept him up-to-date on his contacts with the NCOs. This conclusion suited Dutch interests but also ignored some of the strong signals that the behaviour of the mission may have influenced the NCOs in their actions.

Bomika members Mijnals and Sital denied that Valk was ever involved with their plans to take over the government. Valk himself always claimed that he prioritized the safety of Dutch nationals in Suriname and he only listened to the complaints of the disgruntled members of the SKM.

Although some Surinamers scathe at the idea that 'their' revolution was planned by a foreign power, there are people who believe that entire affair was planned by the Dutch government in order to reassert their control over their former colony. In 2002, when the Netherlands and Suriname were (again) having a difficult time coming to terms about the resumption of development aid, President Ronald Venetiaan bitterly stated: 'The coup was organised in a backroom in the

The members of the NMMS in 1975–1976. From left to right: *Kolonel* H. Valk, Major L.E.A. Oberg, *Kapitein*. A. Clements, Adj P.S. van Dijk, Sergeant Major N.W. Lorwa, Sergeant Van Belsen, Sergeant Major Kejdeniers and *Kapitein*. F.G.W. Steinhorst. Clements, Van Dijk, Lorwa, Van Belsen and Kejdeniers stayed until 1981 – the year the NMMS was disestablished. The other members of the NMMS were Briaire, Kooiman, Maarseveen and Nijs. (Bronbeek Museum)

Netherlands and executed by a certain Colonel Valk'. The role of the Dutch military mission (and Valk in particular) will remain a source of controversy.

By June 1980, *Kolonel* Valk was re-posted to the NATO headquarters in Brussels, a decision made before the *Sergeantencoup*. He was replaced by Lieutenant Colonel Maarseveen, who had originally been requested by the Surinamese government to lead the NMMS. His relationship with the members of the Surinamese army was never as cordial as under Valk. Some of the other members of the NMMS viewed Maarseveen with distrust, leading to a toxic relationship between the head of the military mission and several of his subordinates. Some of them even went as far as openly defying his instructions and making scathing remarks about Maarseveen behind his back – this is explored later in the text.

5
THE CHIN A SEN PERIOD

A New Start ...

After the guns went silent on February 25 and the NMR was formed, Suriname found itself in a vacuum. The NMR, as mentioned before, agreed to form a civilian government. Up until that time, the sergeants were swarmed with questions from entrepreneurs, farmers, journalists, trade union members and other people, who wanted to know what lay ahead and how to act with the curfew in place.

With enthusiasm and vigour, the NMR started to take measures to get Suriname moving again. By the first week of March, the coup was referred to as an *ingreep* (intervention), not a *staatsgreep* (coup d'état).[1] Promoting unity amongst the nation, members of the military went into the streets of Paramaribo to assist the people in cleaning up the rubbish left out, repairing roads, painting houses for senior citizens and fixing streetlights.

NMR members, always carrying their Uzis with them in public, went to visit civil works (such as the water company) to discuss the problems of providing service to the population. In addition, a suggestion box was hung outside the gate of the HQ of the SKM, where members of the public could submit ideas and a consultation hour was established where people could come and discuss ideas and problems with NMR members.

To counter the inefficiency of the civil service system, the NMR mandated that all government employees should show up to work on time and they checked the various departments for absentees. People who did not show up for work, would receive a visit from members of the military.[2]

These measures made the NMR very approachable and initially people welcomed the *ingreep* very much, seeing it as a fresh start to clean Suriname and improve living standards. The signs of appreciation of the people took such forms that news bulletins were sent out urging people to stop giving members of the SKM alcoholic beverages. However, this public enthusiasm would not last.

As the *ingreep* had, for the time being, disarmed and effectively dismantled the Police Corps, the army took over the

In the days following the *Sergeantencoup*, the NMR installed itself in the former headquarters of the SKM commander at MBK and installed a suggestion box outside the gate. In addition, the NMR had daily consultation hours where the general population could discuss problems with the members of the NMR. (Nationale Voorlichtings Dienst Suriname)

The military cracked down hard on crime. Petty criminals were often subjected to public humiliation and received corporal punishment. This later extended to political opponents and members of the press. (Stichting Makmur)

task of maintaining law and order. This meant that on short notice, looters, curfew breakers and small-time criminals were apprehended by soldiers patrolling the streets. These were publicly subjected to beatings, usually performed with a rod called a 'bullepees' (made from pizzle – the hard, dried out penis-bone of a bull). This was not approved by all of the population, many people agreeing that corporal punishment does not belong in a proper civil society.[3]

In addition to the arrests of criminals, the military started a witch-hunt to round up NPK politicians and people deemed to be corrupt. Those caught were jailed until they would be brought to trial. As the Police Corps was not operational, many of the corruption charges were not investigated properly and eventually, many of these people were released without sentencing. Some of them would be rearrested several times, spending more time in jail then they would have done if they had been sentenced for the crime they were originally charged.

… with a New Government

After consultations with various Surinamese politicians, trade union leaders and captains of industry, the NMR decided to form a government out of politicians that had an unblemished record and were not associated with the old parties such as the NPS, VHP and KTPI.[4]

On 15 March, a new government was announced and installed. Henk Chin A Sen was named the new prime minister. Chin A Sen, a popular internist of Chinese origin, was affiliated with the PNR although he was politically inexperienced. The rest of the government was formed out of politicians not affiliated with the old parties while Van Rey and Neede left the NMR to become minister of the army and deputy minister of police respectively.[5]

By April 1980, Korp Braaf had also left the NMR to command the volunteer corps, leaving the NMR with seven members after Sergeant Hardjoprajitno joined. Within the NMR, several factions formed. Joeman, Mijnals and Sital, being leftists, wanted to turn Suriname into a people's republic with people's committees following a Cuban or Nicaraguan model. Horb and Bouterse, on the other hand, preferred to leave the established structure of democracy in place. This caused tension among the council members.

The three leftists within the council had previously demanded that the government followed directives as set by the NMR (instead of the latter performing a controlling function of the former). The fact that the 'capitalist and colonial oppressor' Netherlands had approved the *ingreep* was not much to their liking. In their eyes, the Netherlands was still a colonial power that tried to influence control over Suriname for national gain. Thus, the leftist faction started a public campaign against the Netherlands and its colonial influences.[6]

There was also unrest within the military. A sizeable proportion of the officer cadre had fled the country. Those officers who stayed found themselves being scrutinised by the NMR. Lieutenant Rambocus was initially put in charge of reorganising the army troops but clashed with the NMR as he was of the opinion that the military needed to stay out of the political arena. This caused him to be briefly jailed in April 1980 and held without charge, for several weeks.[7] Lieutenant Rob Behr, who oversaw the financial department of the army and police, was suspended when he brought up questionable receipts for purchases, being informed that the priorities of the 'revolution' would take precedence over his concerns.[8]

Although the *ingreep* was more often referred to as a revolution (or *revo* for short) in Suriname, the events of 25 February 1980 were more inspired by a desire to defeat corruption and remove the governing parties from power, than to change the form of

After the events of 25 February, popular internist Henk Chin A Sen was asked to take the office of prime minister of Suriname. Although he was a member of the PNR, he was politically inexperienced and seen as the right candidate for a fresh start away from the 'old' parties (NPS, KTPI and VHP). (Lucien Chien a Foeng)

government. Thus, although the military started to call themselves revolutionaries, a real ideology or plan on how to govern the nation was missing. NMR members had no 'red book' to base their decisions on – they carried an Uzi instead – leading Surinamese people to say that the country was ruled by '*Ba Uzi*' (Boss Uzi).

Once Chin A Sen's government came to power, one of the first acts of the new government was to pass a law on 2 April 1980 that cleared the sergeants who participated in the coup, from prosecution, therefore legitimising the *ingreep*. The day before, policemen and officers arrested in February (including Chief of Police Walker and Colonel Elstak) were released from prison, although many members of the officer corps were not allowed to return to the SKM.[9]

On 1 May 1980, the cabinet announced that the actions on 25 February were 'a break with a system drenched with injustice, corruption, bureaucracy and nepotism' and that 'the country was liberated and reborn starting a new era for the nation and people of Suriname'. The role of the NMR in governing the country had ended. Chin A Sen promised changes in governing politics, society and education.

The Ormskerk Affair[11]

At the end of April 1980, Fred van Ormskerk was arrested in Albina and jailed for conspiring to organise a coup to overthrow the legitimate government of Suriname. The former warrant officer was a well-known and experienced NCO within the SKM and who had served with the KNIL during the police actions in Indonesia. While there, he served with the Korps Stoot Troepen, the forerunner of the Dutch Commando Corps (KCT) of the KL, where he earned his paratrooper badge. His tough-as-nails attitude towards discipline and the military earned him the nickname '*bikkel*' (Dutch slang for 'die hard' or 'tough guy'). The former TRIS Sergeant had trained Surinamese enlisted men to become NCOs (among them Roy Horb) before the Surinamese TRIS-component became the SKM. Ormskerk carried the flag of the Surinamese Armed Forces during the first parade held on Independence Day.

Reduced Freedom of the Press[10]

Ever since the *Sergeantencoup* of February 1980, one of the things that the members of the military leadership understood, was the importance of the media. The most important sources of news in Suriname came from newspapers, radio and TV.

In 1980, the three main newspapers of Suriname were *De West*, *De Ware Tijd* (The True Times) and *Vrije Stem* (Free Voice). These were the main source of information to Surinamers and were all privately owned. The newspapers supported the *revo* in general, although *De West* was more critical of the actions of the NCOs on strike and was attacked by soldiers on 25 February 1980 (as described in Chapter 4). In addition to newspapers, several editorial magazines were printed serving a wide range of audiences.

At the same time, Suriname counted five radio stations, all based in Paramaribo. These were: Radio Paramaribo (Rapar), Radio Apintie, Radio Radika, ABC and SRS (Surinaamse Radio Stichting). Except for SRS, all were privately owned and served different audiences. SRS was the state owned radio station and together with the only TV station in Suriname (STVS), was run by the government.

In general, all media outlets in Suriname received their news from the SNA (Surinamese News Agency), in addition to a few smaller agencies. As a leftover from Dutch rule, many outlets also received news bulletins via telex from the Dutch news agency, ANP.

Another source of information to people would be the *mofokoranti* ('mouth newspaper' in Sranantongo) otherwise known as gossip. In a time when people did not have access to cell phones or internet, news – especially that from the deep jungles in Suriname – would spread faster than people would be able to read in papers or hear on radio. Often, this form of rumour intelligence (RUMINT) would not be accurate as it had been changed via this game of 'telephone'.

From the first day since the *revo*, the NMR approached the various media outlets and informed them that they would be able to publish freely as they wished, 'as long as they served the interest of the revolution'.

In time, media outlets that became critical of government actions, found themselves at the desks of senior government officials in order to clarify their reporting. In some cases, editors and journalists received imprisonment and harsh physical treatment. As a result, many newspapers imposed self-censorship in order to prevent unwanted attention from authorities.

In addition to Surinamese media, many people in Suriname also read Dutch newspapers that were flown in from the Netherlands and listened to the *Wereldomroep* (Dutch radio world service). As the Surinamese government exerted more control over Surinamese media sources, the Dutch media – free from control by the Dutch government – became to be seen as an alternative (and possibly more truthful) news source than local news outlets.

Over time, the Surinamese government sought to restrict the influence of the Dutch media by expelling and barring journalists. These restrictions resulted in the Dutch media being more critical and sometimes, more hostile to the Surinamese government. The relationship between the Surinamese government and Dutch media would be a love-hate affair – as time would tell.

Often referred to as 'Uncle Fred', Ormskerk retired in 1979 and emigrated to the Netherlands. He tried to settle down but could not find his place outside the military as a pensioner in the cold climate of north-western Europe. As soon as the *ingreep* took place, Van Ormskerk got in touch with Lieutenant Van Rey, proclaiming that he was available to support the new nation. He was quietly brushed aside, being told to 'wait until the time is right as things are turbulent right now' and was never contacted. After meeting up with former SKM members and politicians who had fled to the Netherlands after the *ingreep*, Fred Ormskerk decided to go to Paramaribo.

On 24 April 1980, he arrived in Suriname via French Guiana with letters from the former Minister of Agriculture, Johan Kasantaroeno. These were to be given to other politicians in Paramaribo and discussed the restoration of democracy. Ormskerk was arrested in Albina on April 29 by Sergeant Henk van Randwijk. With the cooperation of the Gendarmerie in St. Laurent du Maroni (across the Marowijne River from Albina), his suitcase and documents were retrieved from his hotel room in French Guiana.

Ormskerk was jailed at Fort Zeelandia and later transferred to the garrison commander's building at the MBK, where he was interrogated for several days, during which he suffered broken ribs and head trauma that led to his death. Once news of his death came out, authorities initially claimed he was shot during an escape attempt, changing the story later to stating that he was found dead in his cell after he hit his head on a table during a struggle while attempting to escape.

Ormskerk's body was shipped to his family in the Netherlands, where the coroner concluded that he died from blunt force trauma. Before closing and sealing his casket before transport, Dutch MP Piet van Dijk placed the blue paratrooper wings that he received from Sergeant Wilfried Hawker (one of the members of the Group of Sixteen) on Ormskerk's chest, as they both were paratroopers.

In the days following Ormskerk's arrest, amid wild speculations of mercenary invasions, weapons caches and death lists, several alleged accomplices were arrested including Lieutenant Jeff Wirth, Kasantaroeno's father and Ormskerk's friend, Cornelis Krol. They were interrogated and suffered beatings by their interrogators.

Krol especially was the focus of interrogation. After a drinking session at a local pub, just before Ormskerk left to retire in the Netherlands, he had told Krol that he might need to come back and take power in a coup. Whether it was the alcohol speaking or not, Krol agreed to help him and was given several sticks of dynamite to use when he came back. Krol, despite being found unsuitable for military service, had claimed to Ormskerk that he was a veteran of the French Foreign Legion and had served in Algeria and Vietnam, among other places.

On 12 May, Krol was brought before cameras at a press conference. He confessed to plotting a coup d'état at bayonet point, appearing weary and drugged. It later transpired that Krol was tortured to extract a forced confession.[12] Evidence was presented, such as weapons, money and lists with names of people that were to be assassinated and additional weapons that were to be purchased.

After the Marmon-Herrington light tanks were taken out of service in 1957, the TRIS received seven or eight GMC Otter scout cars that were armed with a Bren LMG in the top turret. The Otters served until 1972 and were then scrapped in Suriname. At least two survived the scrapyard to be put in a museum, one at Fort Nieuw Amsterdam and the other at the TRIS Museum in Zwijndrecht, the Netherlands. (Artwork by David Bocquelet)

YP408 KN 75-28 was one of the five YP408s delivered to the TRIS in 1972. This machine has a periscope, identifying it as a YP408PWI-PC (Platoon Commander) variant. This YP is equipped with a barbed wire covered screen that was to be used for crowd control operations and a Bren LMG (probably taken off one of the Otters). This YP is now part of the *Pantsermonument* at the Ayoko Barracks near Zanderij. (Artwork by David Bocquelet)

Another one of the YP408 inherited from the TRIS, this YP408 is armed with a .50 M2HB HMG and took part in the *Sergeantencoup* when it was part of the attack on the police headquarters. It was later seen at Fort Zeelandia, when all military personnel had to report in the days following the overthrow of the Arron government. This YP is a standard YP408PWI-S variant. Its final fate is unknown. (Artwork by David Bocquelet)

Between 1975 and 1982 the Netherlands delivered at least four more YP408s to Suriname as part of military aid given to Suriname post-independence. The latecomers can be distinguished from the former TRIS YPs by the larger indicator lights – a modification to the YP408 in the Netherlands that the TRIS YPs never received. This YP408 is a PV-MT mortar tug variant, distinguishable by its hitch to pull a 120mm wheeled mortar – a weapon that Suriname never received. This YP408 was later dubbed *Cobra* and is now located at the NL Museum, part of the Memre Boekoe Kazerne. (Artwork by David Bocquelet)

Another latecomer, this YP408 is a PV-V Cargo carrier that has a shorter exhaust and lacks the hatch clamps that the other YP408 have. During the *Rambocuscoup*, the crew of this YP408 defected to troops loyal to the *Gezag* at Fort Zeelandia. In order to distinguish friend from foe, a white sheet was draped over the front of the YP covering the title NL. This YP408 was later called *Bofroe* (tapir) and is the last known Surinamese YP408 to have been in active service. (Artwork by David Bocquelet)

The NEKAF M38A1 jeep was a Dutch built copy of Willys MD Jeep (derived from the ubiquitous Willys jeep widely used by the Allies in the Second World War) with this variant having bulged indicator lights to comply with Dutch road regulations. Between 1955 and 1962, about 7,500 were built for the Dutch armed forces, finding their way to Suriname as well. The TRIS had at least 15 vehicles in service and used these for liaison, as recoilless rifle mounts and to tow equipment. The M45 Quadmount (seen here mounted on an M20 trailer) was an electrically powered, manually operated, towable anti-aircraft gun that used four .50 HMGs in a single mount (with 200 rounds per gun). The TRIS operated at least four of these but they were mostly seen in parades. After independence, the Surinamese took over these pieces of equipment. (Artwork by David Bocquelet)

S401 was the first of high seas patrol-class boats delivered to Suriname in 1977. Built by Shipyard de Vlijt in Aalsmeer (the Netherlands) it is shown in configuration as when delivered to Suriname without any weapons. The Surinamese government ordered seven SAK-40/L-70-315 40mm Bofors cannons from Sweden and arranged for the installation of two cannons on each of the three vessels. (Artwork by David Bocquelet)

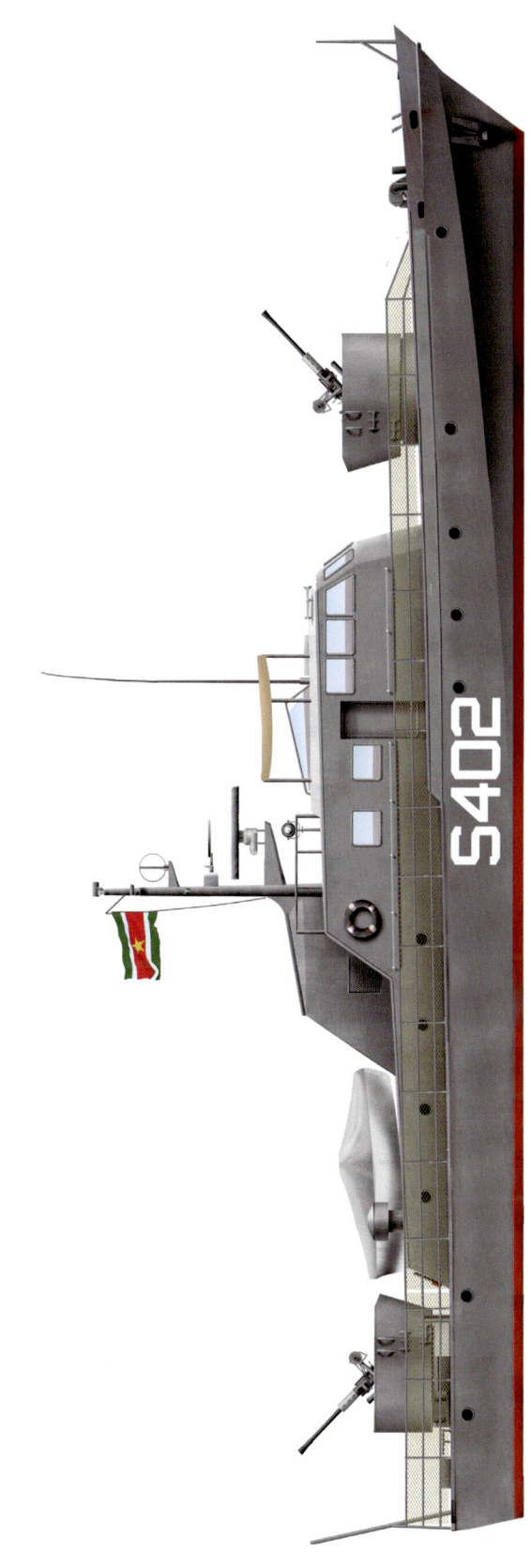

The second of the high seas patrol-class boats, the S402, has become legendary in Surinamese folklore as it was the ship with which the 16 sergeants destroyed the police headquarters on the waterfront of Paramaribo, using one of its 40mm Bofors cannons, most likely the cannon at the stern. The S402 was also used to suppress troops fighting on the side of Rambocus during the coup of 1982. (Artwork by David Bocquelet)

Surinam Airways operated a total of four Dakotas to fly to the various airstrips located within the rainforests in the country. PZ-TAM (c/n 19247), a former USAAF C-47A-70-DL, was one of the Dakotas used to transport TRIS and DEFPOL troops to the Coeroeni outpost. From there, DEFPOL troops then entered the disputed Tigri Area to conduct patrols on foot and by *korjaal*, staying at the various camps set-up in the area. PZ-TAM ended up being scrapped at Zanderij Airport in the 70s. (Artwork by Anderson Subtil)

This Twin Otter DHC-6 Series 200 was one of two aircraft used during Operation Climax by the GDF to attack and capture the DEFPOL post at Tigri on 19 August 1969. This aircraft, registration 8R-GDC, was modified for the attack by the removal of all doors and seats. In addition, the nose was modified by removing the nose cone and cutting four holes in the bulkhead to allow a gunner with an LMG to provide suppressive fire to the assault team. After the operation was completed, the aircraft was restored to its original condition and served with the GAC until it was sold to a Canadian firm in 1974. (Artwork by Luca Canossa)

On 29 August 1980, NF-5A K-3004 was serving with No. 315 Squadron of the *Koninklijke Luchtmacht* (the Royal Netherlands Air Force) and was based out of Twenthe Air Base when it was flown by Lieutenant John Vasilda. That day, he hit and cut three powerlines during a low-level practice flight in Norway. Vasilda was able to land his lightly damaged aircraft safely at Sola but the town of Tollesund was without power for several hours. K-3004 was sold to Turkey in 1990, whilst John Vasilda returned to his native Suriname to become the first commander of the LUMA. (Artwork by Tom Cooper)

The first aircraft in service with the LUMA, this Hughes 369D was leased from Venezuela (previous registration YV-261C). The helicopter was used during the *Rambocuscoup* to prevent the conspirators from taking the ferry at Boskamp. On 28 March, it crashed in bad weather in Guyanese territory when it was flying from Coeroeni to Paramaribo, probably hitting a tree when it was flying low over the Corantijn River. It is unknown whether this helicopter had any markings. (Artwork by Luca Canossa)

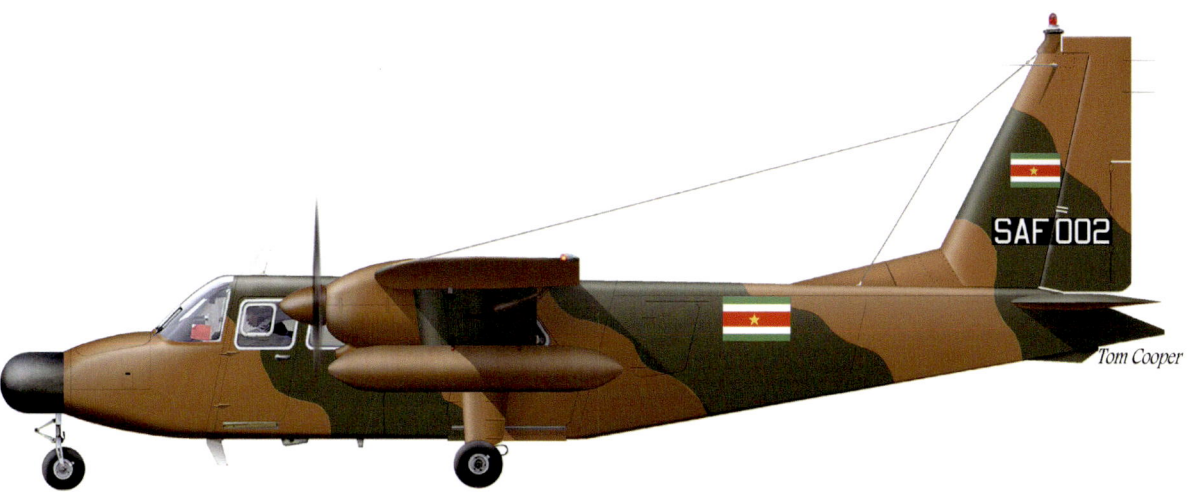

The Britten-Norman BN-2B-21 c/n 2108, eventually marked as SAF002, arrived in Suriname on 25 March 1982. As delivered, all Surinamese Defenders received wrap-around camouflage patterns in Dark Earth (BS381C/350) and Dark Green (BS381C/641). Instead of roundels, they had the Surinamese flag on the fuselage and repeated on the fin. The aircraft is depicted here as seen during its delivery flight from Switzerland to Suriname during a stopover in Reykjavik, Iceland and is equipped with fuel tanks that increase its endurance to up to 12 hours. Eventually, the serial SAF002 was removed and the transfer registration G-BIXE applied on the rear fuselage instead. (Artwork by Tom Cooper)

The third Britten-Norman BN-2B-21 was construction number 2116 and is shown here before delivery, at Luton in the UK, for maintenance by MacAlpine Aviation, in May 1982 – wearing both its transfer registration G-BJEA and the Surinamese Air Force serial SAF003. It was delivered to its customer on 8 June 1982. Although there were minimal differences in the antenna configuration and other equipment between the first two and the second pair of Surinamese BN-21s, they were all outfitted to the military standard of Maritime Defender, had excellent endurance and could have been armed with gun pods and unguided rockets. (Artwork by Tom Cooper)

LATIN AMERICA@WAR VOLUME 31

A typical Dutch conscript, standing on guard with his M1 carbine, wearing khaki shorts and shirt. In the late 1960s, the M1 carbine replaced the M1 Garand as it was easier to carry on jungle patrols, where its longer range was not as useful. (Artwork by Anderson Subtil)

Desiré Jakaoemo (Surinamese police officer with DEFPOL in 1969), armed with a standard Dutch Uzi. He is wearing a second-hand TRIS khaki uniform with cap. DEFPOL consisted of Surinamese volunteers from the Police Corps and the TRIS who patrolled the disputed area known as Tigri. They were trained in jungle survival by former KNIL veteran Sjoerd Lapré and received weapons training at BBZ. Once their training was complete, these men were deployed to Coeroeni from where they would patrol the area on foot and via *korjaal*. (Artwork by Anderson Subtil)

This unidentified soldier is shown as he appeared during the 1982 *Rambocuscoup*, wearing the typical Suriname khaki uniform and armed with an M1 carbine: this was the standard rifle of the NL until the arrival of more modern weapons from Brazil in 1983. (Artwork by Anderson Subtil)

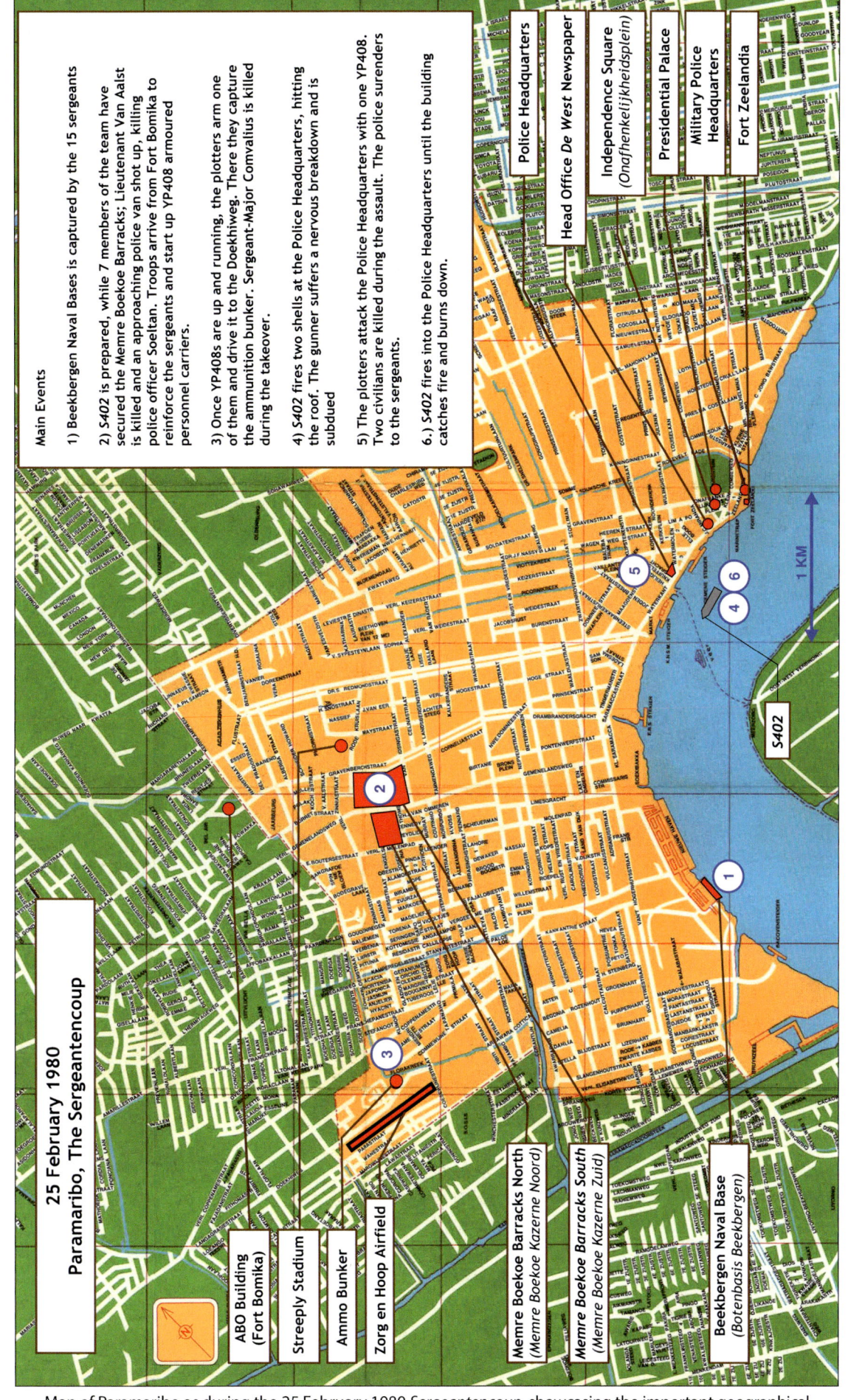

Map of Paramaribo as during the 25 February 1980 *Sergeantencoup*, showcasing the important geographical locations where the main events took place (for details, see Chapter 4). (Map by Sander Peeters)

General overview map of Suriname in 1982, showing the pre-1985 borders, military installations and the aluminium industry. (Map by George Anderson)

Warrant Officer Fred Ormskerk, here standing as the flag bearer on 25 November 1975. Ormskerk was arrested for conspiring a coup in April 1980. He died in custody after receiving severe beatings during interrogation. (Collection Nationaal Archief/Anefo, Bert Verhoeff)

Former Lieutenant Bottse was also implicated, as he had been in touch with Ormskerk before his trip to French Guiana. Krol confessed under interrogation that the Dutch ex-minister of development aid, Jan Pronk, had financed the coup d'état. The incident was used by the NMR to show that the Netherlands was attempting to undermine the revolution by sending in a mercenary army to seize power and restore a democracy made up of politicians from the old guard.

All accused were put on trial. Judge Ramdat Misier gave Krol a two-year jail sentence and other alleged accomplices received sentences ranging from 9 months to several years.[13] The lawyers for the defendants, Eddy Hoost and Harold Riedewald, later defended other opponents of the military leadership –making themselves the target of persecution.

Although news of the death of Ormskerk made headlines in the Netherlands, the allegations of Dutch involvement in the alleged coup did not make as many waves. However, within the Dutch cabinet, members discussed the course of action. Although the accusations of Pronk being involved in a coup were dismissed, the US had requested for the Dutch to maintain cordial ties with Suriname to prevent the military from seizing more power and going on a leftist course, particularly towards Cuba.

Thus, the fates of Dutchmen Ormskerk and Krol were largely ignored by their government and Krol was left to suffer at the hands of those who imprisoned him. In effect, the military leadership got away with torturing opponents and committing its first political murder, whether intentional or not.

Ormskerk was supposedly ordered by Kasantaroeno to commit a coup, together with about 250 mercenaries waiting in French Guiana.

The NMR Falls Apart

Prime Minister Chin A Sen and his cabinet, put together a plan to improve the social-economic, education and political system. By implementing changes on short notice, the plan would last until the next elections were held – planned for October 1982. At the same time, Chin A Sen wanted to resume talks with the Netherlands about the resumption of development aid and requested 500 million for an emergency plan to achieve these improvements. The Dutch Minister of Development aid, Jan De Koning, was invited to Suriname in June to resume talks with the Surinamese government as meetings on development aid had stalled in the previous year.

In the meantime, a small crisis erupted within the military council. The NMR was advised by politicians of small communist splinter parties such as the PALU (Progressive Worker's and Farmer's Union) and RVP (consisting of *Volkspartij* members who split-off as the *Volkspartij* did not want to work with the NMR) that sought to influence the council. They found a listening

The mass of people 'spontaneously' protesting Minister De Koning's decision against adjusting the amount of Dutch development aid for inflation. (STVS)

Members of the NMR (with Ramon Abraham on the microphone) giving fiery speeches and accusations during the demonstration. This did not go well with the government, who were trying to get the Dutch development aid started again. As a result, Bouterse and Horb left the NMR and within weeks, the NMR had lost its political power. (STVS)

ear with Joeman, Sital and Mijnals, who were already leaning to the left.

As the NMR was more involved with the persecution of NPK politicians, former council member Van Rey (now Minister of Defence and Police), requested that Bouterse should become the commander-in-chief of the army. He wanted the NMR to be disbanded so his department could exercise proper control over judicial matters. In addition, he wanted the special privileges (such as a private chauffeur and a large residence) of NMR members, to end. In the ensuing political struggle between Van Rey and the other NMR members, the former was told to resign his post and leave the country. Mediation from André Haakmat (advisor to Prime Minister Chin A Sen) prevented Van Rey from being taken to the MBK by force and possibly be found guilty of treason and shot.[14] The incident sowed distrust between Sital and Bouterse.[15]

At the same time, Bouterse was named official commander-in-chief of the SKM and promoted to the rank of major. In that position, he gained more power as the NMR kept unravelling. In June, the NMR had to recognise that the governing power was with the civilian government so the organisation of people's committees ended.

When De Koning arrived in Suriname for the first high level talks between Suriname and the Netherlands, it became apparent that he would not give-in to the request for additional compensation to the development aid package necessary after the monetary loss caused by inflation. This was a severe disappointment for the Surinamese members of government and again caused a walkout of the Surinamese delegation.[16]

In addition, the leftist members of the NMR had arranged a seemingly 'spontaneous' large public event where the crowd was chanting 'De Koning, Suriname is geen pot met honing!' (Suriname is not a pot with honey!). Several NMR members also made fiery speeches, condemning the Dutch as colonial oppressors and accusing politicians of the traditional parties, of being traitors and counter-revolutionaries, as well as threatening to hold Minister De Koning for ransom, until demands were met.

This went too far for the Surinamese politicians and Bouterse, who were trying to get the Dutch to approve the proposals to donate development aid. After the leftist NMR members refused to withdraw their statements, Bouterse and Horb distanced themselves and left the NMR on 11 June 1980, claiming they needed to focus their attention to run the military as the *bevelhebber* (commander-in-chief) and *garnizoenscommandant* (garrison commander), respectively.

The final straw was when NMR members Sital and Hardjoprajitno, left for Nicaragua to celebrate the first anniversary of their revolution without informing the government. As the celebrations were attended by leaders such as Cuban President, Fidel Castro and PLO leader, Yassar Arafat, Chin A Sen feared that this would send a wrong signal to countries such as the US and the Netherlands. As a result, Sital was forced by Bouterse to step down as NMR chairman.

By the end of July, new elections were held within the military to elect NMR members. Mijnals was voted as chairman whilst new members were voted in, including Bouterse's friend Lieutenant Iwan Graanoogst.[17] Former members Sital, Abrahams and Joeman had not made themselves available for re-election and so most of the left leaning part of the NMR was removed. Abrahams, in the meantime, was promoted to lieutenant and took up his post as head of the military police.

Preventing Another 'Countercoup'

In the meantime, the cabinet members tried to put a budget together to realise the plans set out in the declaration set on 1 May. According to the constitution, all budgets had to be approved by parliament. This was something President Ferrier insisted on and he threatened to resign as president of Suriname if this was not done.[18] The government was also put under pressure from another side – the military.

On August 8, the SKM was officially renamed the *Nationaal Leger* (National Army). The leadership of the NL (*Nationaal Leger*) consisted of *Bevelhebber* Major Bouterse, *Garnizoenscommandant Kapitein* Horb and *Bataljonscommandant* (Battalion Commander) *Kapitein* Fernandes. These three men had, up to this point, formed what was called the '*Militair Gezag*' (military authority). Abbreviated to *het Gezag*, it would become the de facto main ruling authority until the end of the 1980s.

Three days later, NMR members Sital, Mijnals and Joeman, met with several RVP politicians in a hotel outside Paramaribo to discuss changing the political course of the country. NMR member Hardjoprajitno showed up late to the meeting. Being an informer of the military intelligence service, he interpreted the meeting as a plot to overthrow the government.

The following day, Bouterse (acting partly on Hardjoprajitno's report), informed Chin A Sen and Haakmat about a plot to overthrow and eliminate the government. He explained that this grave threat to Suriname must be stopped as it was his duty as *bevel* to protect the nation from bloodshed. Chin A Sen agreed with the threat and decided to counter this by dismissing parliament so that governance could be temporarily transferred to *het Gezag*, at least until a new civilian government would be formed.[19]

The next day – 13 August 1980 – early in morning, Joeman, Mijnals, Sital and the RVP politicians that were at the previous meeting, were arrested along with other people deemed 'a risk to the democracy'. These included Lieutenant Rambocus and Lieutenant Wirth as well as politicians who had served under the Arron government and had previously been arrested and released. A state of emergency was declared and parliament was dismissed.

President Ferrier, who was adamant about the application of the constitution, chose to resign as president of Suriname when informed about the takeover. In effect, the Surinamese government chose to abolish the constitution and have the country ruled by decrees that would be issued by the *Militair Gezag*. Suriname had

Minister André Haakmat. Dubbed Superminister, Haakmat acted as vice-prime minister, minister of foreign affairs, justice and army and police after August 1980 until he was dismissed in January 1981. (STVS)

On the first anniversary of the *Sergeantencoup*, the Monument of the Revolution, built on the place where the police headquarters once stood, was unveiled by *Bevelhebber* Bouterse. (Revokrant)

now taken the first steps of turning the country into a military dictatorship.

With parliament sent home and the constitution abolished, a new government had to be formed. It was decided that Chin A Sen would fulfil the double role of prime minister and president, with Haakmat acting as vice-prime minister, minister of foreign affairs, justice and army and police. The NMR, with Lieutenant Graanoogst now promoted to chairman, would be subordinate to *het Gezag*.

One of the actions Haakmat took, was to have the people recently arrested, tried in court. For this, he formed a special court (consisting of civilian and military members of the judiciary) that would try and convict the accused. Wirth and Rambocus were acquitted and requested to leave the country. Both immigrated to the Netherlands. The NMR members and politicians accused of attempting a leftist putsch, were found guilty (mostly based on Hardjoprajitno's testimony) and sentenced from eight months to three years of prison.[20]

In his function as a minister of foreign affairs, Haakmat was able get support from the Dutch regarding development aid. The Van Agt cabinet approved many of the development aid requests including the earlier mentioned, emergency programme. However, Haakmat was not able to prevent the Dutch from implementing visa regulations for Surinamers which initiated a tit-for-tat campaign between the two countries. The Dutch press criticised the increasingly more authoritarian government of Suriname consistently, slowly souring relations between The Hague and Paramaribo.[21]

In January 1981, Haakmaat was dismissed by Chin A Sen from his post after criticising the government in a radio interview. The criticism came from the fact that he felt that his work was being made difficult by the military. Accused of endangering the 'revolutionary process', he was replaced by RVP politician Harvey Naarendorp.

A year after the events of February 1980, the public support for the *revo* had waned and people noticed the struggle of power that was happening in the country. In addition, the public had reacted negatively to the wave of recent incarcerations which many saw as unjust. Demonstrations were held to protest the curfew, the ban on gatherings and other restrictions on freedom that were imposed after the events of August 1980.[22]

On the first anniversary of the *revo*, celebrations were planned to accommodate 60,000 students. while a monument for the revolution was unveiled at the ruins of the former police headquarters. Instead, 18,000 students arrived and many of them protested against *het Gezag* and demanded that democracy was restored.[23] Bouterse knew he had to act to keep the population involved in the *revo* if he wanted it to succeed.

After consulting with politicians of the old political parties who did not want to make agreements about mobilising their constituencies for the revolution, Bouterse turned to the people he had arrested in August 1980. He visited his leftist NMR members in jail to discuss how to continue the *revo*, rehabilitation and what course to follow, all without informing Chin A Sen and the government. After reconciling with the jailed men, Bouterse released them on 5 March and announced, in a joint press conference, that Suriname would follow the course of socialism.[24]

This move took many by surprise, especially since Bouterse had never been an outspoken supporter of socialism. Henk Chin A Sin, taken aback by Bouterse's announcement, said that he was open to give substance to socialism. This offered an opportunity for the small leftist parties RVP and PALU, as they were normally unable to be elected to parliament due to voting along ethnic lines.[25]

The Hawker Coup and Death of Keerveld

Not only Chin A Sen was displeased with the situation. One of the members of the Group of Sixteen, Sergeant Major Hawker had returned from the Netherlands, after he followed two-and-a-half months of training with the KCT in Roosendaal, in order to learn about the Dutch Commando Corps and implement his training to develop a similar course within the Surinamese army.[26]

Hawker confronted Bouterse that he had not made any personal gains from the *revo* like others had. Upon the release of Sital, Mijnals and Joeman, Hawker was upset that these men had returned to positions of leadership after falling out of grace. He made this known to his team at the commando training school in Paramaribo. Hawker, who like Ormskerk also had the nickname of '*bikkel*', was known as a military hard-ass but was politically inept to change things.[27]

On March 14, Hawker drove back with his driver to Paramaribo after visiting Saramacca. On the outskirts of the capital, he was taken under fire by a team of four men with Uzis that emptied their magazines into the vehicle he was travelling in. Although his driver Weissenbruch, was killed, the sergeant major was heavily wounded

Sergeant Major Wilfried Hawker during his training with the Dutch Commando Corps (KCT) in 1980. Hawker was the second Surinamer to have completed the training, after his good friend and fellow Group of Sixteen member Arthy Gorré. He was going to start a similar corps in Suriname before he was severely wounded on 14 March 1981 when the vehicle he was a passenger in, was taken under fire. He was accused of conspiring to overthrow the government and was sentenced to jail for four years. (De Groene Baret)

On 16 June 1981, Journalist Humprey Keerveld was found dead in neighbouring Guyana. Keerveld had been a vocal opponent of the *Militair Gezag*, having been jailed several times due to printing critical articles in his magazine *Bondroe*. The Guyanese police alleged that he was in Guyana to recruit mercenaries for an invasion of Suriname but this was never proven. (Vrije Stem)

with three shots to his head and neck. The team that executed the hit had left him for dead. Hawker survived after two civilians took him to the hospital.

The next day, the *Militair Gezag* announced that they had prevented a coup that was led by Sergeant Hawker. He was alleged to have conspired with Chinese businessmen to take power by eliminating the members of *het Gezag* and leftist politicians using a team of six disgruntled commandos that he was training. Forty people, including three Chinese businessmen, were arrested on the suspicion of plotting a countercoup, 12 of whom were to be directly involved with the operational part of the coup.[28]

It was claimed that Hawker had originally planned to execute the operation on the evening of 14 March. A fellow conspirator, having doubts about the coup, was said to have informed members of the military police the previous evening, about Hawker's plans. However, it is uncertain whether Wilfried Hawker had any real plans of conducting a coup d'état, as it seemed the ambush was an assassination attempt with the intention of eliminating an element within the armed forces that opposed the leftist turn that Bouterse had taken.

Whatever the case, the sergeant major was sentenced to four years of prison while three other soldiers and one businessman of Chinese descent, received lesser sentences.

Hawker's lawyer, Eddie Hoost, argued that the men had been forced into confessing the crime during their initial interrogation and the authority that Hawker had attempted to overthrow, was illegitimate,[29] These objections were dismissed by the president of the court, Ramdat Misier (who had previously presided over the trials following the Ormskerk affair).

In neighbouring Guyana, Humprey Keerveld was found murdered on 16 June. The journalist and publisher of the magazine *Bondroe*, was a vocal opponent of the government under Chin A Sen. Having been imprisoned for several months in 1981 after being accused of publishing critical articles, Keerveld left the country to campaign for the restoration of democracy in Suriname and the return of the original ethnic parties to politics.[30]

While visiting Georgetown, he was kidnapped and killed by three masked men. According to the police, Keerveld had spent a week in the country trying to recruit mercenaries to overthrow the Chin A Sen government. His 'Central Press Agency Suriname' had a satellite office in Guyana and Keerveld also had good relations with President Burnham.

Although the murder was never solved, some suspected that members of the Suriname military were behind his killing.[31] Whether he intended to commit a coup d'état or not, with Keerveld's death, another vocal opponent of *het Gezag* was silenced. People in Suriname took note.

Turning Left

On 1 May 1981, the Manifest of the Revolution was published by PALU chairman, Krolis. It praised the members of the Group of Sixteen as brave heroes of the people and compared them with Maroons such as Boni that were fighting off the colonial master (see Chapter 2). Filled with anti-colonial rhetoric, the manifest also accused former politicians and well-off Surinamers of being counter-revolutionaries. The confrontational and explicit text of the manifest rubbed many people the wrong way.[32]

A few days later, the chairmen of the radical Left parties entered the advisory council that was set up by *het Gezag* and NMR. This enabled them to control the government under Chin A Sen. This unofficial cooperative body, called the *Beleidscentrum* (Policy Centre), was slowly turning into an alternative government.[33]

Chin A Sen now had to face two leftist members who wanted to turn Suriname into a socialist country like Nicaragua and Cuba. This was in total opposition to his plan to return the country back to a parliamentary democracy and to hold elections within two years.[34]

In line with the turn to the left, the process had restarted of forming people's committees outside of Paramaribo. By August 1981, the hundredth committee was formed and at the event, NMR members and government members confirmed in speeches, that the committees were not only a new dimension of self-government but also a vanguard against colonial and imperial exploitation.[35]

By then, Bouterse had conducted his first foreign visit to Grenada where he met the head of the communist New Jewel Movement,

The National Volunteer Corps was founded after the *revo*. Led by former NMR member Ruben Braaf, the corps coordinated the various improvement projects throughout the country, such as social housing, sanitation and roadworks using the knowledge and manpower of the local *Volkscomitees*. Pictured here is a *Volkscomitee* paving a road in Paramaribo. (Revokrant)

Maurice Bishop. There he received a warm reception and took note of the enthusiasm the Grenadians had for their revolution. Before flying back home, Bouterse made a detour and secretly visited Fidel Castro at his home in Cuba, where he was received as a 'revolutionary brother-in-arms'. Impressed with Castro's knowledge and Bishop's charisma, upon his return, Bouterse announced there would be no short-term elections until the people's committees called for them. This went against Chin A Sen's plan to hold elections by October 1982.[36]

As ties with leftist countries were getting more cordial, several Surinamese soldiers were sent to Cuba in the coming years for specialist military training, including commando training and intelligence. Among those sent to Cuba was a young Maroon soldier named Ronnie Brunswijk, who would make a name for himself in the latter half of the 1980s.

In the meantime, the members of *het Gezag* had promoted themselves in rank with Major Bouterse advancing to the rank of *Luitenant Kolonel* and *Kapiteins* Horb and Fernandes, advancing to

The Surinaamse Luchtmacht

Back in December 1980, *het Gezag* announced they were thinking of an air force.[37] In June 1981, this became reality when Battalion Commander Fernandes announced that Suriname had founded the Surinamese Air Force (*Surinaamse Luchtmacht* or LUMA) and that pilots were being trained in the Netherlands at the Gilze-Rijen airbase.[38] However, the Dutch Minister of Defence later denied that Surinamese officers in-training were being specifically trained as pilots.[39]

The first commander of the LUMA was Lieutenant John Vasilda, a former Royal Netherlands Air Force pilot who had flown F-84F Thunderstreaks with 314 Squadron in Eindhoven and NF-5 Freedom Fighters with 315 Squadron. in Twente. An experienced pilot, in August 1974 he was involved in an accident in Norway where his NF-5 cut several power lines. Despite the damage to his aircraft, he managed to land safely in Sola. Vasilda was one of the Surinamese servicemen who left the Dutch armed forces to join the SKM after independence.[40]

On 11 July, the Minister of Army and Police, Neede signed a contract with the Swiss company Pilatus, for the delivery of four Britten-Norman BN-2B-21 Defenders. These aircraft were to be used for liaison purposes and for maritime patrol, together with the navy's patrol boats.[41]

The first Defender, serial SAF001, arrived at the beginning of March 1982. In addition to the defenders, the LUMA would purchase or lease a helicopter from Venezuela that would arrive before the end of the year. This helicopter, a Hughes 369D built in 1977, was registered as SAF100.[42]

Both aircraft took part in the dramatic events of March 1982.

J.A. Vasilda became the first commander of the LUMA after it was formed in 1981. This picture shows him as a first lieutenant in an NF-5A Freedom Fighter while he served with 315 Squadron of the *Koninklijke Luchtmacht* (Royal Netherlands Air Force) in 1974. (NIMH Collection)

the rank of major. The armed forces of Suriname were expanded with the formation of the *Surinaamse Luchtmacht* (Surinamese Air Force – see box) and a new Military Intelligence Unit was formed.

End of the Dutch Military Mission

Despite an agreement to extend the Dutch military mission in January 1981,[43] relations between both countries were souring. As the members of *het Gezag* started to lean towards the political left, the relationship with the Dutch military mission became strained. Head of the NMMS, Maarseveen, never had ties as good with Bouterse as Valk did, although the other members of the mission (such as Braire and Clements) were still close with members of the NL.[44]

By April, the members of the mission were no longer allowed to enter the barracks and the Surinamese government decided that the Dutch mission to Suriname would be terminated as it was time for the NL to stand on their own feet.[45] Before the end of May 1981, the Dutch military mission had left Paramaribo.[46]

Kolonel Maarseveen continued to stay in Paramaribo in his function of defence attaché to the Dutch embassy. However, the relationship between the disgruntled NMMS members and Maarseveen had soured to the point that the latter was accused of being a spy for the Dutch government, by the former. This resulted in threats to Maarseveen, eventually leading to his repatriation to the Netherlands in July 1981. *Kolonel* Bas Van Tussenbroek took over his role as DEFAT until he was also asked to leave by the Surinamese government, in 1983.[47]

Despite the departure of the military mission, the Dutch would still provide military support to Suriname in the form of equipment (such as old M1 carbines and spare parts for trucks and machine guns) and training of officers and NCOs in the Netherlands.[48] This was as per the previous agreement between both countries.

Starting late 1981, when it became clear that Chin A Sen and his opponents were going their separate paths, the Dutch government ordered the military intelligence to service aid and support the fledgling Suriname Military Intelligence Unit. This was done to keep close ties with the military leadership and to prevent closer military ties with countries of the socialist bloc.[49] The Dutch received support from the US a month later, after the head of the Dutch military intelligence visited Washington D.C. to elaborate their efforts to keep tabs on the Surinamese army. He also complained that the US policy of confrontational politics (what would later be known as the 'Reagan Doctrine') would not work with the Surinamese and hindered Dutch attempts to keep a close watch on the NL.[50]

Chin A Sen Steps Down[51]

As 1981 concluded, tensions between the communist members of the *Beleidscentrum* and Chin A Sen grew. The committee tasked with writing a new constitution had submitted a draft by the end of August 1981. Evaluation of the draft was not made a high priority by most members of the *Beleidscentrum* as they focused on the socialist path to governance, finding the draft not revolutionary enough.

The members of *het Gezag*, together with union leaders, formed a 'Revolutionary Front' designed to restructure the Surinamese form of governance. The front would consist of the various unions,[52] the communist parties, the people's committees as well as the military. The front would be led by a Presidium within which, no positions were occupied by Chin A Sen nor any members of his cabinet. Also missing were the church and women's rights unions, which had a lot of influence in Surinamese society.

On 17 December, the Revolutionary Front was inaugurated by Bouterse at the Monument of the Revolution. Invited to the inauguration were representatives of the various ethnic groups of Suriname as well as delegates from socialist countries and communist parties in the region from Guyana, El Salvador and Trinidad. On the same day as the inauguration, Chin A Sen held a passionate speech in the town of Coronie warning against dark forces that are trying to take over society, making it clear that there was an ideological separation between himself and the Revolutionary Front:[53]

> History has taught us that many people who claim freedom for themselves, will enforce their will and opinions upon others; that there are people who act against wealth, exploitation and idleness and who themselves profit the most and display the greatest self-indulgence, waste and debauchery.[54]

Despite receiving a popular demonstration of support on his birthday in January 1982, Chin A Sen's position was becoming difficult to hold. He would find no support from the old political parties (who saw him as a co-conspirator with the military) and was being undermined by his opponents in the *Beleidscentrum* as well as his former minister Haakmat (who had become active within the trade unions after his dismissal).[55]

Kolonel Maarseveen (left) in a meeting with *Bevelhebber* Bouterse and Minister of Defence and Police E. Ruimveld. Maarseveen had replaced Valk in mid-1980 but had a poor working relationship with most of the men in the NMMS. In addition, relations with the top of the Surinamese military and the NMMS were never as cordial as they were under *Kolonel* Valk. (Vrije Stem)

Garrison Commander Major Horb (left) and Commander-in-Chief Lieutenant *Kolonel* Bouterse announcing that everything is in control after one of the attempted takeovers. (STVS)

After Chin A Sen resigned from his post of prime minister and president, Lachmipersad Frederik Ramdat Misier became the acting president of Suriname on 8 February 1982. Ramdat Misier was the President of the Court of Justice and had previously presided over court cases regarding the Ormskerk affair and the *Hawkercoup* of March 1981. He would remain president of Suriname until 1988. (Public Domain – Wikimedia)

By the beginning of 1982, the Prime Minister's relations with Bouterse worsened significantly. During a cabinet meeting on 4 February, two PALU members presented a speech for him to be delivered, in which he distanced himself from the promise to hold elections in October of that year. Refusing to do so, the PALU members walked out. When Bouterse confronted Chin A Sen about the situation, the Lieutenant Colonel requested the latter step down as prime minister (but to stay on as president).

Chin A Sen confirmed that he would vacate the presidential palace by the next day and ordered his wife to pack up their belongings.[56] After stepping down as president and prime minister, Henk Chin A Sen left Suriname silently, a few months later, to follow training in a medical specialisation in Pennsylvania.[57] It would not take too long before he was involved with Surinamese politics again.

The Military Authority acted fast to replace the president once Chin A Sen left. Judge Ramdat Misier, President of the Court of Justice, was appointed acting president of Suriname on 8 February. Ramdat Misier had previously presided in the court cases concerning the Ormskerk affair and the *Hawkercoup*. With no political affiliation, he would mostly perform ceremonial functions during his tenure as president.[58]

With the functions of president and prime minister separated again, the members of *het Gezag* formed a small council that included Bouterse, Horb, Krolis and Haakmat. The latter two would act as advisors to *het Gezag* in setting up a new government and in the weeks to follow, more politicians and NMR members would be added to this council.

By the end of the month, Bouterse announced that the country would be governed by a Revolutionary Council, consisting of members of *het Gezag* and appointed revolutionaries officially turning Suriname into a dictatorship. In addition, Bouterse had announced that an intermediate constitution would be installed by 15 March, which would be referred to as the 'basic rules of the revolution'.[59]

Dutch and Domestic Response

In the Netherlands, the dismissal of Chin A Sen had not gone unnoticed. Following the installation of Ramdat Misier as president and the announcement of the Revolutionary Council, the Dutch government under Prime Minister Van Agt decided to limit development aid to Suriname. The funding of approved development projects that were in progress would continue (as would the pay supplements for Surinamese military personnel) but new projects would not be paid for until there was an outlook that democracy would be restored.[60]

Although Horb threatened to file an international complaint against the Dutch government, *het Gezag* did not take any measures against the Netherlands except issuing verbal rhetoric. Former NMR member Sital, now Minister of Healthcare, expressed his dissatisfaction with the Dutch decision and wondered why the Netherlands had no problem sending development aid to Nicaragua, while aid to a similar socialist country as Suriname, was now being reduced.[61]

In Suriname, the departure of Henk Chin A Sen did not change the unpopularity of the current form of government with the population. The curfew, a ban on political gatherings and the state of emergency were still in effect and promises to improve prosperity had not been fulfilled. In addition, the government censorship of the media was still in effect, leading to people not being able to vent their frustration.

On 13 February, the memorial service for NPS propagandist Lemmer was attended by at least 1,000 people, including Chin A Sen and Henck Arron. The funeral turned into a demonstration against the Military Authority, with speeches being held and people voicing their opinions before news cameras:

> It is oppression in the purest form! [The Military Authority] says there has never been as much freedom but [in reality] there never has been as much oppression [as now]. If you want to talk openly you are apprehended or can't find employment. Do you know what NMR stands for? *Nog Meer Rotzooi* (even more rubbish).[62]

In addition, organisations such as the Committee of Christian Churches (CCK) and university students disagreed with the path followed as there was no way to speak out except via the people's committees. Since there was little input and accountability, 'the chances of underhand deals and corruption were enormous' (as per CCK communique).[63]

If *het Gezag* had thought that the discontent had limited itself to the civilian population, they were seriously mistaken.

6

1982 – A MOST VIOLENT YEAR

In the early morning of Thursday 11 March 1982, citizens of Paramaribo who lived around the Memre Boekoe Kazerne, were awoken to the sound of gunfire. People who turned on their radio heard Major Horb's voice on SRS calling all soldiers to report to MBK as 'several adventurers and irresponsible elements' had caused problems in the barracks. The broadcast was then abruptly cut off. Other radio stations only broadcast music until 0630, when Radio Radika announced that Right-wing military forces, supported by high-ranking policemen, had taken power. What had happened?[1]

The three members of the *Militair Gezag* together at Fort Zeeland on 11 March 1982. From left to right: Commander-in-Chief Lieutenant Colonel Bouterse, Garrison Commander Major Horb and Batallion Commander Major Fernandes. According to a Dutch military intelligence report, the commissioning of Horb and Fernandes was a disappointment to the Surinamese troops, especially after Rambocus and Wirth were dismissed. (Nationale Voorlichtings Dienst Suriname)

The State of the National Army[2]

According to a Dutch military intelligence report from 1981, the situation in the NL was characterised by low morale, defeatism and frustration ever since the *Sergeantencoup* in 1980 had taken place. Although the army had expanded in strength, it had lost quality, partly when the officer corps had been thinned out by purges and departures.

Many members of the military were disappointed when the NMR was at the helm. Despite being promised participation, the NMR did not involve the rest of the military when making important decisions. Members of the NMR had even gone as far as stating that the council was not accountable to anyone and decisions were made according to their own insights.

Another disappointment came when Sergeant Major Fernandes and Sergeant Horb were elected battalion and garrison commander respectively. Within military circles the former was known as a frustrated military man prior to the 25 February coup, in addition to being a slow learner and guilty of serious dereliction of duties. The dismissal of lieutenants Rambocus and Wirth (see Chapter 5), which occurred before Horb's appointment, was a shock to the average soldier and went accompanied with lies and deception.

After the *Militair Gezag* took over command of the army from the NMR, things did not improve when Sital, Mijnals and Joeman were jailed by Bouterse. The army command was guilty of deceit in trying to excuse the jailing of the popular former members of the NMR. Finally, bad blood was formed when in January 1981 various members of the military were passed over for promotion and other promotions being based on loyalty and connections with *het Gezag*.

Many soldiers, most of them professionals, were looking to leave the service for other job opportunities. *Het Gezag*, however, had prohibited larger companies from employing active-duty personnel. This was a hypocritical measure, as many members of the army leadership had their own side jobs (for example, Bouterse had a pig farm) to make extra income (on top of their pay supplementation) courtesy of the Dutch state.[3]

Keeping intimidations, extreme unresponsiveness of the army command and heavy disciplinary punishments in mind, it is not surprising that many kept their criticism to themselves. With Chin A Sen dismissed and Suriname turning into a military dictatorship, several members of the military decided to act.

Planning for a Change[4]

A week after Chin A Sen was dismissed, a group of Hindustani civilians and soldiers started meeting in secret to hatch a plan to overthrow *het Gezag*. Their plan was to seize power and form the *Nationale Bevrijdings Raad* (National Liberation Council – NBR)

Promotion ceremony for conscripts on 21 January 1982. The SKM had started out with about 1,000 men in 1975. By 1982, the NL had grown to about 2,000 men. This was done by stricter enforcement of conscription – before the 1980 coup a lot of draftees were absent. (Azemalie Panchu)

At the same ceremony, newly promoted Sergeant A. Panchu (centre) receives congratulations while *Bevelhebber* Bouterse stands to the right of the line. When the military started to exercise more control over the country, Sergeant Panchu joined the plot to overthrow the *Militair Gezag* with the intent to restore democratic rule. (Azemalie Panchu)

to rule Suriname until free elections could be held and democracy could be restored.

The group met in secrecy at Professor Baal Oemrawsingh's house, where details were worked out. Oemrawsingh was a VHP member of parliament, who, as a Professor of Biochemistry, regularly held lectures at the prestigious Harvard University in the US. As such, he had close contacts with the US and Dutch embassies, which could come in handy once the NBR was in power.

Lieutenant Surendre Rambocus would assume leadership of military operations. He had returned to Suriname in May 1981 to complete his training as a social studies teacher, after receiving permission from *het Gezag*. Sergeant Sheombar, who was an instructor of the army cadet class and enjoyed the trust of many of the troops, would also take part in the coup. Besides members of the military and parliament, the group consisted of three civilians, two medical students and a warden of Santo Boma prison making a total of about 20 people.[5]

In order to prevent the coup from being seen as a Hindustani-only affair, several people from other groups of society were invited to meetings to ensure that the coup would have a large base of support. Creole Cyrill Daal, head of the trade union *Moederbond* and André Haakmat, were among those invited by Professor Baal but declined to meet as Daal felt that he was being watched by the intelligence service.[6]

After an earlier attempt on 8 March failed due to bad reconnaissance,[7] it was decided that the coup would be executed in the early hours of 11 March, the day after the Hindu Phagwa (or Holi) festival. It was expected that security at MBK would be lax since many soldiers would be recovering from the festivities or suffering from a hangover. The coup would be known as the *Rambocuscoup*.

A Turbulent Morning in March

Early in the morning, a lightly armed group of men led by corporal Mahabier arrived at the NMR headquarters on the Wilhelminastraat. After pointing his Uzi at the three guards, Mahabier forced the men to lie down and surrender their weapons. Aided by corporal Birbal, the group managed to quickly capture weapons that would be used for the next steps of the takeover.[8]

In the morning of 11 March, two MPs went to the MBK to check on reports of a takeover. They were fired upon by the conspirators posted at the gate. Both MPs managed to escape and report to Lieutenant Abrahams that the *Memre Boekoe Kazerne* had been taken over. The damage done to their NEKAF Jeep is pictured here. (Vereniging van Progressive Media Werkers)

Fully armed, the group broke into the southern part of the Membre Boekoe complex, where the fire department and vehicle fleet of the army were located. At around 0200, the facility was broken into and swiftly taken over. Two YPs were started and then used to crash through the gate of the northern complex of the MBK.[9] After an exchange of gunfire, the sentries on duty were overpowered and the complex was swiftly taken over.[10]

In the meantime, a group of conspirators including Warden Mangal and parliament member Mahadewsingh went to the Santo Boma prison and released several soldiers imprisoned there. This was done without resistance as the sleeping guard was awoken and told that Paramaribo was taken over and no resistance should be offered.[11] Sergeant Major Hawker and the men implicated in the March 1981 coup, were released.[12] Hans Lachman, a sergeant in the military police who had befriended Hawker during their time in jail, was also released and joined the group. His role in the *Rambocuscoup* would turn out to be pivotal.

As reports of gunfire reached the military police, a jeep with two MP corporals was sent to investigate the situation at the MBK. Arriving at the gate, soldiers at the sentry post opened fire with Uzis on the two military policemen. When the jeep was blocked in by a YP, the two men fled on foot. The injured MP Corporal Osran was able to alert his commander by radio, while lying in the front yard of one of the homes close to the barracks.[13]

The MP Commander, Lieutenant Abrahams, having been notified of the shooting at MBK, sped to the MP headquarters next to Fort Zeelandia, picking up Marcel Zeeuw and Arthy Gorré on the way. By the time they reached the Fort Zeelandia complex, Fernandes and Horb, who lived nearby, had arrived.[14]

The men turned the MP HQ into a temporary command centre and frantically started calling officers and NMR members to prevent them from reporting to the MBK barracks and ordering them to report to Fort Zeelandia instead. Not everyone could be reached so runners were sent out to alert officers at their homes, with Bouterse being reached just as he was about to leave for *Memre Boekoe Kazerne*. Horb had also sent out a tape to the radio station SRS to warn the members of the armed forces that MBK had been taken over by unknown personnel. As previously mentioned, his tape was abruptly cut off at 0430. The army leadership and their followers were unable to further communicate with the rest of the armed forces.[15]

As soldiers started arriving at MBK to report for duty, officers and NCOs who were unaware of the situation in MBK, were incarcerated and thrown into the stockade. Soldiers arriving at MBK Zuid were gathered in the courtyard and put to work as more YPs were started up and armed with .50 machine guns. With the soldiers following orders from Lieutenant Rambocus, the troops went out through the city, set-up roadblocks at strategic points and captured the various radio stations in the city. The patrol tasked with capturing the ammunition bunker at the Dhoekhiweg arrived at 0430, only to find that Sergeant Major Hawker had already arrived and taken it over.[16]

In the MBK, the public address speakers blared out announcements that the *Nationale Bevrijdings Raad* had taken power and new elections were to be held in three months. Names of prominent Surinamese military and police members were mentioned as being members of the council including Hawker and Rambocus.[17] The soldiers present at the MBK cheered upon hearing that the army leadership had been eliminated, with only a few soldiers choosing to leave the barracks and not participate.[18] During the day, politician Paul Somohardjo of the Javanese Pendawa Lima, went to the MBK and joined the conspirators.

At this point, troops under NBR command were in control of all military installations of the country. These included the outposts in Nickerie, Zanderij and Albina, the ammunition bunker and MBK, in addition to all radio and television stations. Only the military police and the naval detachment (with its powerful high sea patrol boats) were still reporting to the *Militair Gezag* with the latter all located at the MP HQ. At the time that Paramaribo would normally come to life, schools, offices and shops remained closed. One of the S-class patrol boats left the naval base and patrolled the Suriname River off Fort Zeelandia.[19]

Lieutenant Rambocus (left) with his troops at the MBK. The YPs pictured right are ready to move to attack Fort Zeelandia. (STVS)

At the fort, the men gathered there discovered it was Rambocus and Hawker who had launched the coup. The men at the HQ, including the MP force, military leadership, the NMR members and the members of the Group of Sixteen (minus Hawker) had access to limited amounts of weapons including carbines from the police and personal sidearms.

Some of the men at Fort Zeelandia were not surprised to hear about the coup as Lieutenants Dihal (Deputy Battalion Commander) and Birdja (MP Deputy Commander) had been in contact with the NBR prior to the coup being launched. If the coup attempt was successful, Birdja agreed to take on an important role in the army after the elimination of the military leadership. Dihal on the other hand, stayed ambivalent, not committing himself to giving any support. They had disagreed to participate in the coup d'état itself

Soldiers following Rambocus are moving forward towards the Independence Square. The ad hoc nature of the attack is illustrated by the use of a pickup truck instead of army lorries. (Collection Nationaal Archief/Anefo, Rob C. Croes)

and would not command forces against *het Gezag*.[20]

At 0700, Rambocus called the leadership at the fort demanding them to surrender. Fernandes responded that Rambocus would have to come get them and they would be waiting. The battalion commander did not have to wait long.[21]

By 0730, soldiers following Rambocus and supported by YPs, started making attacks with machine guns and 81mm mortars on the Fort Zeelandia complex from the area around the *Mamabon*, west of Independence Square. The men at the HQ retreated to the old fortress in the complex, where the defenders established a perimeter.[22] Their defence was assisted by Ernst Gefferie who was onboard patrol boat S402 and used its 40mm Bofors cannons to attack any forces trying to reach the fort. Most of the mortars fired on the fort landed in the Suriname River.[23]

A NBR-manned YP408 standing guard at the Court of Justice. Although grainy, the picture shows that this is one of the newer YPs delivered between 1975 and 1982 as it has the larger indicator light. It could be the PV-V mortar tug, that would later be called *Cobra*. (Collection Nationaal Archief/Anefo, Rob C. Croes)

During the fighting, several soldiers were injured and taken to *het Militair Hospitaal* (the military hospital). During one of the attacks of the NBR on the fort around 1130, Soldaat Badal collapsed and died of a heart attack. He was the only death that occurred during the fighting around Fort Zeelandia.[24] A woman was injured during the exchange of gunfire and was taken to *het Academisch Hospitaal* (the Academic Hospital) for treatment. At this point, Bouterse and his men were holed up in the fortress and a stalemate ensued. With the battle on the ground halted for the time being, a battle of the airwaves started.[25]

The Information War

Following Radio Radika's announcement at 0630 that the NBR had taken power, around 0900 the ANP released a message that Chief of Police De Vrij refuted the claim that he supported the coup attempt. The SNA released a message that the members of *het Gezag* were not liquidated as claimed but were alive and well and set-up in Fort Zeelandia.[26]

Besides reaching out over the airwaves, the NBR also reached out to the Dutch embassy. The Dutch DEFAT was contacted by Hawker and informed that the NBR had the situation under control, except for light resistance at Fort Zeelandia. 'Bikkel' informed Van Tussenbroek that the NBR would disclose their plans within 24 hours but he could already announce that elections were planned to be held within three months. The embassy personnel could clearly hear the fighting taking place and see two patrol boats moored in the Suriname River.[27]

At 1230, Radio Radika went off air and the SRS started transmitting NBR announcements. The NBR made it known that there would a curfew from 1900 to 0400 and that gatherings larger than three people were forbidden. Furthermore, schools would be closed the following day.[28]

This was countered by an SNA communique at 1400 that stated that all military objects were under the control of *het Gezag* (with the exception of MBK and the ammo bunker). The army leadership was present at Fort Zeelandia, supported by the NMR and other prominent military personnel. But the battle for control was still underway and had taken a turn against the men under Rambocus.[29]

At 1000 two YP408s arrived at Fort Zeelandia. These were instructed by Rambocus to go to the fort and capture or take out the army leadership.[30] The first YP was driven by Hans Lachman, who had been released from Santo Boma prison in the morning, on the insistence of Hawker. A few weeks prior to his release, he had been convicted of murdering a peasant farmer named Mahes over a drug deal and had been sentenced to 10 years in prison.[31] Being a sergeant in the military police, he had received training on driving the YP. Together with gunner Ramkhelawan, he drove to the fort with the second YP in tow commanded by Corp Francis. After arriving at the fort, it is unclear what exactly happened.

YP408 drives down the Gravenstraat towards Fort Zeelandia. Part of the presidential palace at the *Onafhankelijkheidsplan* can be seen in de background. (STVS)

11 & 12 March 1982
Paramaribo, The Rambocuscoup

Blue = actions by troops that sided with NBR
Green = actions by troops that sided with Gezag

[99] = broadcasts
(99) = military operations

12 March 1982
23) 04.00: Troops siding with het Gezag attack the MBK complex from two sides. Hawker is seriously injured by a mortar bomb and sent to the hospital.
24) Hawker is captured at the Academic Hospital and brought to Fort Zeelandia.
25) 07.45: Shots fired at Radio SRS and all NBR broadcasting ceases.
26) 09.00: Interview with Hawker is broadcast on STVS.
27) 09.30: Second attack on the MBK is repulsed.
28) 12.00: Rambocus and closest conspirators flee the MBK in two YP408s and a car in direction of Nieuw Nickerie.
29) MBK and Ammo Bunker secured by het Gezag and officers locked in the brig are set free.
30) The LUMA scrambles its BN-2 and helicopter to search for Rambocus.

By 17 March 1982, the conspirators have been captured by het Gezag; Corporal Mahabir escaped.

Main Events
11 March 1982
1) **01.30:** NMR Building entered and weapons captured
2) **02.00:** MBK South captured and YP408s started.
3) **02.00-02.30:** MBK North captured without bloodshed using YP408s.
4) **02.00-02.30:** Warden Mangal and Mahadewsing go to Santo Boma and free Sergeant-Major Hawker.
5) Jeep with MPs arrives at the MBK and is shot at. The fleeing MPs manage to warn the MP HQ at Fort Zeelandia.
6) MP Commander warns members of het Gezag and 'Group of Sixteen' about the coup and the MPs assemble at Fort Zeelandia, taking refuge inside.
7) **04.00-04.30:** A tape sent by Major Horb to the SRS announces that 'adventurers and irresponsible elements' are causing trouble and that all soldiers are to report at the MBK. It is cut off when soldiers siding with Rambocus arrive.
8) Men arriving at the MBK are informed that the members of the Militair Gezag are dead or captured and that the Nationale Bevrijdingsraad (NBR) will hold elections in three months. Officers are locked up in the brigade. Troops siding with the NBR leave the barracks to set up roadblocks throughout the city and capture all radio stations.
9) **04.30:** A patrol sent to capture the ammo bunker at the Dhoekiweg finds out that Hawker had already captured the installation.
10) S402 and one of river patrol boats cast off from the naval base and set up off Fort Zeelandia to support the men inside.
11) **06.30:** Radio Radika announces that the NBR has toppled het Gazag and that they have taken power.
12) **07.00:** Rambocus calls the men in Fort Zeelandia to surrender. They refuse.
13) **07.30:** First attack on Fort Zeelandia with APCs and 81mm mortars.
14) **09.00:** NBR claims of leadership being captured are proven wrong by ANP bulletins.
15) **10.00:** Rambocus sends several APCs led by Lachman to Fort Zeelandia to capture the Militair Gezag. However, Lachman ends up defectring, taking his APCs with him.
16) **11.30:** Troops siding with the NBR attack the For Zeelandia again. Solider Badal dies of heart attack during the shooting.
17) **12.30:** The NBR announced a curfew over SRS, a ban of gatherings, and the closure of schools.
18) **14.00:** Using radio and with Telesur assistance, het Gezag and NMR at Fort Zeelandia are able to set up a transmitter and announce that they are in control of all military installations except the MBK and ammo bunker. This is confirmed by a telephone call to the Wereldomroep and by the SNA.
19) **14.30:** Soldiers siding with the NBR attack Fort Zeelandia again. The attack is repulsed.
20) **17.00-17.45:** Interviews from Fort Zeelandia broadcast on SRS and STVS, making it clear that het Gezag is not beaten.
21) **20.45:** The last attack on Fort Zeelandia with APCs and mortars is unsuccessful.
22) **22.45:** Hawker and Rambocus appear on TV to announce that, 'Suriname has been liberated from an unbearable yoke'.

Lieutenant Hans Lachman was jailed in Santo Boma for the murder of a farmer when he was broken out of prison by Wilfried Hawker. Being a member of the military police, he was ordered to command a force of YP408s to capture the *Militair Gezag* at Fort Zeelandia. Instead, he ended up surrendering his APCs to Bouterse's men. (Vrije Stem)

According to the SNA, Lachman had stopped at the fort. Instead of attacking or capturing the members, he went into discussion with the military personnel and was convinced by Arthy Gorré to side with the army leadership and to hand over his APC. According to people who took part in the coup attempt, Lachman was approached by Paul Bhagwandas to surrender as he was the only person in the military who supported him during his trial for murder. According to the *mofokoranti* (RUMINT), Lachman's .50 machine gun jammed and he was only then approached by the besieged army personnel at Fort Zeelandia. For whatever reason that Lachman surrendered, the results were the same. The soldiers at Fort Zeelandia loyal to Bouterse were now in possession of two armoured personnel carriers, leaving the troops supporting the NBR with at least three YP408s to silence the opposition in Fort Zeelandia.[32]

The YPs were immediately put to good use. Manned by members of the MP and 'Group of Sixteen', the APCs took up defensive positions in front of the fort and near the presidential palace. In order to distinguish these YPs from the ones in hands of the NBR, a white cloth was wrapped over the front end of the vehicles to cover the title NL As it took a while for the news of Lachman's surrender to reach Hawker and Rambocus, the men at the fort (now totalling about 75 men), went out to re-establish communications with the outside world. Troops loyal to Bouterse were able to get an emergency transmitter set-up with help from personnel of the radio services and the head of the Surinamese phone company (John Neede). Broadcasting on the frequency of Rapar, Bouterse's group started broadcasting messages at 1400. Additional communication equipment was brought to the fort by soldiers loyal to the leadership, thanks to the confusion on the complotters' side.[34]

In the meantime, one member of *het Gezag* called the *Wereldomroep* in the Netherlands, to explain that the army leadership was intact and in control of the situation. As many people in Suriname (including the army) regularly tuned in to the *Wereldomroep*, this news was taken at face value due to the fact that the Dutch news channel was not controlled by any of the fighting parties.[35]

Rambocus Loses Control

After realising what happened to the two YPs, Rambocus sent out another attack on Fort Zeelandia around 1430. Using two YP408s and mortars, soldiers on both sides exchanged fire without any significant results. Due to the fact that stores remained closed and the civilian population stayed off the streets, casualties amongst the population of Paramaribo during the coup attempt were low.[36]

By 1700, announcements made by Bouterse were broadcast on Rapar, followed by a TV broadcast on STVS at 1745 that the military leadership was intact. They confirmed they were back in control of all military installations except the munitions bunker and MBK. Soldiers were asked to stop the pointless fighting, side with the army leadership and report to the fort. Amazingly, STVS kept broadcasting interviews from both sides that day via tapes delivered from Fort Zeelandia as well as interviews held at the TV station itself.[37]

SRS announcer Sajadsingh vehemently countered these reports. Combined with the reports from the *Wereldomroep*, it became clear to the Surinamese people that the *Militair Gezag* was certainly not defeated, never mind captured or killed. For many of the soldiers at the MBK this was the final straw. Troops started defecting to Fort Zeelandia en masse, some taking equipment with them. By the end of the day, forces loyal to *het Gezag* were in possession of at least three YP408s.[38]

Around 2045, another attack was conducted by soldiers fighting for the NBR side. After firing several 81mm mortars at the fort with limited results, attacks ceased for the night and all remained calm as the people of Paramaribo followed the curfew.[39]

Contrary to the silence on the streets, both forces kept

An YP408 placed on the north side of Independence Square from where it could cover the Fort Zeelandia complex. (STVS)

More YP408s for Suriname?[33]

Upon independence, the Surinamese army inherited five YP408s from the TRIS. These were used during both the *ingreep* and the *Rambocuscoup*, where they played a prominent role. However, press reports talked about six vehicles in 1982 and even reported nine vehicles being in service in 1986.

Observations by tank enthusiasts noted that some of the YPs were equipped with a different set of indicator lights to the ones that served with the TRIS. These different lights were part of a modification performed on Dutch YPs after 1972, modifications which the TRIS YP408s did not receive. This meant that more YPs were delivered to Suriname, somewhere between independence and before military cooperation between Suriname and the Netherlands was halted after the events of December 1982. These were possibly shipped to Suriname with the intention to supply them for spare parts. At least two of these were taken into active service.

Pictures of YPs taken at the maintenance depot at MBK in 2009 and during military parades show that at least four YPs were delivered after independence. One of these was a YP408 PW-MT named *Cobra*, another a YP408 PW-V named *Bofroe*. Which type of variant the two remaining YP408s were, cannot be determined.

The PW-MT had a baseplate for a hitch at the rear end, distinguishing it from the standard PWI. In Dutch service, these were used for pulling wheeled 120mm Hotchkiss-Brandt Rayé mortars (not available in Suriname). For this purpose, they could carry a five-man crew (driver, gunner and the three-man mortar crew) and had a cargo deck in the back to transport mortar shells.

The PW-V was a version designed for carrying 1,500kg of (infantry) weapons and stores on the battlefield. It was therefore equipped with a loading floor and a gate to separate the crew of the APC from the cargo. Other differences were the shortened exhaust to reduce the risk of sparks in the cargo bay and the absence of levers on the top hatches as there was no infantry to operate these. The PW-V was also not equipped with radios and only had a crew of two (driver and gunner). This did not mean, however, that *Bofroe* was never spotted without soldiers riding in the cargo compartment (as seen during parades).

In order to distinguish the YP408s of the NBR from the ones under control of *het Gezag's* control, a white sheet was put onto the front of the YP to cover the title of NL. This YP408 is of the PW-V cargo carrier version, which arrived after independence. Its shortened exhaust, lack of catches for the top hatches and large indicator light distinguishes it from the YP408 that were given to the SKM when the TRIS left. (Copyright inheritors of Jul M Dubois)

transmitting messages into the airwaves. Sajadsingh continued making pro-NBR broadcasts throughout the night, having interviews with religious leaders and other pundits while at the same time making verbal assaults on *het Gezag*. From Fort Zeelandia, the army leadership kept transmitting messages until at around midnight, power was cut to their transmission equipment.[40]

At around 2245, Hawker and Rambocus appeared on television. This time the duo stated that Suriname had been liberated from an unbearable yoke. They claimed that the police and the NBR were maintaining order in the streets and all strategic locations were in their control. In addition, all treaties with friendly nations would be adhered to.[41]

In the evening of 11 March, Rambocus and Hawker appeared on STVS, with the latter announcing that Suriname had been released from 'an unbearable yoke'. By this time, the forces under Bouterse were substantial, putting the success of their coup in doubt. (STVS)

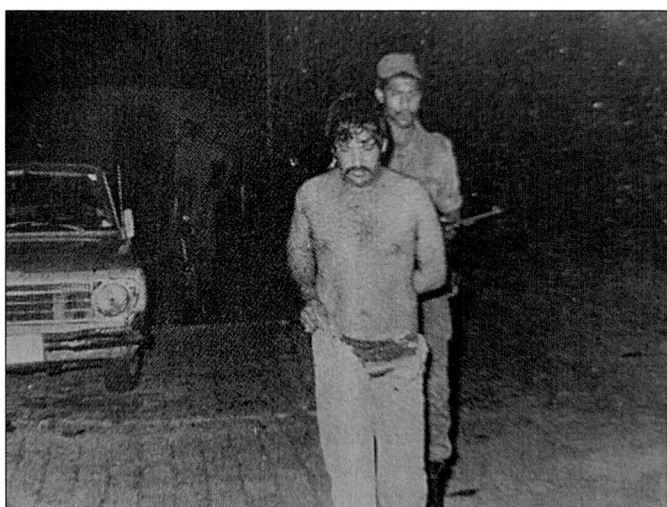

Warden Mangal had gone with VHP Member of Parliament Mahadewsing to Santo Boma prison to release Sergeant Major Hawker. He was captured and sentenced to 4 years of prison. (Stichting Makmur)

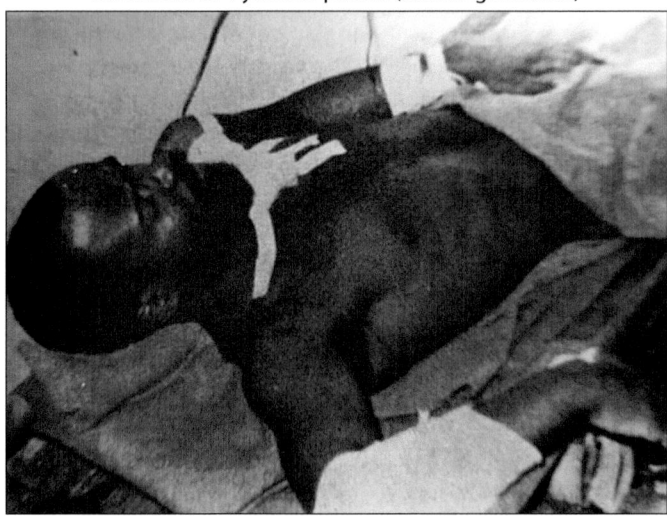

On 12 March, Hawker was injured by an exploding mortar shell at the MBK. He was captured by loyalists in the hospital and taken to Fort Zeelandia. There he was put on TV and requested Rambocus' men to put down their arms. A member of the 'Group of Sixteen', Hawker was probably executed that morning. (Stichting Makmur)

Realising that they had lost a significant amount of support from the bulk of the soldiers, the complotters attempted to get more political support behind them. In the evening, Professor Oemrawsingh, Rambocus and Hawker visited the chairman of the VHP, Jaggernath Lachmon, at his home to ask for public support for his cause. The chairman refused, stating that he was against any form of violence.[42]

Hawker and Rambocus would have to keep on fighting with the troops they had – and with no political party speaking out in support of their coup attempt, they had no alternative but to keep going with the meagre resources at their disposal.

Bouterse Strikes Back
Around 0400 on 12 March, forces loyal to *het Gezag* marched on the *Memre Boekoe Kazerne* and attacked with the support of several APCs, targeting the northern complex in two groups from the east and north. Each group consisted of at least one YP and attacked the MBK with mortars and machine guns. The attack was repelled by the NBR forces holding the MBK but it came at a heavy cost to the defenders.[43]

During or before the attack, Sergeant Major Hawker was demonstrating the use of an 81mm mortar to some of his men. In his enthusiasm he dropped a round into the tube, firing the mortar round into a low overhanging concrete roof. The mortar round bounced off the roof, exploded and showered him with shrapnel, severely injuring him in the process. In the confusion of the attack, medic Sergeant Kolf treated Hawker and had him quickly sent away for medical care, ending up in *het Academisch Ziekenhuis*.[44]

After arriving at the hospital, a sympathiser of *het Gezag* informed Fort Zeelandia that Hawker was there undergoing treatment. Wasting no time, a YP408 was sent to capture the sergeant major while he was in a vulnerable spot. Troops arrived and dragged the heavily bandaged Hawker into the YP, injuring a protesting healthcare employee in the process.[45]

Around 0700, a communique from SNA announced the capture of Wilfried Hawker. In addition, Warden Mangal had been captured as well when he showed up to work in the morning. Sajadsingh countered these claims over SRS, requesting all military personnel to stay at home and informing them that the army leadership had fled the country. By 0745, shots were fired at the SRS building and the radio channel went off the air. This left all media outlets in Suriname in control of *het Gezag*.[46]

Concurrently, the *Wereldomroep* announced the capture of Hawker. Any doubt of the legitimacy of this claim ended at 0900 when he appeared on television, heavily bandaged on a stretcher at Fort Zeelandia. During the interview, Hawker said that he was forced to participate with the conspirators. He also called on Rambocus and his men to surrender to the military authorities.[47]

After another failed attack by army soldiers at 0930, the forces loyal to Bouterse waited to commence any further attacks.[48] This was done in order to save the lives of the officers that were captured during the initial takeover,[49] although probably more so because the forces loyal to *het Gezag* were low on ammunition. Around noon, word reached Fort Zeelandia that Rambocus and his men had fled the Memre Boekoe Kazerne.

When soldiers captured the MBK, they freed the 15 officers and NCOs that were held in the stockade. The captured men claimed that Rambocus panicked after Hawker had been captured and hastily planned his escape. After going through the armoury and taking a large number of weapons, Rambocus and his men left the

MBK with two YP408s and a car, taking off westwards towards Nieuw Nickerie on the border with Guyana.[50]

Chasing Rambocus
After leaving the MBK, one of the YPs taken by Rambocus first stopped at the ammunition bunker at the Doehkiweg, before leaving Paramaribo. Rambocus' men also shot up the police post at Kwatta (a town west of the capital).[51] Despite the border with French Guiana being closer to Paramaribo, getting there would be impossible as the ferry across the Suriname River to Meerzorg was closed due to the fighting in the city. For the fleeing men to reach Nieuw Nickerie, they had to cross the Coppename River by ferry between Boskamp and Jenny at Coppenamepunt. The lead YP, commanded Rambocus, was followed by Mahabier in a second YP, manning the .50 machine gun on top of the APC.

Meanwhile back in Paramaribo, the men under Bouterse had retaken the munitions bunker. In total, 15 participants of the coup were captured when the bunker and the MBK fell back under control of the *Militair Gezag*. The NL had now retaken all military installations and could now focus on finding and capturing Rambocus and his men.[52] In order to persuade Lieutenant Rambocus to surrender to the authorities, a message from his brother Jhai was recorded and broadcast on SRS multiple times that afternoon.[53]

The burnt-out wreckage of one the YP408s that Rambocus and his men used to escape. It was set on fire after it broke down. It now serves as a gate guard at the MBK. (De Ware Tijd)

Battalion Commander Fernandes instructed the air force to take to the air and locate the fleeing group of men. The LUMA used both of its aircraft in service – a light aircraft (Defender BN-2 SAF001) and a helicopter (Hughes 369D SAF100) flown by a US civilian pilot. On their way to Coppenamepunt, the YPs were approached by the Defender. Mahabier fired on the aircraft but the BN-2 was not hit.

Near Caledonië (5km from the ferry at Coppenamepunt), one of the YPs broke down. After disconnecting the fuel line, the YP was set on fire by tossing a grenade into the main compartment. As the YP was filled for three-quarters with weapons and ammunition, the resulting explosion and fire burnt-out the vehicle. Of the

The Surinamese Defenders were the first aircraft ordered for the LUMA. All were delivered in 1982, with SAF001 being used to locate Rambocus' men as they fled Paramaribo. Here SAF003 (with temporary registration G-BJEA) is seen at Luton Airport, UK in May 1982 before its delivery to Suriname. (Frank McMeiken)

men present, seven decided to press on while the rest returned to Paramaribo.[54]

Upon learning of Rambocus' flight towards the Guyanese border, the army leadership sent out the helicopter to Boskamp and instructed the ferry to sail to the other side of the river at Jenny, cutting off Rambocus' escape route.[55] The conspirators were trapped between two rivers with their remaining APC and car.

Confused and realising that he could not reach Nieuw Nickerie by vehicle, Rambocus and his group decided to head to the rainforest of Saramacca to hide. Heading eastwards, the BN-2 Defender of the LUMA approached the remaining vehicles and swept in low to investigate. As the YP driver swerved to avoid the aircraft, one of the men riding on top of the APC, lost their balance and fell off of the YP. The resulting fall severely injured the man and he was taken back to Paramaribo for treatment. In the end, only three conspirators – Rambocus, Mahabier and Ramsandjal – continued on to the forests of Saramacca.[56]

As *het Gezag* announced the recapture of the Memre Boekoe Kazerne, it informed the public that the army was still on the lookout for Rambocus and his co-conspirators and requested information on their whereabouts. In addition, the curfew would remain in place until further notice. Despite the search for Rambocus carrying on for the following days, the people of Paramaribo went back to their normal lives that afternoon now that the fighting was over. That evening, acting President Ramdat Misier held a speech on TV in which he urged the fighting parties to lay down their arms to prevent further bloodshed and to report themselves to the authorities.[57]

Rambocus and his two fellow conspirators were still on the run. After a passer-by brought them in his vehicle to an acquaintance of Ramsandjal, the driver reported the trio to the authorities. The army responded by arriving in force with several APCs and started to comb out the areas, swiftly capturing Ramsandjal.

Rambocus had been severely injured during the fighting at the MBK. Mahabier helped the lieutenant until he could no longer carry him. Forced to leave his commander behind, Mahabier eventually escaped Suriname via Guyana and fled to the Netherlands. After nearly a week on the run, Lieutenant Rambocus was finally captured by the authorities on 17 March. He was immediately brought over to Fort Zeelandia for interrogation. By then, his co-conspirators Baal and Hawker were dead.[58]

The Execution of Wilfried Hawker

On the morning of the following day, Saturday 13 March, all members of the military were called for assembly on the parade grounds at the Memre Boekoe Kazerne. With many civilians gathered at the fence to watch the activity, Lieutenant *Kolonel* Bouterse held a speech, starting off praising the military and the civilian population for their heroic actions in the previous day.[59]

However, the tone changed quickly when the commander-

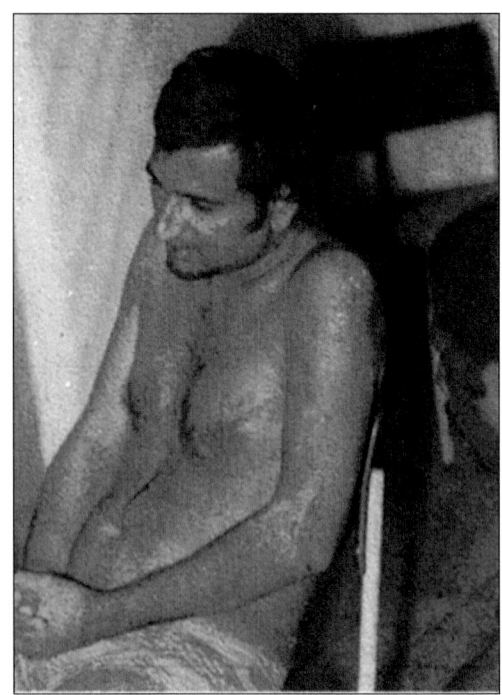

Lieutenant Soerendre Rambocus after his capture. He was severely beaten by his interrogators at Fort Zeelandia and would have likely been executed if it were not for the protests from Surinamese society and abroad, against Hawker's execution. (Stichting Makmur)

in-chief announced that high treason had been committed and that considering that crime, Sergeant Major Hawker had been executed by firing squad at 0600 that morning. This news was received with cheers from the soldiers present. By contrast, the civilians at the fence were shocked. News of Hawker's death spread like wildfire. During the flag parade, several of the captured conspirators were brought out and humiliated in front of the attending soldiers.

When asked at the afternoon press conference if Hawker had been given a trial by a military court before his execution, Bouterse responded by saying: '[…] Hawker was a soldier and knew what the consequences [of his irresponsible actions] would be and had to accept them'. It did not take long for society to respond. The fact

Arrested conspirators brought out at the MBK during the flag parade on the morning of 13 March. The men were marched out in their underwear and publicly humiliated. (Stichting Makmur)

Sergeant Sheombar was an instructor with the NL and had thus the trust of many of the men. His participation in the *Rambocuscoup* was severely punished, leading to a jail term of 7 years. (Stichting Makmur)

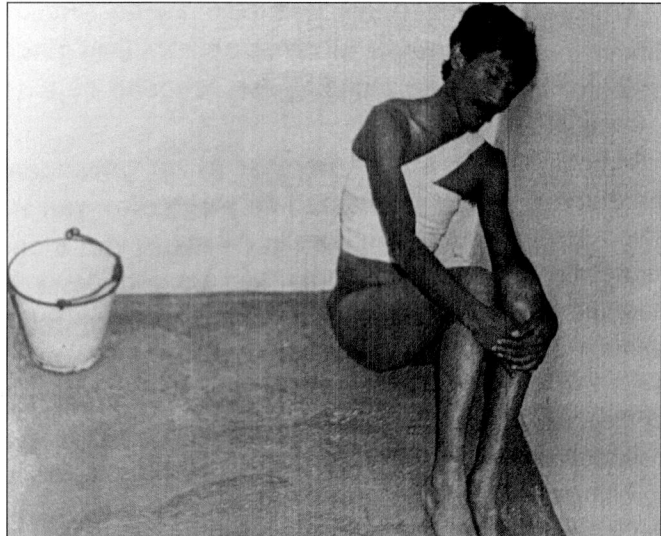

Paul Somohardjo was a parliament member for the Javanese Pendawa Lima party. He went to the MBK after the coup was started and supported the NBR. He was later arrested and jailed by the *Militair Gezag* but escaped after attending a funeral in December of that year. (Stichting Makmur)

that Hawker had been executed without trial, while being heavily wounded and lying on a stretcher, had caused major indignation. Hawker was most likely executed the previous day, not long after giving his interview on TV.

The following Monday, the CCK responded first condemning the use of violence. This was soon followed by protests from trade unions, the bar association, the medical associations, the Red Cross and student organisations, amongst others. In addition, Dutch Prime Minister Van Agt called it 'a despicable act'. This outrage probably prevented the same from happening to Surendre Rambocus after he was arrested.

While the army had surrounded Saramacca in search of Lieutenant Rambocus, the military police had started an investigation into the failed coup d'état by doing house searches and issuing warrants for arrests. On Sunday 14 March, MP Commander Abrahams announced in a press briefing that four members of parliament (from the VHP and Pendawa Lima) were suspected of organising the coup and that arrests had been made including those of industrialists, politicians, students and (ex-) military personnel.[60] Of these, several were still on the run, including korp Mahabier, Lieutenant Rambocus and Professor Oemrawsingh.

Furthermore, Abrahams announced that the group of coup plotters had attempted to assassinate the members of *het Gezag* and NMR on two occasions. The first attempt was at a temple celebration on 7 March, where the targets would be taken out by Sergeant Sheombar (one of the soldiers captured after he returned to Paramaribo). This failed when only two NMR members showed up. The second attempt was alleged to be at a Phagwa celebration at Professor Oemrawsingh's house on 10 March. When the invited guests (Bouterse and Hardjoprojitno) did not show up, the coup was planned for the next day.[61]

On 22 March, the military police held a briefing in which evidence for the coup was presented. Various captured weapons were shown and several suspects, including Mahadewsingh and Somohardjo, were shown with their heads shaved but otherwise unharmed. In addition, Sergeant Sheombar explained on a chalkboard how the assassination murders at the Hindu temple and Oemrawsingh's house, were to have been carried out.[62]

Despite claims in several books and by various politicians after the failed countercoup, the group of conspirators never made use of any mercenaries nor was there any foreign involvement. The coup of 11 March 1982, later known as the (*Hawker-*)*Rambocuscoup*, was an all-Surinamese affair.[63]

Death of Professor Baal Oemrawsingh

On the morning of 15 March, Professor Oemrawsing's dead body was found in a polder near Aloepi outside Nieuw Nickerie, the district he represented in parliament. An autopsy later reported he died due to poisoning by a pesticide.[64] Nevertheless, rumours went around that he was murdered on order of *het Gezag*.

Seeing the upheaval caused by Hawker's execution and threats by the Dutch government to suspend development aid,[65] the authorities decided to put Rambocus in prison while awaiting trial for treason. On the day of the MP briefing, services were held for Hawker and Oemrawsingh which were attended by many members of the public. These were closely watched by the military to ensure the occasions were not used for demonstrations.

With hostilities over, Jaggernath Lachmon reported himself to the authorities to inform them that the conspirators had requested him for political support. He expected that someone would report that Hawker, Rambocus and Oemrawsingh had visited his home. Bouterse reached out to the VHP chairman and requested they held a speech together on TV to calm things down. Lachmon agreed on the condition that he would be given insight to the speech. In the end, Bouterse declined and had President Ramdat Misier hold a speech that evening in which he called for Surinamers to join together and for reconciliation.[66]

Professor Baal Oemrawsingh was the mastermind behind the *Rambocuscoup*. A VHP member of parliament representing Nickerie, he was found dead after the coup in his home district with his death ruled as a suicide by poisoning. (Vrije Stem)

The first aircraft of the LUMA was this Hughes 369D. It was registered as SAF100 but unfortunately, no particular markings can be made out in the picture. (Copyright inheritors of Jul M Dubois)

The wreckage of SAF100 as found in the rainforest on Guyanese soil. (Gerda Tjien Foe via Dave Edhard)

On 18 March, the *Militair Gezag* issued two decrees that retroactively declared a state of war starting at midnight on 11 March 1982. Anyone who undermined the legal authority would receive a court martial in the fields and sentenced to death. With the latter decree, the members of *het Gezag* tried to legitimise the execution of Sergeant Major Wilfried Hawker. Due to the domestic and international outcry the execution of Hawker had received, *het Gezag* ended the state of war by decree again on 23 March which meant that all suspects in the coup attempt would be judged by a normal military court. With this move, *het Gezag* successfully prevented sanctions from the Netherlands – for now.

In the meantime, Suriname was still without an official government despite the announcement of a Revolutionary Council. Due to the upheaval caused by the latest coup attempt, all work on forming a new government was halted while the members of *het Gezag* fought for survival. With the conspirators arrested and the situation calmed down, the *mofokoranti* and Dutch press speculated on who would become the new prime minister and in what form the military would exert control over the new government.[67]

On 31 March 1982, a cabinet was formed under Henry Neijhorst. The new prime minister was a politically non-affiliated economist and would lead the civilian government consisting of 12 ministers, half of whom had served under the Chin A Sen government previously.[68] The military and the NMR would exert control over the civilian government via a 'new' *Beleidscentrum*,[69] a council that seated two members of the military (Bouterse and Horb) and two ministers from the civilian government (Neijhorst and Naarendorp).[70] The name 'Revolutionary Council' had been quietly dropped.

The Loss of Helicopter SAF100 [73]

With all the upheaval caused by the *Rambocuscoup* in Paramaribo, the logistical effort to resupply the small military outposts in the hinterland was disrupted. With the lack of resupply, food stores in the Coeroeni camp (close to the disputed Tigri Area – see Chapter 4) ran low. In order to get some extra food, the camp commander allowed several of his men to go out into the rainforest to hunt game.

Two of his soldiers, Soldaat Kowid and Soldaat Tjon A Kon, became lost in the dense jungle and caused great concern. A search party was sent out to find the men but was unsuccessful in locating them. With passing of time, the chances of these men returning became slim. The men based at Coeroeni consulted a local obia, a shaman who practices a system of spiritual healing and justice, common amongst the Maroons living in the rain forest. On his recommendation, the soldiers at the outpost made a sacrificial offer of food to satisfy the forest spirits. Not long after, both missing men emerged from the jungle, famished and tired but alive.

The army headquarters had been informed of the missing men. On 28 March they sent over the LUMA's helicopter to Coeroeni to assist in the search, together with Major Fernandes and 2e Lieutenant Norman de Miranda. When the men were found, it was decided to repatriate the soldiers back to Paramaribo so they could recover from their ordeal. Major Fernandes offered the camp commander his seat on the helicopter but the commander declined as he wanted to return at a later day. This decision would be a fateful one.

Due to the bad weather and low hanging clouds, pilot William Forster decided to return to Paramaribo by flying north along the Corantijn River and to turn east after reaching Nieuw Nickerie, following the east–west road to Paramaribo. The helicopter left for the capital but sadly, never arrived at its destination.

Several hours after it was due, the Surinamese army started a search for the missing helicopter, assuming that the pilot had landed the aircraft and waited for the weather to clear. The LUMA Defender was sent out to look along the route but bad weather hampered the search. Two days later, the missing helicopter was found in the jungle on Guyanese soil.

Soldier Gerold Franklin Tjon A Kon, one of the two soldiers (the other being Ronald Orlando Kowid) who became lost in the rainforest. He was killed in the crash of SAF100. (via the Kowid family)

Major Henk Fernandes was also killed in the crash. He was slated to become the new Minister of Defence in the Neijhorst cabinet. After his death, Iwan Graanoogst took over that position, while Lieutenant Etienne Boerenveen became the new battalion commander. (De Ware Tijd)

Flying low, under and through the clouds, the helicopter had followed the river along the rapids. Due to poor visibility, the helicopter had probably hit the jungle canopy and crashed on the Guyanese side of the river. Sadly, all five occupants – including the two soldiers who had been lost in the rainforest – perished in the crash.

As Major Fernandes had been slated to become the new Minister of Army and Police in the Neijhorst cabinet, his death meant this post would be filled by NMR chairman Lieutenant Graanoogst. In April 1982, Etienne Boerenveen became the new *bataljonscommandant* and the latest member of the *Militair Gezag*.

Expansion of the Armed Forces

The coup attempt in March revealed that *het Gezag* was vulnerable to uprisings from within the military. Thus, the military was reinforced with several more elements that were established in the months following the March coup.

First of all, a new elite unit – Echo Company – was founded and was led by KCT alumni (and Group of Sixteen member) Arthy Gorré. In contrast to the other army units that were based at the MBK, Echo Company would be based in the fortress at Fort Zeelandia, where *het Gezag* had held out against the conspirators. Echo Company consisted of about 50 to 100 members, from which a number were selected to form a group of bodyguards for the ministers and army leadership, the latter group led by Roy Esajas.[74]

In addition to the regular army units, a people's militia (*Volksmilitie*) was formed after the curfew was abolished in the summer of 1982. The first 40 members of the *Volksmilitie* started their training at the BBZ in July.[75] Consisting of volunteers who received a short military training, this group was made up of several hundred operational troops (about 300) with a similar number of members in supporting roles for a total of 600 to 700 members.

The *Volksmilitie* was built up around a small group of intellectuals (mostly RVP members) leading the rest of the force. Plenty of members of the *Volkscomitees* joined this group. This group of part time soldiers would be used in a policing role. In general, they were armed with M1 carbines and grenades.[76]

Although the military usefulness of the people's militias was limited, they did act as the eyes and ears for the Army Intelligence service. As such, the general population feared the *Volksmilitie* as they would snitch on dissenters. Union leader Daal found this a dangerous development and scornfully wondered 'against whom is defence necessary?'[77]

In May, Bouterse left Suriname to go on a vacation to Grenada and to visit Maurice Bishop. Together with foreign minister Naarendorp (who had visited Havana to arrange this meeting), Bouterse also secretly visited Cuba again. There he visited the four Surinamese members of the armed services undergoing military training and had a meeting with Fidel Castro. During the meeting, it was agreed that both would set up embassies in each other's countries. Bouterse requested and received arms, which were brought to Suriname.[78] During the months that followed, ties with Cuba were discretely strengthened in order not to risk cutting off Dutch development aid.

Bouterse was now again taking another political path since he had still failed to locate a political power base. The moderate path had failed, the old political parties did not support him and the majority of the Surinamese did not seem to warm up to socialism. Now that he was in bed with the communists of the PALU and RVP, the Revolutionary Front did not seem to warm the Surinamers' hearts either. Having been impressed with the reception he received from Bishop and Castro, he felt nudging Suriname on a slightly leftist course was the answer. For this, he requested Cuban support.[79]

With his shifting in political allegiances, Bouterse was dubbed a 'wakaman' (Sranantongo for hussler) as he was willing to change his allegiances for pragmatic purposes. The more he did this, the less the Surinamers felt in touch with *het Gezag*.[80]

Opposition from the Trade Unions

At the beginning of August, the judge advocate general released officers Birdja and Dihal (accused of having prior knowledge about the *Rambocuscoup*), pending their trail. The officers were immediately arrested again at the behest of the commander-in-chief and thrown into prison, while Bouterse accused the men of being enemies of the state.[81]

The barrister association, the court of justice, the public prosecutor, the association of Surinamese businesses and the CCK sent a strong letter of protest to Bouterse expressing their deep concern over this development. After a week, *het Gezag* relented

The Fort Zeelandia Complex [71]

Fort Zeelandia in 1837–1840, drawn in 1842 by H.J. Backer. At the time, the fort complex was used to garrison colonial troops. (Public Domain)

Fort Zeelandia is a key landmark of Paramaribo. Located in the heart of the city, Fort Zeelandia is a pentagonal shaped, stone fort located on a high plot of land in a bend of the Suriname River. The fort originally consisted of five bastions, located at each point of the pentagon, of which three pointed out to the river. The fort was surrounded by a moat and a wall with a gate between the two bastions which pointed to land inwards. Over time, these two bastions, the wall and the moat disappeared.

The fort was originally built by the French in 1640, near an Arawak village. When the British arrived in 1650, they reinforced the fort and named it Fort Willoughby. It was used to guard the capital of Thorarica located 50km upstream. When Abraham Crijssen's fleet arrived in 1667, he captured the fort after a three-hour battle and renamed it Fort Zeelandia.

After Cassard's raid in 1712 (during which the French did not attack the fort but raided the plantations), the strategic value of the fort declined, especially after the new fort at Nieuw Amsterdam was built in 1747. The area around the fort instead was used as barracks and headquarters

During the second half of 1982, the conspirators of the *Rambocuscoup* were put on trial. These court cases drew nationwide attention and publicly questioned the legitimacy of the *Militair Gezag* as well. (STVS)

and 'released' both men from prison but confined them to the MBK. This development was seen as a victory for independent judicial powers but at the same time, it clearly indicated that many leading organisations in Suriname did not agree with the policies of *het Gezag*.[82]

As the freedom of the press was still restricted and elections were curtailed, the main opposition power in Suriname shifted to the trade unions. In Suriname, the two largest ones were the AVVS *De Moederbond* and C-47. The former, led by Cyrill Daal was more or less allied with the traditional political parties, whereas C-47 under Fred Derby, was allied with the PNR and a member of the Revolutionary Front.

The *Federatie van Arme Landbouwers* (FAL, Federation of Poor Agriculturalists), another one of the trade unions that were part of the Revolutionary Front, had been in negotiation with *het Gezag* about raising minimum guaranteed purchasing prices of rice for some time. With the negotiations in a deadlock, farmers in Nieuw Nickerie got frustrated by the lack of progress. On 16 August, they blocked the roads around the city and the runway of the local airport, with tractors. A detachment of the army came in with troops and YPs to restore order and made arrests, including 10 board members of the FAL (including chairman J. Sital). This was the first time that Surinamese troops were deployed against their own civilians, something that *het Gezag* had vouched against.

Major Horb announced in a press conference that the FAL members were guilty of organising actions to disrupt public order. Journalists responded aggressively, with one calling the actions fascist. The other trade unions (including *Moederbond* and C-47) released their own press statements demanding the immediate release of the FAL board members.[83] These demands were met and the board members were released from the MBK.

It became clear afterwards that *het Gezag* had acted upon rumours that a coup was underway in Nickerie. They reacted in force because the *Dr. R. Ali kampement* had been cut off during the blockade when military convoys could not reach the barracks.[84]

The Fort Zeelandia complex on the Suriname River consists of multiple buildings which included the fort, a prison, barracks, residences, stores and guard houses. By the early 1980s, several members of the *Militair Gezag* resided there with the prison (called 'Devil') and military police headquarters also being in use. The fort itself was turned into the *bevelhebbers* office after the *Rambocuscoup*. (Google Maps)

The Devil prison shown in 2018. The *Militair Gezag* held many of its political prisoners in the old cellblock on the Fort Zeelandia complex, including the conspirators of the *Rambocuscoup*. (Nationale Voorlichtingsdienst Suriname)

for troops garrisoned in Paramaribo, with residences for the commanders and officers, a guardhouse, prison, along with space for weapon storage and a food warehouse built on the premises. The fort itself was used as a prison.

By independence, the complex had changed. The military police were headquartered at the complex. 'Building 1970' – the former foodstuff warehouse, was turned into a government building to house the Ministry of Education. The garrison had moved to the *Memre Boekoe Kazerne* further in the city, away from the Suriname River and the ammunition storage had been moved to the bunker at the Doekhiweg.

Once the prison was moved to Santo Boma outside the city in 1968, the fort was renovated and turned into a museum in 1972. After the *Rambocuscoup* of 1982, the fort was turned into the HQ of the *Militair Gezag* and Echo Company. It would be the scene of some of the most shocking events in Suriname modern history in December of that year.

The Devil prison was used to incarcerate political opponents of the *Militair Gezag* during the 1980s, such as journalists, dissidents and conspirators of the failed *Rambocuscoup*. Many of the inmates were severely mistreated by their captors' hands.[72]

The trade unions and *het Gezag* were now opposing each other, as the former became more critical of the poor economic decisions taken by the latter. More and more demonstrations were organised by the unions as trials were held against the plotters of the *Rambocuscoup* in March. The Revolutionary Front fell apart in the process, as the various participants now openly opposed each other.

On 21 August, Birdja and Dihal were sentenced to five months of prison and dismissed from the army.[85] The trial against Rambocus and the other plotters started on 12 October when they were subpoenaed. The judge advocate general demanded a sentence of 15 years against Surendre Rambocus for his part in the coup.[86] The trial would last until the beginning of December, by which time tensions in Suriname reached boiling point.

High Level Meeting by Candlelight[87]

As the month of October progressed, demonstrations and protests by the various trade unions became larger and noisier. The various unions started demonstrations, leading to strikes in the ports, the hospitals and in education. The unions spoke out against the unfair division of wealth in Suriname, demanding better pay and less government involvement.

When the Prime Minister of Grenada, Maurice Bishop, came to visit Paramaribo on 28 October, his timing could not have been more unfortunate. The trade union for air traffic controllers went on a wildcat strike due to disagreements with the ministry of economic affairs, not knowing about Bishop's flight.

Although Daal had managed to broker a timely agreement with the controllers to end the strike, the union leader was summoned to Fort Zeelandia, where Bouterse accused Daal of sabotaging Bishop's visit on purpose and threatened to lock him up and throw the key to his cell away if he did not end the strike by 1800. Daal, fuming at the threats, went to the office of the *Moederbond* and announced a general strike in a meeting that was broadcasted live on ABC.

In the middle of the meeting, an army motorcyclist delivered a telegram from the *bevelhebber* to Daal. The leader of the *Moederbond*, expecting it to be a letter of apology, was annoyed to find out that it was an official invitation to the reception held in the honour of the Grenadian prime minister. In no uncertain terms, Daal told the soldier that he could tell his boss to use the invitation as toilet paper. As this all was broadcast live on the airwaves, the commander-in-chief had Daal arrested and taken to Fort Zeelandia.[88]

Upon hearing of Daal's arrest, a mob assembled outside the fort to protest his incarceration. In an emergency meeting held by the Policy Centre and the other trade union leader, Fred Derby of C-47 was able to convince Bouterse to release Daal in order to restore order.

In the meantime, Bishop's plane was able to land despite the ongoing strike of the air traffic control workers. As the utilities companies had gone on strike, the members of the Policy Centre had to receive Bishop at his hotel in Paramaribo without running water and by candlelight. The prime minister was not amused but did inform Bouterse during a long discussion about revolutionary politics, that Grenada had similar problems and the Suriname revolution was well on its way. In admiration of his words, Bouterse asked Bishop if he could tell this to a large crowd during a mass meeting organised in his honour on 31 October.

Maurice Bishop is warmly received by *Bevelhebber* Bouterse at Zanderij Airport. The plane was able to land, despite the air traffic controllers being on strike. (STVS)

During a meeting at Fort Bomika, Bishop warns the crowd that 'a revolution is not a tea party' and that opposition must be eliminated. (STVS)

The ultimate humiliation for Bouterse occurred during the mass meeting that was organised to welcome Prime Minister Bishop at 'Fort Bomika'. This meeting was attended by up to 1,500 people. However, at the same time, the *Moederbond* had organised a demonstration against the *Militair Gezag* that was visited by more than 15,000 people. This was not how the Lieutenant *Kolonel* had planned to receive the revolutionary that he adored so much.

On stage, Bishop made it clear that: 'A revolution is not a tea party. The Surinamese revolution is too friendly. Reactionary forces are strong. You have to eliminate those that are not with you, otherwise they will eliminate you'.

Bouterse, speaking in Sranantongo, made it clear what he wanted to do.

> Up until today we have taken a defensive stance but tomorrow, we shall go onto the offensive. Because Mr. Daal has presented me the bill [...] I have taken a look at it and wonder, shall I pay it by cash or bank transfer? I can't do by bank transfer as the banks are going to be closed. Therefore I shall pay him back in *CASH*!

At the mass meeting held by the *Moederbond*, the crowd made it clear that they rejected the current government's policy. There, Daal demanded in a speech, that the military must return to the barracks, the power of governing needs to return to the people and that the state of emergency and restrictions of the press need to be lifted. In addition, Daal also announced that strikes would continue until *het Gezag* met all those demands and that C-47 would also join the general strikes. A long, enthusiastic applause from the crowd followed Daal's speech.

When asked by Haakmat how he got Derby to go along with the strikes, Daal made it clear that had yet to discuss the matter with the C-47 union leader, who was known to disagree with Daal's path of confrontation.

Daal and Derby discussed going on strike but failed to reach an agreement. Derby announced that the C-47 agreed with the demands made by the *Moederbond* but that instead of going on strike, he proposed a phased plan that would introduce a new parliament, a new constitution, a reconstruction plan for the economy and a plan that would allow political parliaments to restore democracy.[89]

His phased plan was not something new as in September of 1982, Bouterse and Haakmat had held a secret meeting in the plantation of Katwijk. There, it was agreed there would be a phased return of the military to the barracks. As certain stipends of the agreement were not upheld, Daal had increased the protests, especially after foreign minister Naarendorp had proclaimed on 24 September that the 'Cuban model' did not fit Suriname but no further information was given on how Suriname would proceed.[90]

As not all unions went on strike, the impact of the general strike was not big enough for the members of *het Gezag* to yield to Daal's demands. Horb, however, reached out to Haakmat and Daal and started a series of negotiations between Bouterse and Daal to reach an agreement. The following day, the *Moederbond* agreed to curtail any strikes as they were unaware that a plan had been set-up to return to democracy. Unfortunately, Horb had undermined his own position by visiting Henk Chin A Sen in the US, returning just before Maurice Bishop left Paramaribo on 1 November.

Foreign Influences

In September 1982, Chin A Sen briefly returned to Suriname to collect personal belongings. The former president and prime minister had spoken with several politicians during the visit and had invited the *garnizoenscommandant* over.

After returning from a state visit to North Korea on 17 October, Horb went to Pittsburg together with his political advisor and a journalist, all accompanied by Horb's bodyguards. This group went to see the head office of Alcoa (Suralco's parent company) to discuss the future of the aluminium industry in Suriname. This was followed by a visit to the US State Department, where he was briefed on operating methods of communism, Cuba's influence and the strategic end-goal of world domination. As soon as he heard of the unrest back home, he flew back to Paramaribo.[91]

After Horb agreed with Daal to end the strikes, Horb fell out of favour with Bouterse and he was removed from the *Beleidscentrum*. While information about the agreements between trade unions and the government remained sketchy and the 'mofokoranti' went into overtime with rumours, it seemed that Horb was accused of seeking contact with the CIA during his visit to the US.[92] Bouterse and Horb did appear on STVS together about a week later, stating that everything was in order. However, Horb would rarely be seen in public after this date.

Tensions were not eased either by the accusation from Prime Minister Neijhorst that the US was 'stirring the pot' as two local diplomats were accused of egging on the labour union leaders to go on strike. One of the diplomats involved, LaRoche, was present at the US Embassy in Chile during the downfall of President Allende in September 1973. The Netherlands, also accused of criticising the Surinamese ministry of Finance and Planning, denied any involvement with trade unions.[93] The *Militair Gezag* would remain paranoid that foreign powers would try to intervene in Surinamese affairs.

The Militair Gezag vs the Surinamese Population

In the early morning of 6 November, André Haakmat's residence was shot at while he was at home, leaving him shaken but uninjured. Not taking any chances, Haakmat fled the country to French Guiana as he thought that members of the *Volksmilitie* had made the attempt on his life. The *Moederbond* had to keep on going without its main advisor.

Talks did not seem to lead to any concrete steps to introduce democratic reforms. On 15 November, Bouterse announced that the 'guidelines for new democratic structures' would only be announced in March 1983. The request of other associations (such as the bar association) for involvement in the new plans, was denied.[94]

The trade unions felt betrayed by het *Beleidscentrum*. The five main trade unions (including FAL, C-47 and AVVS) issued a joint statement accusing Bouterse of breaking his promise to introduce reforms before the year was out. The number of demonstrations slowly started to increase and by the end of the month, the trade unions had been joined by other organisations.[95]

The Association for Democracy, a spokes group that represented various religious and professional organisations, sent Bouterse a letter on 23 November in which he was articulately criticised of his governing in a fundamental way.[96] Student organisations also joined the association and announced demonstrations. Additionally, the media disregarded the restrictions and freely spoke out in support of the strikes and the restoration of democracy. Basically, the majority of the population of Suriname was now opposed to the *Militair Gezag*.

In the last months of 1982, the labour unions and student organisations organised regular demonstrations against *het Gezag*. (STVS)

Although demonstrations were plentiful, the fact that not all trade unions took part in the demonstrations, limited their effectiveness. Nevertheless, they were a strong signal to the world that the population of Suriname strongly disagreed with the policies of the *Militair Gezag*. (STVS)

Kamperveen's radio station ABC was destroyed on the night that he was arrested. A hole made by a recoilless rifle is visible on the left. Radio Radika was the other radio station that was set on fire that night. (STVS)

The print shop of the newspaper, *Vrije Stem* was destroyed as well. Owner Wilfried Lionarons was out of the country when the arrests of his fellow journalists took place and thus escaped a similar fate. (STVS)

The ruins of the head office of trade union, AVVS *de Moederbondc*. After the night of 8 December, the trade union ceased their protests overnight due to fear. (STVS)

On December 3, the trial of Rambocus and his fellow conspirators came to an end. Rambocus was sentenced to 12 years of hard labour in prison. Corporal Mahabier, who had managed to escape to the Netherlands, was sentenced to 15 years in absentia. In his closing argument, Rambocus held a long passionate monologue about restoring democracy in Suriname. He ended his speech by saying:

'The temporary and fleeting judgement we leave to you; the historical judgement we leave to history; the final judgement we leave for God'.

A large cheer erupted from the crowd in the courtroom and people started singing the national anthem. Upon leaving the court under police escort, the crowd outside threw confetti over Surendre Rambocus, in effect protesting against *het Gezag*.[97] His lawyers (John Baboeram, Eddy Hoost, Kenneth Gonçalves and Harold Riedewald) stated in an interview that they would file for an appeal. This never happened due to events described later.

A day before the closing statement of Rambocus' trial, a student protest numbering 3,000 demonstrators was held to demand a solution to the strikes from the college staff at the university. The police violently quelled the protests, injuring four students and arresting six.[98] On 7 December, students marched to Revolutionary Square where they ran into military forces. After throwing stones and attempting to set an YP on fire, the square was cleared and crowd was dispersed.[99]

That evening, Cyrill Daal and André Kamperveen went to Fort Zeelandia to discuss the student demonstrations – after which they left. Little would they know that they would return later that night, under very unfriendly circumstances.

Rounding up 'Counter-revolutionaries'

Late in the evening of 7 December 1982, the members of the Group of Sixteen assembled at Fort Zeelandia. The *bevelhebber* ordered his men to arrest a number of 'counter-revolutionaries, who have tried to frustrate the revolution'.[100] The members of the group were reinforced with some trusted bodyguards and headed out to the homes of these prominent Surinamers. Among them were journalists, trade union leaders, lawyers, professors and businessmen. These had led the demonstrations against Bouterse's rule and many were part of the Association for Democracy.

In the early hours of 8 December, people were awoken by soldiers knocking on their front door. If not answered promptly, doors were knocked down with brute force and several houses were ransacked. Occupants were threatened at gunpoint as soldiers apprehended the men they were looking for and then left. They often left a few soldiers behind to make sure the other occupants stayed put and did not contact anyone – even going as far as cutting phone lines.

The people arrested were all outspoken critics of the *Militair Gezag* and included two trade union leaders, three lawyers, five journalists, the dean of the barrister association, the dean of the faculty of economics, the head of the University Mathematics Centre and an entrepreneur (see Appendix V).

In addition to the arrests, soldiers were also sent out to the office of *AAVS de Moederbond*, radio stations Radio ABC, Radio Radika and the printing office of the newspaper, *De Vrije Stem* Around 0345, explosives and recoilless rifles were heard throughout Paramaribo and the buildings were set on fire.[101] The fire brigade of Paramaribo was ordered by the *bevelhebber* to not extinguish the fires, resulting in their destruction.[102] By early next morning, only smouldering ruins remained.

During the night, the arrested men (14 in total) were taken to the MP headquarters and the old fort at Fort Zeelandia. Rambocus and Sheombar, who were still in prison at the MBK and Santo Boma respectively, were transferred to Fort Zeelandia as well. All men had been beaten up during or after their arrests. Several Surinamers who were to be apprehended, were either abroad or not at home.[103] These men escaped the fate of those who were detained.

In the morning of 8 December around 0700, SRS reported that the army was 'forced to intervene on behalf of the revolution'. This was followed by an announcement that the army had started an investigation to determine the arsonists and their motivation.

That day, offices, schools and the university remained closed as all telephone and telex communications were shut down. The international borders and airspace were closed as well, isolating Suriname from the outside world. Except for the state TV and radio (STVS and SRS respectively) and newspaper, *De Ware Tijd*, all media were prohibited from publication. Paramaribo was buzzing with rumours, the *mofokoranti* working overtime, about what had happened the previous night.

The council of ministers gathered at the cabinet at Bouterse's request in the morning as the *bevelhebber* had some announcements to make. Minister of Army and Police Graanoogst, who was not a member of the Group of Sixteen, arrived late at the meeting but had no idea what was going on. During the hour-long meeting the council was informed that the army had intervened and arrested counter-revolutionaries. When the names of the detainees were given, Prime Minister Neijhorst requested that Daal and Derby were released, seeing the labour unrest in the country. Bouterse responded that he would check at the fort to find out what was possible. After the *bevelhebber* left, the ministers discussed how to free the prisoners and whether they should resign or not.[104]

'Shot on the Run'[105]

What precisely happened during that day at Fort Zeelandia is not exactly known. Only, the following can be stated with certainty:

At 2100 on 8 December, Lieutenant *Kolonel* Bouterse appeared on STVS and made an announcement that a coup which would have caused massive bloodshed, had been prevented. He further announced that the coup was aimed to restore the situation that a small elite would be in power (as before *the revo*) and that the interests of the farmers, labourers and a large part of the population would be trampled upon. Several suspects had been arrested and would be presented for questioning.[106]

As evidence, an interview was shown between Roy Horb and Jozef Slagveer, in which the latter read a declaration stating that he was part of a conspiracy founded in October to overthrow the *Militair Gezag*. He disclosed that André Haakmat was the ringleader who had planned to get the military back into the barracks by means of a popular uprising or civil disobedience, together with foreign military help. It was clear on TV that Slagveer had been physically abused (as the left side of his face was swollen) and that he was reading the statement under duress. Hence, many people did not believe his confession to be true.[107]

A similar interview by André Kamperveen was not shown on TV but was broadcasted on SRS, as Kamperveen was so badly beaten up that his injuries made him unsuitable to be shown on television. Slagveer's interview was also broadcasted over the radio.[108]

During that night, shots were fired throughout Paramaribo. It was reported the next day that the army had held successful live fire exercises.[109] Shots were also heard coming out of Fort Zeelandia. Fred Derby, the C-47 labour leader, was released from the fort and arrived home at around 2100. He remained silent about what took place at Fort Zeelandia until 2001.[110]

In the morning of 9 December, trucks from the NL were seen bringing over a dozen body bags to the mortuary at the *Academisch Ziekenhuis*. These were kept under guard by the military. Rumours went around quickly that these were the bodies of the people arrested on 8 December. During the day, hundreds of people gathered outside the hospital to find out what happened.

On 8 December 1982, Bouterse informed the population that a 'coup that would cause massive bloodshed' had been prevented. This was followed by Slagveer's taped confession. (STVS)

In the presence of Lieutenant *Kolonel* Bouterse, a beaten-up 'Ampie' Kamperveen confesses to conspiring to overthrow the government. As he was visibly abused, Kamperveen's confession was not televised on 8 Dec but broadcast on radio instead. This video was used in the murder trial that started in 2007. (Screenshot of confession video via OGV)

Together with Major Horb, Jozef Slagveer confessed to having conspired to overthrow the government of Suriname together with journalists, lawyers, teachers and trade union leaders. Slagveer was beaten up as well, although he looked more presentable than Kamperveen. (Screenshot of confession video via OGV)

The same morning, Bouterse met up with the members of the cabinet again. The *bevelhebber* informed Neijhorst and his ministers that the 15 men had been shot while the guards in the fort were

On 12 December, a demonstration against the murder of the 15 victims was held at The Hague in the Netherlands. Surinamers and Dutchmen of Surinamese descent took part in the protest which included a march to the Surinamese embassy. The Dutch and US government responded to the December murders by freezing all aid to Suriname, cutting off one of the two major sources of income for the country. (Collection Nationaal Archief/Anefo, Marcel Antonisse)

shooting at unknown aircraft attacking the fort. Bouterse told the members that he was not in the fort when the shooting took place, having given command over to Bhagwandas and Gorré, who must have panicked. Upon hearing that the rumours were true, the members of the cabinet were stunned. Not wanting to bear any responsibility for the bloodbath, Neijhorst handed the resignation of his cabinet to Bouterse, who passed it on to President Ramdat Misier.[111]

During the evening news, an announcement was made that the suspects who were involved in the most recent coup attempt, had tried to escape Fort Zeelandia. After firing warning shots, all suspects were fired upon and were 'shot on the run', resulting in their deaths. By that time, the family members of the deceased had been informed about their death by the army chaplain.

The After Effect of the December Murders

In a country where everyone knows everyone, the news of the deaths of the 15 deeply shocked Surinamese society. Many stores and businesses remained closed for several days until *het Gezag* ordered them to reopen. This measure was enforced by the members of the *Volksmilitie*.[118]

All demonstrations by the trade unions and universities stopped overnight, except for a silent protest march that saw people calling out for help to Dutch Ambassador Hoekman as he stood on the balcony of the embassy when the march passed by. Despite the ban on gatherings, thousands of people joined the march that ended at Independence Square. Demonstrators attempted but failed, to burn the Cuban flag and lower the Surinamese flag to half-mast.[119]

On 10 December, family members were allowed to visit the mortuary at the *Academisch Hospitaal* to identify the human remains of their loved ones. Upon seeing their bodies, it became clear that they had been tortured. This contrasted with the statement that they had been shot while escaping. A report from the Dutch Judicial Committee for Human Rights, concluded that the 15 men had been badly beaten with blunt objects and that all had been shot from afront and that attempts had been made to camouflage the injuries.

The bodies were released to the families on Monday 13 December and all 15 men were buried that day under great public interest. Their bodies had not been embalmed. In addition, no autopsies had been performed. The military and police guarded the cemeteries day and night for the rest of the week.

The *Decembermoorden* (December murders), as the events on 8 December would become to be known, started another emigration wave of Surinamers to the Netherlands. Although not as big as the wave before Independence Day, many Surinamers with ties to the trade unions and media, left the country to settle in the Netherlands. Surinamers arriving at Amsterdam airport were afraid to speak out, fearing their statements would affect friends and family back home.

Once communications were re-established and it became clear what had actually happened, the news shocked the Surinamers in the Netherlands as well. The Surinamese Ambassador to the Netherlands, Henk Herrenberg, closed the embassy as soon as he received the news. Surinamese expatriates held demonstrations during the weekend of 11 and 12 December at the Surinamese

The December Murders – What Happened at Fort Zeelandia?

Not long after the events of 8 December, plenty of wild rumours spread regarding the number of people killed, who had been present at Fort Zeelandia and what exactly took place. In 1983, after Roy Horb's death, a book on the December murders was published as an eyewitness report of the events. Some statements appear to be sensationalised but the book reports that the following events took place that fateful night.

On the evening of 8 December, a meeting was held between Bouterse, Bhagwandas, Horb, Naarendorp, Sital and Alibux. During the meeting, it was decided that the recently arrested 'criminal elements' were to be executed. The main proponent of eliminating the dissidents appeared to be PALU leader Alibux. He asserted that Surinamese society was not shocked enough by the *revo* of 1980 to subdue counterrevolutionary elements and thus, had to be cleared of these elements.[112]

In order to be able to 'sell' the elimination of the dissidents internationally, their death would have to be whitewashed by stating it occurred while attempting to escape. Echo Company would cause a distraction by firing weapons throughout the night to mask the shots of the firing squad. Fred Derby, who had always supported Bouterse (and also was part of the Revolutionary Front), was to be spared. Horb, in trying to save his friend Daal, had tried to argue that either both union leaders had to be shot or be released but was overruled by Bouterse. After Derby was sent home, the executions began.[113]

The arrested men were brought in one by one before Bouterse, Horb and Bhagwandas where they were informed of their pending execution. Their responses varied from crying to hurling insults at the *bevelhebber,* to being silent. However, they were sent out to the platform of Bastion Veere of the Fort. There, the men were executed by a firing squad consisting of 16 soldiers led by Bhagwandas and Dendoe, using Uzi machine pistols, Browing Hi-Power pistols and Kalashnikov assault rifles to shoot the condemned.[114]

Bouterse claimed he was not there because he was with a mistress, that Bhagwandas had acted on his own and summarily executed the 15 men after Fred Derby was released. As Bhagwandas had possibly saved his life during the 1980 coup (when he shot Lieutenant Van Aalst), Bouterse felt obligated to cover for him, as the conspirators had sworn an oath to protect each other (see Chapter 4).[115] It is also claimed that it was never intended for the 15 men to be executed. They were to have been deported instead, with some people claiming that Bouterse had arranged for an aircraft to be ready at Zanderij.[116]

A documentary released by the Organisation for Justice and Peace (OGV – Organisatie voor Vrede en Gerechtigheid), showed the confession videos of Kamperveen and Slagveer. As Bouterse and Horb were shown in Fort Zeelandia interviewing the two men, it seems that Bouterse was present at the fort. The documentary also stated that both men had witnessed the execution of Rambocus and Sheombar first, before being ordered to read the confessions.[117]

Whatever may have happened at Fort Zeelandia, Bouterse later claimed that he was politically responsible for what happened that night but denied any wrongdoing on his part. It would take almost 25 years before he was brought to trial for the murders.

A collage of the 15 prominent Surinamers who were killed on 8 December 1982. For more details, see Appendix V. (Jessica Dikmoet)

On 8 December 2009 (the 27th anniversary of the *Decembermoorden*), President Venetiaan unveiled a monument for the victims at the Bastion Veere at Fort Zeelandia. (Thomas Kautzor)

Embassy in The Hague. A wake was held for the 15 dissidents who were shot and the building was defaced with graffiti.

The Dutch government actively protested against the killing of the 15 men (of whom one, Wijngaarde, was a Dutch citizen). On 11 December, Ambassador Hoekman handed Lieutenant Colonel Bouterse a letter from the Dutch government that stated that all development aid to Suriname was halted immediately. The US also withdrew all economic and military aid, valued at one and a half million dollars, that was to be given to Suriname in 1983.[120]

In addition to cutting off development aid, the Netherlands would stop representing and assisting Suriname with international matters, as the young country lacked an experienced diplomatic corps with an established set of international contacts. All military cooperation between the Dutch armed forces and the NL would stop as well, meaning that all pay supplementations to Surinamese military personnel that had previously served in the Dutch armed forces, would stop at once. Dutch military support personnel were withdrawn from Suriname and Surinamese army cadets undergoing courses at military school in the Netherlands, were sent back to their home country immediately.

Thus, at the end of 1982 – a year filled with violence and bloodshed in a country that is known for its peacefulness and relaxed pace of life – Suriname started 1983 as a country isolated from its greatest supporters with a bleak economic outlook and home to a society shaken with fear.

Appendices

I

SURINAMESE POPULATION IN SURINAME AND THE NETHERLANDS AND THEIR ETHNICITY

Table 8A: Ethnic Composition of the Surinamese population (Source: Algemeen Bureau voor de Statistiek Suriname)					
Group	1972		1980*	2004	
Hindustani	142,300	37.0%	n/a	135,117	31.3%
Creole #	118,500	30.8%	n/a	87,202	20.2%
Maroon	39,000	10.3%	n/a	72,553	16.8%
Javanese	58,900	15.3%	n/a	71,879	16.7%
Amerindian	10,200	2.7%	n/a	18,037	4.2%
Chinese	6,400	1.7%	n/a	8,775	2.0%
European	4,000	1.0%	n/a	2,899	0.7%
Other/Mixed/Unknown	5,400	1.3%	n/a	34,843	8.1%
Total	379,607		354,860	431,305	
# Included in the numbers for the Creole population are people of mixed descent. * in 1980, ethnicity was not recorded as part of the nationalist agenda of the *Militair Gezag*					

Table 8B: Ethnic Composition of Surinamers in the Netherlands[1]				
Group	1972**	1980**	2004	
Hindustani	N/A	N/A	110,000	33.6%
Creole	N/A	N/A	129,000	39.4%
Maroon	N/A	N/A	35,000	10.7%
Javanese	N/A	N/A	43,000	13.1%
Other	N/A	N/A	10,000	3.1%
Total	40,000	145,000	327,000	
** Ethnicity of Surinamers was not recorded at the time of the census				

Between 1973 and 1980 a large group of Surinamers emigrated to the Netherlands in fear of a civil war between the various ethnic groups. In addition, Surinamers could freely immigrate to the Netherlands without a visa, until 1980.

From this information, the following conclusions can be drawn:

- The total population of Surinamers in both the Netherlands and Suriname nearly doubled between 1972 and 2004.
- By 1980 about 30 percent of the Surinamese population lived in the Netherlands (vs approximately 10 percent in 1972).
- Between 1972 and 1980 the population of Suriname shrank by 25,000 or about 7 percent.
- The largest growing population group between 1972 and 2004 are the Maroons (by 250 percent).
- The majority of the people that emigrated to the Netherlands were Hindustanis and Creoles.

Note that Surinamers who emigrated to other countries, such as the US, Canada, Brazil and French Guyana, were not taken into account.

11
ATTEMPTED, SUCCESSFUL AND ALLEGED COUPS IN SURINAME UP TO 1982

The *revo* was initially supported by many Surinamers. Mementos, cards and posters were designed. One of these shows an 'updated' Surinamese coat of arms, where the Amerindians have been changed into Uzi-wielding soldiers and the colonial ship is replaced by patrol boat S402. (Authors collection)

Table 9: Coups in Suriname		
Date	(Claimed) Perpetrators	Results and consequences
14 May 1910 The *Killingercoup*	7 police officers under Inspector Killinger	Coup thwarted due to betrayal. Conspirators were jailed for 2 to 5 years.
6 November 1947 The *Sanchescoup*	15 plotters, mostly former KNIL soldiers, under Simon Sanches	Coup was prevented due to betrayal. Sanches was released after trial and deported to the Netherlands.
25 February 1980 The *Sergeantencoup*	The Group of Sixteen	Coup successful. Government overthrown. NMR founded and new government installed.
May 1980 The Ormskerk affair	Mercenaries under *Adjudant* Fred Ormskerk	Ormskerk and co-conspirators apprehended before coup was to be executed. Ormskerk died in custody, others convicted and sentenced to prison.
13 August 1980 The Leftist coup	Three former NMR members and several RVP politicians	Alleged Leftist coup thwarted. State of emergency declared with the constitution abolished and president replaced.
March 1981 The Hawker coup	Commandos under Sergeant Major Wilfried Hawker, supported by Chinese businessmen	Alleged coup thwarted. Hawker was injured during an ambush which killed his driver, Weissenbruch. Conspirators sentenced to prison.
June 1981 The Keerveld affair	Mercenaries under Humphrey Keerveld	Keerveld was murdered in Guyana before he was able to recruit mercenaries for a plot to overthrow the Surinamese government.
11–12 March 1982 The *Rambocuscoup*	Approximately 20 soldiers and civilians under Lieutenant Rambocus, masterminded by Baal Oemrawsingh	Countercoup was almost successful but failed when army leadership was able to convince the bulk of the army to defect.
7–9 December 1982 The December Murders	16 men, including lawyers and union leaders	Conspirators apprehended and 15 'shot while attempting to escape'.

III
COUP PLOTTERS OF THE SERGEANTEN COUP

The members of the Group of Sixteen in a staged post-coup picture. (Lucien Chien a Foeng)

Table 10: Members of the Groep van Zestien (Group of Sixteen)				
#	Name	Rank	Role in Coup*	Notes
1	Bhagwandas, Paul	Sergeant	Attacked MBK	KMS-alumni, battalion commander, known as *the Executioner of Fort Zeelandia*. Dismissed from the service in 1986. Passed away in 1996. Final rank: Lieutenant
2	Bouterse, Desi Delano	Sergeant Major	Attacked MBK, went to HQ after	KMS-alumni, commander of the Armed Forces until 1993. President of Suriname from 2010 to 2020. Final rank: *Kolonel*
3	Brondenstein, Benny	Sergeant	Part of S402 crew	Member of the Surinamese Navy until dismissed due to drug-related charges. Final rank: unknown.
4	Dendoe, Steven	Sergeant	Attacked MBK	Founder of the security service. Following military intelligence training in Cuba and became vice-consul of Suriname in Miami. Final rank: unknown.
5	Esajas, Roy	Sergeant		Founder of the security service. Jailed for atrocities committed during the civil war of 1986–92. Passed away in 2012. Final rank: Major
6	Gefferie, Ernst	Sergeant	Part of S402 crew	Became District Commander of Western Suriname. Adjutant to President Shankar. Final rank: Lieutenant
7	Gorré, Arthy	Sergeant		KCT & KMS-alumni, served with the *Mariniers* before switching to the KL. Became commander of Echo Company in 1982. Left the armed service in 1986. Returned to become commander of the NL in 1993 until 1995. Passed away in 2018. Final rank: *Kolonel*

8	Hardjoprajitno, John	Sergeant	Captured before coup, prisoner in Fort Zeelandia	Member of NMR in March 1980. Became Minister of Culture, Youth and Sports until jailed in Jan 1983 on charges of plotting a coup with Horb. Left the military after serving 16 months and emigrated to the Netherlands in 1996. Final rank: Lieutenant
9	Hawker, Wilfried	Sergeant	Attacked MBK	KCT alumni, following internship with the Dutch Commandos in late 1980. Led countercoups in 1981 (allegedly) and 1982. Executed in March 1982. Final rank: Sergeant Major
10	Horb, Roy	Sergeant	Organised the men at Fort Bomika after capture of the naval base, went to HQ after	Garrison commander. Rumoured to be a CIA informant. Found dead in his cell on 2 February 1983 while awaiting trial for coup plotting. Final rank: Major
11	Leeflang, Ewoud	Sergeant	Attacked MBK	Killed during the *Binnenlandse Oorlog* in 1986. Rumoured to have been executed by Maroon insurgents. Final rank: Sergeant Major
12	Mahadew, Guno	Sergeant		Drowned during vacation in Brazil (May 1988). Final rank: Sergeant Major
13	Nelom, John	Sergeant	Attacked MBK	Founder of the security service. Jailed for atrocities committed during the civil war of 1986–92. Passed away in 2014. Final rank: Lieutenant
14	Tolud, Roy	Sergeant	Part of S402 crew	Commanded patrol boat during the coup, became naval commander. Missing since 1989, rumoured to have been killed and buried in his car. Final rank: Lieutenant
15	Rozendaal, Ruben	Sergeant	Attacked MBK, participated in the attack on the munitions bunker and police HQ	Head of the military security service. Committed suicide in 2017. Final rank: Major
16	Zeeuw, Marcel	Sergeant	Assisted Horb and participated in the attack on the police HQ	Became head of MP. Passed away in 2015. Final rank: Lieutenant *Kolonel*
*All participated in the attack on the naval base at Beekhuizen, except for Hardjoprajitno				

IV
THE NATIONALE MILITAIRE RAAD (NMR)

The founding members of the *Nationale Militaire Raad* (NMR). (Lucien Chien a Foeng)

Table 11: Founding Members of the Nationale Militaire Raad (National Military Council)			
#	Name	Rank (26 February 1982)	Notes
3	Desi Bouterse*	Sergeant Major	Left NMR in July 1980. Part of the *Militair Gezag*.
4	Horb, Roy*#	Sergeant	Left NMR in July 1980. Part of the *Militair Gezag*.
5	Abrahams, Ramon#	Sergeant	Kicked out of NMR in July 1980. Minister of Public works (2010-2013).
6	Joeman, Stanley	Sergeant	Kicked out of NMR in July 1980. Briefly jailed in Aug 1980 to March 1981 for allegedly planning Leftist coup.
2	Mijnals, Chas	Sergeant	Kicked out of NMR in July 1980. Briefly jailed in Aug 1980 to March 1981 for allegedly planning Leftist coup. Joined *het Gezag* in 1987.
8	Neede, Laurens#	Sergeant	Vice-Chairman. Left NMR in March 1980 to become the Deputy Minister of Army and Police (1980-1982).
7	Rey, Michel van	Lieutenant	Left NMR in March 1980 to become Minister of Army and Police. Left Suriname in May 1980 after being dismissed, later became a military advisor of insurgents during the civil war of 1986-1992.
1	Sital, Badrissein#	Sergeant Major	Kicked out of NMR in July 1980. Chairman of NMR. Briefly jailed in Aug 1980 to March 1981 for allegedly planning Leftist coup. Became Minister of Public Health (1981-1982). Joined *het Gezag* in 1987.
9	Braaf, Ruben#	Kpl	Left NMR in March 1980 to lead the volunteer corps.
* Member of the Group of Sixteen			
# Bomika board member at time of February 25 Coup			

The Members of the NMR at the time of the 1982 *Rambocuscoup*. (Nationale Voorlichtings Dienst Suriname)

Other members of the NMR that joined later, were John Hardjoprajitno (joined March 1980), Cederboom, Nankoesing, Cairo, Olfers and Graanoogst (July 1980). The NMR disbanded after the elections of November 1987.

V
8 DECEMBER 1982: THE DECEMBER MURDERS

Table 12: The List of Victims

Name, age, notes

Baboeram, John, 38, lawyer, defended the conspirators of March 1982 during their court-martial

Behr, Bram, 31, journalist, communist paper *Mokro*

Daal, Cyrill, 46, leader of AVVS *de Moederbond* (trade union)

Gonçalves, Kenneth, 42, lawyer, Dean of the Barrister Association

Hoost, Eddy, 48, lawyer, defended the conspirators of March 1982 during their court-martial

Kamperveen, André, 58, lawyer, owner of ABC Radio and former minister and vice-president of the FIFA

Leckie, Gerard, 39, Dean of the Faculty of Economics at the University of Suriname

Oemrawsingh, Sugrim, 42, mathematician and physicist, former Member of Parliament and brother of Baal Oemrawsingh – alleged mastermind of the countercoup of March 1982

Rahman, Lesley, 28, journalist, de Ware Tijd newspaper

Rambocus, Surendre, 29, officer, led countercoup of March 1982

Riedewald, Harold, 49, lawyer, defended the conspirators of March 1982 during their court-martial

Sheombar, Jiwansingh, 28, soldier, took part in the countercoup of March 1982

Slagveer, Jozef, 42, journalist and director of Informa news agency

Sohansingh, Robby, 37, entrepreneur

Wijngaarde, Frank, 42, journalist, editor and radio announcer, ABC Radio – Dutch citizen

BIBLIOGRAPHY

Books

Anon., *Gevangen van Desi Bouterse – vluchtelingen vertellen hun ervaringen* (Uitgave Makmur – Stichting Van Surinaamse Vluchtelingen/Landbouwers Rotterdam: Rotterdam, 1984)

Anon., *De Decembermoorden in Suriname – Verslag van een ooggetuige* (Het Wereldvenster (Unieboek Bv), Bussum, 1983)

Anon., *De Revolutie Overwint! – de Contra-Revolutionaire Poging tot Staatsgreep in Suriname op 11 en 12 Maart 1982* (Vereniging Van Progressieve Mediawerkers: Paramaribo, 1982)

Bram, Behr, *Terreur op* Uitkijk (Surinaamse Arbeiders Publikaties: Paramaribo, 1982)

Boom, Henk, *Staatsgreep in Suriname – De Opstand van de sergeanten op de voet gevolgd* (Uitgeverij L.J. Veen Bv, Utrecht/Antwerpen: 1982)

Buddingh', Hans, *De geschiedenis van Suriname* (Uitgeverij Rainbow, 2017, 5th Edition)

Couhat, J.L. (Ed.), *Combat Fleets of the World 1980/1981: Their Ships, Aircraft and Armament* (Naval Institute Press, 1980, 1st Edition)

Dew, Edward M., *The Trouble in Suriname, 1975–1993* (Westport, Ct, Usa: Praeger Publishers, 1994)

Dubois, Jul M., *11 Maart 1982 – De mislukte coup in beeld* (Uitgeverij Dubois, Paramaribo, 1982)

Dubois, Jul M., *Suriname in ontwkkeling (foto's spreken de waarheid) 25 Februari 1980 – deel 1* (Uitgeverij Dubois, Paramaribo, 1980)

Dubois, Jul M., *Suriname in ontwkkeling (foto's spreken de waarheid) 25 Februari 1980 – deel 2* (Uitgeverij Dubois, Paramaribo, 1980)

Grant, A., *Tigri – Erfenis van een verraad* (Ralicon, 2008, 2nd Edition)

Groen, P. Et Al, *Krijgsgeweld en Kolonie – Opkomst en Ondergang van Nederland als koloniale mogendheid* (Amsterdam: Uitgeverij Boom, 2021)

Haakmat, André, *De Revolutie Uitgegleden – Politieke Herinneringen* (Amsterdam: Uitgeverij Jan Mets 1987)

Hoogbergen, Wim & Dirk Kruijt, *De oorlog van de sergeanten – Surinaamse Militaire in de Politiek* (Uitgeverij Bert Bakker, 2005)

Janssen, Roger, *In search of a path – An analysis of the foreign policy of Suriname from 1975 to 1991* (Kitlv Press, 2011)

Kagie, Rudie, *Bikkel – het verhaal van de eerste politieke moord van het Bouterse-Regime* (Amsterdam: Uitgeverij Bert Bakker, 2012)

Klinkers, Ellen, *De TRIS – De Nederlandse Defensie in een veranderende koloniale wereld 1940 – 1975* (Amsterdam: Uitgeverij Boom, 2015)

Marshall, E.K., *Ontstaan en ontwikkeling van het Surinaams nationalisme* (Delft: Eburon Uitgeverij, 2003)

Ishmael, Dr. Odeen, *The Guyana Story – from Earliest Times to Independence* (Xlibris, 2013)

Pinas, Lucien, *De Woelige Dagen van Maart 1982* (Paramaribo: Apollo's Reklame & Uitgeversburo, 1982)

Reeser, Pepijn, *Desi Bouterse – Een Surinaamse Tragedie* (Amsterdam: Uitgeverij Prometheus Bert Bakker, 2015)

Slagveer, Jozef, *De Nacht van de Revolutie – De staatsgreep in Suriname op 25 februari 1980* (Paramaribo: Uitgeverij C. Kersten & Co NV, 1990)

Stichting Triscontakten, *Verliefd op Suriname 1947–2009* (Triskontakten Zwijndrecht, 2009)

Verhey, Elma & Gerard van Westerloo, *Het Legergroene Suriname* (Amsterdam: Weekbladpers, 1983)

Vries, Ellen dee, *De Mediastrijd om Suriname – Van mythemakers tot nieuwsverduisteraars* (Zutphen: Walburg Pers, 2017)

Vries, Ellen de, *Hans Valk – Over een Nederlandse Kolonel en een coup in Suriname (1980)* (Zutphen: Walburg Pers, 2021)

Interviews

Azemalie Panchu, Sergeant in the NL – Participant in the *Rambocuscoup*

Jules Vasilda, Veteran of the NL – Mechanic in the Surinamese Air Force

Websites

USAF Historical Research Agency website: http//www.afhra.af.mil/

CIA FOIA Electronic Reading Room: https//www.cia.gov/readingroom/

DAF YP408 Forgotten Hero? https//www.dafyp408.nl

Netherlands department of defense: http//www.defensie.nl

Court of Justice Suriname https//rechtspraak.sr

Stabroek news: http//www.stabroeknews.com

Starnieuws: https//www.starnieuws.com/

Tris Online: http//www.trisonline.nl/

Magazine Articles

Anon., *Surinamese Airforce 1981–2009*, Scramble Magazine, Issue 361, 2009

Anon, *Revokrant, 24 Februari 2020 40 jaar dag der bevrijding*, Published by the NDP, 2020.

Beekers, H.J., *De huidige TRIS*, Militaire Spectator Magazine, Issue 147, 1960, pp. 386–401

Kagie, Rudie. *De Verzonnen Contracoup*, Parbode Surinaams Magazine, Aug 2018, No. 134, pp.46–49

Karbaat, J., *De militaire geschiedenis*, Militaire Spectator Magazine, Issue 146, 1960, pp.377–385.

Klinkers, Ellen, *De opbouw van de Surinaamse Krijgsmacht, Symbool van onafhankelijkheid en ontreddering*, OSO Tijdschrijft voor Surinamistiek en het Carabisch gebied, 2016, pp.245–260.

Meel, Peter, *Henck Arren en de staatsgreep van 25 februari 1980*, OSO – Tijdschrift voor Surinaamse taalkunde, letterkunde en geschiedenis, Issue 34, 2015, pp.10–24.

Velde, Richard van de, *Jodensavanne, Nederlands laatste concentratiekamp*, Parbode Surinaams Magazine, February 2021, No. 178, pp.68–73.

Velde, Richard van de, *Het Prinses Irene Detachement in Suriname*, Parbode Surinaams Magazine, February 2021, No. 178, pp.38–42.

Vries, Ellen de, *Ik vind: moord is moord, Suriname 30 jaar na de Staatsgreep, Wordt Vervolgt Magazine*, Amnesty International, Issue 2, 2010

Woerlee, M.G. and Ir. F. Roodenburg, *De taakvervulling van de Troepenmacht in Suriname in de laatste periode voor de onafhankelijkheid, Militaire Spectator Magazine*, Issue 145, 1976, pp. 475–496

Online Articles

Anon., *Combined package of various declassified reports and cables received by the Dutch Ministry of Defence concerning the Rambocus coup and Suriname in the years 1975 to 1983*, <https://respubca.home.xs4all.nl/pdf/mindeframbocus.pdf/>, accessed 12 September 2021.

Anon., *Wijlen Fred Derby over de Decembermoorden*, https//www.waterkant.net/suriname/2006/12/08/wijlen-fred-derby-over-de-decembermoorden/, accessed 23 September 2022.

Chan-A-Sue, Michael, *The Guns of August: Retaking the New River Triangle*, <https//guyana.hoop.la/topic/the-guns-of-august>, accessed 21 September 2022.

Granger, David, *Defence of the New River, 1967–1969*, Starbroek News, <https//www.stabroeknews.com/2009/02/15/features/the-defence-of-the-new-river-1967-1969/>, accessed 21 September 2020.

Jardim, Philip, *Guyana defends itself*, <https//guyanathenandnow.wordpress.com/british-guiana-airways-limited/>, accessed 16 Jul. 2020.

Newspapers

Various articles from the following newspapers (see Endnotes)

Algemeen Dagblad
Amigoe
De Ware Tijd
De West
Leeuwarder Courant
Nederlands Dagblad
Nieuwsblad van het Noorden
NRC Handelsblad
Reformatorisch Dagblad
Het Parool
Provinciaalse Zeeuwse Courant
De Telegraaf
De Volkskrant
Starnieuws
Trouw
Turbantia
Vrije Stem: Onafhankelijk weekblad van Suriname

News Bulletins

ANP News bulletins – Copies from TELEX messages.

Reports

Nederlandse Juristen Comité voor de Mensenrechten, *De Gebeurtenissen in Paramaribo 8 – 13 December 1982: de geweldadige dood van 14 Surinamers en 1 Nederlander*, Leiden, 14 February 1983 < https://njcm.nl/wp-content/uploads/2015/12/NJCM-rapport.pdf>, accessed 21 September 2022.

Verdict of Steven Dendoe (case 3979, verdict 51) as issued bij de *Krijgsraad* on 29 November 2019, <https://rechtspraak.sr/wp-content/uploads/2020/05/KRG-2019-51.pdf>, accessed 25 September 2022.

TV Programmes/Documentaries

11 Maart 1982, Nationaal Informatie Instituut, Paramaribo, March 2018.
<https//www.youtube.com/watch?v=bzM3ba50xi8>, accessed 23 September 2022.

Andere tijden: Bouterse aan de macht, Dirk Kagenaar, NPS-VPRO, 2009
< https//anderetijden.nl/aflevering/279/Bouterse-aan-de-macht>, accessed 21 September 2022.

Bewijs voor coup of bewijs voor moord?, De Organisatie voor Gerechtigheid en Vrede (OGV), 2022
< https//www.youtube.com/watch?v=xn5KN1oVnTo>, accessed 27 October 2022.

De Zonen van Suriname deel 1, René Roelofs, IKON, 2001
<https//www.2doc.nl/speel~WO_VPRO_032075~zonen-van-suriname-de-decembermoorden-2~.html>, accessed 21 September 2022.

De Zonen van Suriname deel 2, René Roelofs, IKON, 2001
<https//www.2doc.nl/documentaires/2012/04/zonen-van-suriname.html>, accessed 21 September 2022.

Het Drama van Fort Zeelandia, Amnesty International, 1996.
<https//www.youtube.com/watch?v=TufWkYYZjmg>, accessed 23 September 2022.

Lo Fo Sang haalt herinneringen coup op in Santo Boma, Starnieuws, 2011
<https//www.youtube.com/watch?v=Xqe8ufz6_Xs>, accessed 21 September 2022.

Suriname 1973–1982, Jessica Dikmoet et al, MTV-Amsterdam, 1985.<https://www.youtube.com/watch?v=_lmaUMXWePg&list=PLIzDo7qRyYmy8M65uFSDzPxdd7CVs_r9a&index=13>, accessed 21 September 2022.

NOTES

Author's notes

1 Dutch abbreviations used in this table and throughout the text were taken from the monument for the soldiers killed during the *Binnenlandse Oorlog* located at the *Gravenbrechtstraat*.

Chapter 1

1 Suriname is the official name of the country. It was spelled Surinam in the English language until 1978. Some companies, such as Surinam Airways still use this spelling. In addition, some sources still refer to Suriname as Dutch Guiana. This is technically incorrect as Dutch Guiana at one point used to comprise of the Dutch colonies of Essequibo, Demerara, Berbice, Suriname and Cayenne.

2 Although French Guiana is smaller, it is an overseas department of France and fully integrated into the European Union.

3 Suriname has four seasons. The short rainy season runs from the beginning of January to the beginning of February, followed by the short dry season until the end of April. The long rainy season runs until half August, followed by the long dry season that runs until the end of the year. Surinamers, with

their sense of humour, often refer to the dry seasons as the 'wet dry season' as rain is still plentiful.
4 The borders with Guyana and French Guiana are both in dispute. While France and Suriname agree on the Marowijne River and the Lawa River forming the border, both countries disagree on what river is the source of the Lawa. Suriname recognises the eastern Marowini as the headwater, whereas the French recognise the Litani as the source. This issue has not been resolved to this day and the area formed between the Litani and Marowini Rivers and Brazil is currently administered by France, although investments in the area have been minimal. The border dispute between Guyana and Suriname will be discussed in detail in Chapter 3.
5 Hans Buddingh', *De Geschiedenis van Suriname* (Uitgeverij Rainbow, 2017, 5th edition), pp. 17–18.
6 The Guianas encompass the area that is now formed by the nations of Guyana, Suriname and French Guiana.
7 This and the next few paragraphs refer to Buddingh', *Suriname*, pp. 13–15.
8 The Dutch origins of New York are still apparent today. For example: Brooklyn and Harlem are named after the Dutch cities of Breukelen and Haarlem, respectively.

Chapter 2

1 Over the years of slave trade, the Dutch would transport about half a million slaves (out of an 11 million total) across the Atlantic, of which 200,000 would end up in Suriname. These slaves came mostly from the African coast (from the area between Ivory Coast and Nigeria). Buddingh', *Suriname*, p. 82.
2 Du Casse would cause later serious damage to the Dutch possessions at Berbice and Pomeroon (in current day Guyana), Buddingh', *Suriname*, p. 37.
3 Fort Sommelsdijk (named Fort Cottica at first) was located at the Commenwijne River. These garrisons held about 200 European soldiers in 1700. Ellen Klinkers, *De Troepenmacht in Suriname – De Nederlandse Defensie in een veranderende koloniale wereld 1940-1975* (Amsterdam: Uitgeverij Boom, 2015), p. 13.
4 Buddingh', *Suriname*, p. 39.
5 Klinkers, *Troepenmacht*, p. 13–14.
6 Indeed, the number of troops sent to Suriname had increased from 200 in 1700 to 600 in 1750. Klinkers, *Troepenmacht*, p. 14.
7 The Boni maroons are now known as Alukus.
8 Buddingh', *Suriname*, pp. 146–149.
9 The members of the *Vrije Neeger Korps* would be free men after serving their time with this unit. As these men fought against former slaves, the term *redimoesoe* (red cap) is synonymous with traitor in Suriname.
10 Buddingh', *Suriname*, pp. 226–228.
11 Buddingh', *Suriname*, p. 218.
12 Buddingh', *Suriname*, pp. 219–223.
13 Buddingh', *Suriname*, pp. 224–226.
14 Klinkers, *Troepenmacht*, p. 15.
15 Klinkers, *Troepenmacht*, p. 15–16.
16 For all information on the Dutch military units in Suriname up until the Second World War, refer to J. Karbaat, *De militaire geschiedenis*, *Militaire Spectator Magazine*, Issue 146, 1960, pp. 377–385. Additional information added from Petra Groen et al, *Krijgsgeweld en Kolonie – Opkomst en ondergang van Nederland als koloniale mogendheid* (Amsterdam: Uitgeverij Boom, 2021), pp. 426–427.
17 During these riots, troops killed 24 people. Klinkers, *Troepenmacht*, p. 17.
18 Klinkers, *Troepenmacht*, pp. 18–20.
19 Klinkers, *Troepenmacht*, p. 21.
20 Buddingh', *Suriname*, pp. 262–271.
21 Buddingh', *Suriname*, pp. 272–273.
22 The *Goslar* sank and capsized in the Suriname River. Today, its wreckage is one of the most visible landmarks of Paramaribo.
23 Klinkers, *Troepenmacht*, p. 24.
24 Klinkers, *Troepenmacht*, p. 25.
25 High octane fuel was used for aviation and powered British aircraft, including Royal Air Force fighters that fought in the Battle of Britain.
26 Klinkers, *Troepenmacht*, pp. 27–31.
27 Richard van de Velde, *Het Prinses Irene Detachement in Suriname*. Parbode 178, February 2021.
28 With the troops came 4-inch naval guns, USAAF aircraft and air defences. By early 1942, the US had established an air base at Zanderij Airport and thus, Dutch plans to station 9 Brewster fighters and pilots in Suriname, were put on hold. Klinkers, *Troepenmacht*, p. 32.
29 Deployment information found on the USAF Historical Research Agency website <www.afhra.af.mil>, accessed 18 September 2021.
30 The entire crew was killed, except for one survivor who was rescued by a US destroyer after 10 days at sea. <https://uboat.net/boats/patrols/patrol_1127.html>, accessed 18 September 2022.
31 *Chaos op Zanderij door Bijlmer-Expres*, Vrije Stem, 9 November 1974.
32 Richard van de Velde, *Jodensavanne, Nederlands laatste concentratiekamp*, Parbode 178, February 2021.
33 The constitution stated that conscripts could not be sent overseas unless they volunteered. As the Dutch parliament-in-exile was not allowed the change the constitution, these decisions were in the hands of local governments. After the war ended, this law was temporarily changed and conscripts from the Netherlands could be sent to serve in Indonesia during the so-called '*Politionele Acties*' (Policing Actions) from 1947 to 1949.
34 Racial segregation was not unique to the Dutch armed forces. For example, the US armed forces also enforced racial segregation until it was officially abolished in 1948.
35 Fifteen (some sources say fourteen) Surinamers went to Europe directly with the Princess Irene Brigade to serve with the Dutch armed forces and the RAF. About 200 Surinamers served as gunners on convoys of which 29 perished. The number of Surinamers that fought with the KNIL in 1941–1942 is unknown. Klinkers, *Troepenmacht*, pp. 45 and 41 respectively.
36 Anton de Kom was the author of '*Wij slaven van Suriname*' (Us slaves of Suriname) – a book about the history of slavery in Suriname and a protest to the Dutch government. He was imprisoned and deported to the Netherlands in 1933. When the Second World War broke out, he joined the Communist resistance. He was captured and executed by the German authorities just before liberation in April 1945.
37 The monument to Surinamese victims of the Second World War (unveiled in 1950) and the memorial to Surinamese Jews murdered during the Second World War (built in 2016), list a total of 12 Surinamers that were killed serving with the Dutch resistance, 105 Surinamese Jews that were killed in concentration camps, 30 seamen that were killed in the Atlantic and 13 soldiers that were killed in action.
38 There were rallies in Suriname organised by the Javanese party (the KTPI). Klinkers, *Troepenmacht*, pp. 68–70.
39 The Korean War Monument (1950–1953) lists the names of the 102 Surinamers who served in Suriname, together with the names of Herbert Seedorf and Jacques Bandison who were killed on 10 October 1951, during attacks on Hills 605 and 905 of Heartbreak Ridge.
40 In total 4,748 Dutch troops served in the Korean War, of whom 121 perished and four are still missing in action. Netherlands Ministry of Defence website on military missions of the Dutch armed forces <https://www.defensie.nl/onderwerpen/historische-missies/missie-overzicht/1950/korea-oorlog>, accessed 18 September 2022. For more details on the Surinamese contribution to the NDVN, please refer to Klinkers, *Troepenmacht*, pp. 95–105.
41 This is not the first coup attempt in Suriname. In 1910, police inspector Frans Pavel Killinger (a Hungarian who had served in the KNIL), had conspired with six others (including police members) to overthrow the Governor and to form a free state. His plot was betrayed before it could be carried out and was a reason the Dutch did not fully count on the police to maintain order during political unrest. Buddingh', *Suriname*, pp. 240–241.
42 Klinkers, *Troepenmacht*, pp. 73–74.
43 Klinkers, *Troepenmacht*, pp. 80–81.
44 Klinkers, *Troepenmacht*, pp. 82–91.

Chapter 3

1 Buddingh', *Suriname*, pp. 289–294.
2 Buddingh', *Suriname*, pp. 309–310.
3 Buddingh', *Suriname*, p. 315.
4 Buddingh', *Suriname*, pp. 315–318.
5 Klinkers, *Troepenmacht*, pp. 108.
6 For comparison, the standard time of conscription for Dutch soldiers serving in the Netherlands was 18 months in the 1960s. Conscripts volunteering for Suriname would serve for a shorter time but would serve a year in Suriname after four months of training. TRIS officers typically served for three-year deployments. The Netherlands armed forces became a professional army in 1996, ending conscription.
7 Klinkers, *Troepenmacht*, pp. 108.
8 Klinkers, *Troepenmacht*, pp. 127–131.
9 Klinkers, *Troepenmacht*, pp. 112–119.
10 Klinkers, *Troepenmacht*, pp. 115–117, M.G. Woerlee and Ir. F. Roodenburg, *De taakvervulling van de Troepenmacht in Suriname in de laatste periode voor de onafhankelijkheid*, *Militaire Spectator* Magazine, Issue 145, 1976.

11 Information gathered from discussions with TRIS veterans on the Facebook groups *TRIS Online* and *TRIS Troepenmacht in Suriname*.
12 Most of these weapons are found described on the TRIS Online website, <http://www.trisonline.nl>, accessed 18 September 2022. The PIAT anti-tank weapon was also used by the support platoons (see H.J. Beekers, *De huidige Troepenmacht in Suriname (TRIS), Militaire Spectator Magazine*, Issue 147, 1960, pp. 386–401).
13 TRIS Online website, <http://www.trisonline.nl>, accessed 18 September 2022.
14 TRIS Online website, <http://www.trisonline.nl>, accessed 18 September 2022.
15 Stichting Triscontakten, *Verliefd op Suriname 1947–2009* (Triskontakten Zwijndrecht, 2009), pp. 186 and 405.
16 More information on Guyana's history up until independence, can be found in the book *The Guyana Story (From Earliest Times to Independence)* by Dr. Odeen Ishmael (see references).
17 Called Nieuwe Rivier by the Dutch and Surinamers since it was discovered in 1871. A. Grant, *Tigri – Erfenis van een verraad* (Ralicon, 2008, 2nd edition), p. 24.
18 This area is referred to as the New River Triangle by the Guyanese.
19 In 1933, while a commission was working out the frontier between the Brazil and British Guiana, the Netherlands proposed that the tri-nation border be the point where the Koetari River crosses the Brazilian border. The agreement was brought up in 1939 but never signed due to the outbreak of the Second World War.
20 Immediately after Guyana claimed independence, relations with Venezuela were not very cordial as Caracas laid claim to the territory west of the Essequibo River (rejecting previous boundary agreements from 1899 and 1932). In October 1966, Venezuelan troops and newly built installations were discovered on the Guyanese half of Ankoko Island (formed by the confluence of the Coyinu and Wenamu Rivers). Despite Guyanese protests, Venezuelan troops are still occupying the island to this day.
21 Despite Pengel denying this, there were speculations that he sought Venezuelan support for Suriname's border dispute. Grant, *Tigri*, p. 29 and CIA Library document CIA-RDP08C01297R000700070013-6 – Cable US Consul to US Department of State (dated 21 Dec 1967, declassified 2 October 2012).
22 Grant, *Tigri*, p. 29.
23 Grant, *Tigri*, p. 30 and David Granger, *The defence of the New River*, 1967–1969, <https://www.stabroeknews.com/2009/02/15/features/the-defence-of-the-new-river-1967-1969/>, accessed 16 July. 2020.
24 This was confirmed by a low pass with a civilian SLM aircraft. Klinkers, *Troepenmacht*, p. 146.
25 Klinkers, *Troepenmacht*, pp. 143–145.
26 CIA Library document CIA-RDP08C01297R000700070008-2 – Research memorandum Department of State (dated Mar 29, 1968, declassified 12 December 2012).
27 The TRIS initially supplied 25 Uzis and 70 second-hand uniforms. Klinkers, *Troepenmacht*, pp. 145 and Grant, *Tigri*.
28 Klinkers, *Troepenmacht*, pp. 147–148, Triskontakten, *Verliefd*, pp. 265–266.
29 The type of weapons delivered is still unknown but these are suspected to be LMGs or rifles delivered from Venezuela. Klinkers, *Troepenmacht*, p. 149, Grant, *Tigri*, pp. 61–62.
30 Grant, *Tigri*, pp. 63–65.
31 Policeman Grant claims that the patrol consisted of 25 men. Grant, *Tigri*, p. 68. The Guyanese claimed that their engine had broken down (Granger, *New River*).
32 Klinkers, *Troepenmacht*, pp. 150–151, Grant, *Tigri*, pp. 70–72.
33 Klinkers, *Troepenmacht*, p. 151.
34 Klinkers, *Troepenmacht*, pp. 152–153.
35 CIA Library document CIA-RDP08C01297R000700070007-3 – Intelligence note from US Dept. of State (dated 22 Aug 1969, declassified 2012/12/12).
36 On January 2, 1969, Amerindian tribe members in Rapanuni revolted against the local government in protest of Burnhams policies. The 200 troops of the GDF were airlifted to successfully quell the uprising. Philip Jardim, Guyana defends itself, <https://guyanathenandnow.wordpress.com/british-guiana-airways-limited/>, accessed 21 September 2020.
37 Jardim, *Guyana*.
38 Granger, *New River*.
39 This and the next few paragraphs refer to Jardim and Michael Chan-a-Sue, *The Guns of August*, <https://guyana.hoop.la/topic/the-guns-of-august>, accessed 21 September 2022.
40 Surinamese sources claim that a group of GDF special forces had arrived at Tigri several days before and hid in the jungle near the airstrips. Just before the aircraft arrived, they removed the drums from the airfield without getting noticed by the DEFPOL troops and allowed the Twin Otters to land. Triskontacten, *Verliefd*, p. 264, *Terwijl Suriname slaapt, rooft Guyana*, Vrije Stem, 26 August 1969.
41 Klinkers, *Troepenmacht*, pp. 153, Triskontacten, *Verliefd*, p. 268.
42 Grant, *Tigri*, p. 85. Ellen Klinkers claims Van Dams was received triumphantly (Klinkers, *Troepenmacht*, p. 153). Whatever the case, Gerrit van Dams received recognition for his plight when he was awarded the Order of the Palm on 25 February 2016 by President Desi Bouterse.
43 CIA Library document CIA-RDP08C01297R000700070023-5 – Telegram from US Embassy in Georgetown to US State Department (dated 21 Aug 1969, declassified 2 October 2012).
44 For this and the following paragraph, see *Suriname en Guyana botsen*, Algemeen Dagblad, 11 November 1981.
45 Grant, *Tigri*, p. 87.
46 Klinkers, *Troepenmacht*, pp. 157–160.
47 Klinkers, *Troepenmacht*, p. 164.
48 Klinkers, *Troepenmacht*, p. 166, Buddingh', *Suriname*, p. 297.
49 Buddingh', *Suriname*, p. 303.
50 Buddingh', *Suriname*, p. 305.
51 From 1966 to 1968, 12,000 Surinamers immigrated to the Netherlands, followed by a further 25,000 from 1969 to 1972. E.K. Marshall, *Ontstaan en ontwikkeling van het Surinaams nationalisme* (Eburon Uitgeverij, Delft, 2003), p. 193.
52 Buddingh', *Suriname*, p. 305.
53 Marshall, *Nationalisme*, p. 193.
54 Buddingh', *Suriname*, pp. 301–302, Klinkers, *Troepenmacht*, pp. 197–199.
55 Klinkers, *Troepenmacht*, p. 170.
56 Woerlee, *Taakvervulling*, p. 480–487 and Klinkers, *Troepenmacht*, p. 173.
57 Woerlee, *Taakvervulling*, p. 495.
58 YP-408 Forgotten Hero? <https://www.dafyp408.nl>, accessed 23 September 2022.
59 The five YP-408 had the serial numbers KN 75-28 (PWI-S PC version), KN 75-32, KN 88-45, KN 88-46 and KN 88-48. See <https://www.dafyp408.nl/suriname.htm>, accessed 23 September 2022.
60 Klinkers, *Troepenmacht*, pp. 181–183.
61 Klinkers, *Troepenmacht*, p. 173.
62 The KMA is the Royal Military Academy in Breda which trains officers for the Army and Air Force, the KMS is the Royal Military School in Weert, which trained NCOs for the Army. The OCOSD is a shortened officer training course, meant to train reservists or NCOs to the rank of officer.
63 Woerlee, *Taakvervulling*, pp. 492–493 and Klinkers, *Troepenmacht*, p. 184.
64 Klinkers, *Troepenmacht*, p. 190.
65 This and the next paragraph refer to Klinkers, *Troepenmacht*, pp. 168–176.

Chapter 4

1 Roger Janssen, *In search of a path – An analysis of the foreign policy of Suriname from 1975 to 1991* (KITLV Press, 2011), p. 54–55.
2 Janssen, *Search*, p. 55.
3 Vrije Stem, *Cirkus Stupido: Komproe zet Lachmon eruit. Rufus vraagt om vergiffenis voor Jack*, 27 April 1978 and documentary, *Andere Tijden – Bouterse aan de macht*.
4 Janssen, *Search*, p. 40 and Buddingh', *Suriname*, p. 308. It is important to note that of the 55,000 Surinamers who immigrated to the Netherlands, approximately 19,000 left in 1980 – the year of the *Sergeantencoup*. It is also important to note that between 1976 and 1980, about 20,000 Surinamers remigrated to the Netherlands – a net result of 35,000 leaving Suriname in that period.
5 Many of the facts in this section are described in more detail in Janssen, *Search*, pp. 48–54.
6 Buddingh', *Suriname*, p. 325.
7 Buddingh', *Suriname*, p. 325.
8 These were Captain H. Jesserun, 2nd Lieutenant H Rodriguez, sergeants Vonsee, W. Rusland and R. Fredison – *Patrouille boten nog zonder kanonnen*, Vrije Stem, 12 June 1978.
9 J.L. Couhat (ed.), *Combat Fleets of the World 1980/1981: Their Ships, Aircraft and Armament* (Naval Institute Press, 1980, 1st Edition), pp. 600–601.
10 *Kustwachtpatrouilleboten voor Suriname*, Reformatorisch Dagblad, 22 April 1975.
11 Often mistakenly written as 'Beaufort' in newspapers and publications.
12 *High Seas Patrolboats 12.5 miljoen te duur*, Vrije Stem, 8 June 1977.

13 Jozef Slagveer, *De Nacht van de Revolutie – De staatsgreep in Suriname op 25 februari 1980* (Paramaribo: Uitgeverij C. Kersten & Co NV,1980), p. 179.
14 Rudie Kagie, *Bikkel – het verhaal van de eerste politieke moord van het Bouterse-Regime* (Amsterdam: Uitgeverij Bert Bakker, 2012), p. 64. Ellen Klinkers has the date as January 1977 (Klinkers, *Opbouw*, p. 255).
15 Ellen Klinkers, *De opbouw van de Surinaamse Krijgsmacht, Symbool van onafhankelijkheid en ontreddering, OSO Tijdschrijft voor Surinamistiek en het Carabisch gebied*, 2016, p. 253.
16 Klinkers, *Opbouw*, p. 256.
17 Kagie, *Bikkel*, p. 64.
18 Valk and Elstak had both served in the Juliana barracks in Den Daag together and were known to despise each other – although Valk in an interview says he had a 'normal working relationship with him'. Kagie, *Bikkel*, p. 95. Video – *Andere Tijden: Bouterse aan de macht*.
19 Elma Verhey & Gerard van Westerloo, *Het Legergroene Suriname* (Weekbladpers, Amsterdam, 1983), p. 131 and Kagie, *Bikkel*, pp. 95–96. The Minister of Army, Defence and Police, Eddy Hoost informed Valk in February 1976 that the SKM was focusing on becoming a development army, there to support civil projects (in contrast to what was agreed with the Dutch government). Only in March 1976, did the members meet Elstak and they were allocated an office in the *Memre Boekoe Kazerne* in Paramaribo.
20 Wim Hoogberg & Dirk Kruijt, *De oorlog van de sergeanten – Surinaamse Militaire in de Politiek* (Uitgeverij Bert Bakker, 2005), pp. 25–27.
21 This Mamabon or Greenhart tree, was planted on a grass field in front of the old Parliament building in 1954. It has been a well-known assembly point for demonstrations in Suriname.
22 The report was not published because it accurately described the problems within the SKM and would be an embarrassment for the government to publish during the election campaign. The report also proposed solutions for the government to solve these. Among them, it recommended that the government employed all SKM volunteers at the naval base but it also recommended that 'all forms of trade union activities in the classic sense, by military personnel are deemed not acceptable'. This was the only advice in the report that the Arron government followed. Slagveer, *Nacht*, pp. 109–208.
23 This and the next few paragraphs refer to Henk Boom, *Staatsgreep in Suriname – De Opstand van de sergeanten op de voet gevolgd* (Utrecht/Antwerpen: Uitgeverij L.J. Veen BV, 1982), pp. 57–61.
24 Police officer Danny Lo Fo Sang, who was present at the stand-off, denied that the chief of police ever gave this order. Video interview with Lo Fo Sang, Starnieuws, 2011.
25 See Ellen de Vries, *Hans Valk – over een Nederlandse Kolonel en een coup in Suriname (1980)* (Walburgpers 2021), pp. 138–143, Verhey, *Legergroene Suriname*, pp. 50–53 and Slagveer, *Nacht*, 21–48.
26 Lieutenant Rambocus' first name is spelled in various ways including Surindre, Surendre & Soerendre. The author decided to use Surendre as this is how his family refers to him in correspondence to the Suriname military court when they pleaded for his release in 1980.The other officers were 2nd Lieutenant Wirth, Cairo and Dihal. It is of interest to note that Rambocus was a KMA alumni who graduated on the subject of 'coup d'état'. Verhey, *Legergroene Suriname*, p. 50.
27 De Vries, *Hans Valk*, p. 116, Verhey, *Legergroene Suriname*, pp. 50–51.
28 Slagveer, *Nacht*, pp. 46–48.
29 *Mijnals doet boekje open over Coup*, De West website, <https://dagbladdewest.com/2015/12/11/mijnals-doet-boekje-open-over-coup/?fbclid=IwAR0PMEc6HkM4_5Av6bYnO62ZewTwYRms7bsPYH7lkB2KpixiP3u5zr8KZ4A>, accessed 30 September 2022.
30 Boom, *Staatsgreep*, pp. 106–110.
31 Pepijn Reeser, *Desi Bouterse – Een Surinaamse Tragedie* (Uitgeverij Prometheus Bert Bakker, Amsterdam, 2015), p. 155.
32 Confirmed participants are Bouterse, Hardjoprajitno, Nelom, Mahadew and Zeeuw. Slagveer, *Nacht*, pp. 36–37.
33 Slagveer, *Nacht*, pp. 46–48.
34 Slagveer, *Nacht*, pp. 53–56.
35 Documentary – *De Zonen van Suriname deel 1*.
36 Slagveer, *Nacht*, pp. 56–57.
37 Ellen de Vries, *Hans Valk*, pp. 143–144. Hardjoprajitno and his team had actually managed to capture weapons during the raid on the ammunition bunker. The weapons cache was also confiscated during his arrest.
38 Ellen de Vries, *Hans Valk*, p. 25.
39 The following paragraphs refer to Slagveer, *Nacht*, pp. 65–66.
40 Bouterse claimed a warning shot was fired but the police bus did not stop. Slagveer, *Nacht*, p. 66.
41 Ellen de Vries, *Ik vind: moord is moord*, *Suriname 30 jaar na de Staatsgreep*, *Wordt Vervolgd Magazine*, Amnesty International, Issue 2, 2010 and V. Boejharat, *De wond is nog niet geheeld*, Starnieuws, 26 February 2015.
42 Bouterse also claims that he ordered the YPs to be armed with Bren guns. This has not been confirmed in any of the pictures taken around and after the coup, although this is technically still possible. Slagveer, *Nacht*, p. 68.
43 Slagveer, *Nacht*, pp. 66–67.
44 Boom, *Staatsgreep*, p. 115–119.
45 Slagveer, *Nacht*, p. 98.
46 Sgt Ernst Gefferie claimed that man even threatened to jump overboard which posed a risk of revealing the coup operation. It is doubtful whether it would have made a difference because at that time, the naval base and the MBK were in the coup plotters' hands. Slagveer, *Nacht*, p. 95.
47 Slagveer, *Nacht*, pp. 68–69.
48 Triskontacten, *Verliefd*, pp. 161–162.
49 Boom, *Staatsgreep*, p. 118.
50 The two people killed were Joseph Bacchus, an employee in a jewellery store and an unknown man, probably from Guyana. (De Vries, *Ik vind: moord is moord*) and Boom, *Staatsgreep*, pp. 125 & 129–130.
51 Slagveer, *Nacht*, p. 83
52 Slagveer, *Nacht*, p. 69.
53 Boom, *Staatsgreep*, p. 125–126.
54 Bouterse claims that the fire was started by a phosphorus round (Slagveer, *Nacht*, p. 72). Bofors 40mm cannons do not have that type of ammunition and it is therefore more likely that this was a high explosive incendiary (HE(I)) round.
55 Slagveer, *Nacht*, p. 87.
56 Slagveer, *Nacht*, p. 97.
57 It seems that the destruction of the police headquarters was a part of the plan, despite the fact that Bomika council members were released and the police had surrendered. S402 was not told to hold fire, which was clearly possible when Roy Tolud was informed to cease firing on Fort Zeelandia. Boom, *Staatsgreep*, p. 126.
58 Boom, *Staatsgreep*, p. 134, Reeser, *Desi Bouterse*, p. 160.
59 Boom, *Staatsgreep*, pp. 136–138.
60 Bomika council member De Rhamdhanie, was not selected for a seat in the NMR as he was uncovered as being an informant for the military intelligence service. Reeser, *Desi Bouterse*, p. 166.
61 Boom, *Staatsgreep*, pp. 139–142.
62 Boom, *Staatsgreep*, pp. 153–154.
63 Boom, *Staatsgreep*, pp. 160–161.
64 Peter Meel, *Henck Arren en de staatsgreep van 25 Februari 1980*, OSO – Tijdschrift voor Surinaamse taalkunde, letterkunde en geschiedenis, Issue 34, 2015, pp. 16–18.
65 Boom, *Staatsgreep*, pp. 171–172.
66 Janssen, *Search*, pp. 58–59.
67 This section refers to the documentary *Andere tijden: Bouterse aan de macht* and the books by Verhey, *Legergroene Suriname*, pp. 123–162, Reeser, *Desi Bouterse*, pp. 161–166 and Ellen de Vries, *Hans Valk*.
68 Operation *Zwarte Tulp* is declassified and currently available in the TRIS Archives to view to the public. According to Ellen Klinkers, the plan is a set of operational instructions to evacuate Dutch nationals from Suriname in case of ethnic violence and unrests. It was written after a meeting between COTRIS Woerlee and the Commander Landzaat of the naval forces in the Antilles. Klinkers, *Troepenmacht*, p. 199.

Chapter 5

1 *Niets is geheel zeker en zelfs dat niet – de Ingreep*, NRC Handelsblad, 3 March 1980.
2 The latter showed how many 'ghost' civil servants were actually on government payroll. Servants, who had barely showed up in the previous months, all arrived at work to crowd the offices clearly illustrating that the departments did not have enough workplaces and were overstaffed. Boom, *Staatsgreep*, p. 175.
3 See documentary *Zonen van Suriname*, part 1.
4 Boom, *Staatsgreep*, p. 160.
5 This government also consisted of the first female ministers in a Surinamese cabinet. Jul M. Dubois, *Suriname in ontwkkeling (foto's spreken de waarheid) 25 Februari 1980 – deel 2* (Paramaribo: Uitgeverij Dubois, 1980), p. 46–60.
6 Hoogbergen, *Sergeanten*, p. 48–49.
7 Letter from Rambocus to Dutch Ministry of Defence. Part of document package of the Dutch Ministry of Defence concerning the Rambocus coup.

<https://respubca.home.xs4all.nl/pdf/mindeframbocus.pdf/>, accessed 21 September 2022.
8   See documentary *Zonen van Suriname, part 1*. Robby Behr would later flee Suriname in early 1982. See *Surinaamse Officier vraagt asiel*, Het Parool, 13 March 1982.
9   Hoogbergen, *Sergeanten*, p. 48.
10 See Ellen de Vries, *De Mediastrijd om Suriname – Van mythemakers tot nieuwsverduisteraars* (Zutphen: Walburg Pers, 2017), Chapter 3, pp. 79–130 for a very detailed description of the Surinamese and Dutch media landscapes as they existed between 1980 and 1992.
11 This section refers to the book *Bikkel* and the Parbode artikel *De Verzonnen Contracoup* by Rudie Kagie, the journalist who was able to break the news of Ormskerk's death to the world.
12 Krol was reported to have been severely beaten and had a knife put into his genitals during interrogation. A report about the ill-treatment of Krol was released by the archives of the Amnesty International Office in London.
13 Kasantaroeno and Roy Bottse were sentenced to five and four years in absentia. Kasantaroeno's father received two-and-a-half years of prison time.
14 André Haakmat, *De Revolutie Uitgegleden – Politieke Herinneringen* (Uitgeverij Jan Mets, Amsterdam, 1987), pp. 46–50.
15 *Suriname – Rol militairen vrijwel uitgespeeld*, Provinciaalse Zeeuwse Courant, 1 Aug 1980.
16 Janssen, *Search*, p. 60.
17 The 'new' NMR consisted of Sgt Mijnals (chairman), Sgt1 Hardjoprajitno (vice-chairman), Adj Cederboom, Sgt1 Nankoesingh, Lt Graanoogst, 2nd Lt Cairo, Sgt Maj Olfers – *Nieuwe Militaire Raad treedt in Suriname*, Amigoe, 30 July 1980.
18 Haakmat, *Revolutie*, pp. 64–65.
19 This and the next few paragraphs, refer to the book by Haakmat, *Revolutie*, pp. 65–67.
20 See Haakmat, *Revolutie*, pp. 88–100. The special court was credited with preventing bloodshed and allowing tens of people to regain their freedom. For example, Haakmat claimed he was approached by Bouterse with the suggestion to have Joeman, Mijnals and Sital perish in a transport accident. When a shocked Haakmat responded that was out of the question, Bouterse was said to have replied, 'Ok, then, we will cancel this' and passed the message on to an accomplice with whom Bouterse had visited Haakmat's office.
21 Janssen, *Search*, pp. 61–62.
22 Hoogbergen, *Sergeanten*, pp. 49–50 and Buddingh', *Suriname*, pp. 332–333.
23 Vrije Stem, *Suriname binnen twee jaar naar democratie*, 26 February 1981.
24 Reeser, *Desi Bouterse*, pp. 184–185.
25 Buddingh', *Suriname*, pp. 333–334.
26 Amigoe, *Sergeant-Majoor Hawker was in Nederland opgeleid*, 18 March 1981. In addition, Arthy Gorré and Hawker also followed an internship with the KCT. Gorré had already completed the course in 1970 before joining the SKM.
27 This and the next paragraph refer to 'Terug naar oude structuren of nieuwe chaos', Nieuwsblad van het Noorden, 16 May 1981.
28 *Nieuwe coup in Suriname verijdelt*, Nieuwsblad van het Noorden, 17 March 1981.
29 *Straffen hoger dan eis*, Algemeen Dagblad, 19 October 1981.
30 For this and the next paragraph, see *Bestrijder regime Suriname vermoord*, De Volkskrant, 16 June 1981.
31 Edward M. Dew, *The Trouble in Suriname, 1975–1993* (Westport, CT, USA: Praeger Publishers, 1994), p. 69.
32 Hoogbergen, *Sergeanten*, p. 64 and Reeser, *Desi Bouterse*, p. 193.
33 Dew, *Trouble*, p. 64. The council included the President (Chin A Sen), Chairman of the Liberation and Development Front (Bouterse), the Garrison Commander (Horb), Chairman of the Advisory Council (Krolis) and Foreign Minister (Naarendorp). They would advise the council of ministers (led by Chin A Sen) who would execute the policy.
34 Vrije Stem, *Suriname binnen twee jaar naar democratie*, 26 February 1981.
35 Dew, *Trouble*, p. 64.
36 Hoogbergen, *Sergeanten*, p. 57
37 Amigoe, *Suriname denkt aan luchtmacht*, 11 December 1980
38 Amigoe, *Suriname krijgt eigen luchtmacht*, 24 June 1981.
39 Trouw, *Surinaamse officier in Luchtmacht opleiding*, 17 July 1981.
40 Vrije Stem, *John Vasilda – Straaljagerpiloot*, 5 Aug 1969 and Twentse Straaljager vloog kabels stuk, Turbantia, 30 Aug 1974.
41 Amigoe, *Luchtmacht Suriname schaft vier vliegtuigen aan*, 13 July 1981.
42 *Surinamese Airforce 1981-2009*, Scramble Magazine, Issue 361, 2009.
43 *Militaire overeenkomst met Suriname Verlengt*, Nederlands Dagblad, 28 January. 1981.
44 Klinkers, *Opbouw van der Surinaamse Krijgsmacht*, p. 258.
45 Leeuwarder Courant, *Nederlanse Militaire Missie uit Suriname*, 21 April 1981.
46 Interestingly, Clements would, after his return to the Netherlands, retire from the Dutch Army and return to Suriname as a civilian, becoming an advisor to the *Nationaal Leger*.
47 Ellen de Vries, *Valk*, pp. 39–51.
48 *Toch militaire bijstand aan Suriname*, NRC Handelsblad, 12 June 1981.
49 Hans van Mierlo, who was the Dutch Minister of Defence between September 1981 and November 1982, later admitted that his department continued providing support at the request of the US as the Reagan administration was concerned that Suriname would turn towards communism, *Van Mierlo Steunde in 1981 Regime Bouterse met Wapens*, NRC Handelsblad, 23 April 1996.
50 Buddingh', *Suriname*, p. 336.
51 This section refers to Dew, *Trouble*, pp. 70–75.
52 The C-47 and FLA trade unions would take part in the Revolutionary Front. Absent were other unions such as the *Moederbond*.
53 Buddingh', *Suriname*, p. 335.
54 Hoogbergen, *Sergeanten*, p. 58.
55 Hoogbergen, *Sergeanten*, pp. 58-59.
56 Hoogbergen, *Sergeanten*, p. 59 and Haakmat, *Revolutie*, pp. 148–149.
57 Haakmat, *Revolutie*, p. 150.
58 According to a provision in the Constitution of Suriname, the (Vice) President of the Court becomes acting President of the Republic in case of an unexpected resignation of a State President. It is unknown whether this was the case with Ramdat Misier, but in his memoirs, Haakmat writes that either he or court member Waalwijk proposed Ramdat Misier as a candidate for President. Haakmat, Revolutie, p. 150
59 *In Suriname macht blijvend bij militairen*, NRC Handelsblad, 27 February 1982.
60 *Nederland staakt ontwikkelingshulp Suriname*, NRC Handelsblad, 20 February 1982.
61 *Waarom wel Nicaragua en niet wij?* het Vrije Volk, 17 February 1982.
62 Video *Suriname 1973 to 1982 – part 4*.
63 Dew, *Trouble*, p. 75.

Chapter 6

1   Lucien Pinas, *De Woelige Dagen van Maart 1982* (Paramaribo: Apollo's Reklame & Uitgeversburo, 1982), p. 3, Anon., *De Revolutie Overwint! – de Contra-Revolutionaire Poging tot Staatsgreep in Suriname op 11 en 12 Maart 1982* (Paramaribo: Vereniging van Progressieve Mediawerkers, 1982), p. 12 and ANP, *foreign news bulletin 14*, 11 March 1982.
2   This section refers to an undated report sent to the Dutch ministry of defence about the political situation in Suriname since the Sergeantscoup of 1980, <https://respubca.home.xs4all.nl/pdf/mindeframbocus.pdf/>, accessed 12 September 2021.
3   Hoogbergen, *Sergeanten*, p. 47.
4   This section refers to *Rambocus had Suriname in handen, maar wilde geen bloedvergieten*, De Telegraaf, 15 January 1983.
5   The following (ex-)military personnel plotted to take part in this coup: Lieutenant Rambocus, Sergeants Maharadjien and Sheombar, Corporals Birbal and Mahabier and Soldiers Oedit, Djarab, Gayadeen, Ramkhelawan and Ramililawan. Correspondence and interview with Sergeant A. Panchu in July 2021, January 2022 and September 2022.
6   See Haakmat, *De Revoltie Uitgegleden*, pp. 150–151.
7   As per correspondence with Sergeant Azemalie Panchu, September 2022.
8   Corporal Birbal worked at the NMR office (Pinas, *Dagen*, p. 18).
9   The following conspirators took part in the attack on MBK North: Rambocus, Mahabier, Sheombar, Ramlakhan, Gayadeen, R. Kasi, Doerga, S. Panchu, Djorai, W. Sital and Oedit. As per correspondence with Sergeant Azemalie Panchu, September 2022.
10 *De Revolutie Overwint*, p. 10 & Pinas, *Dagen*, p. 18 & ANP, *foreign news bulletins 10 and 11*, 14 March 1982 & Jul M. Dubois, *11 Maart 1982 – De mislukte coup in beeld* (Paramaribo: Uitgeverij Dubois, 1982), p. 83.
11 *Rambocus had Suriname in handen, maar wilde geen bloedvergieten*, De Telegraaf, 15 January 1983.
12 Besides Winfried Hawker, corporals Waldi Sedoc, Francis and Lloyd Bahalwankhan, who were also accused of participating in the Hawker Coup of March 1981 were also released. *Jongste coup Suriname louter militaire zaak*, Amigoe, 21 Maart 1981.
13 *De Revolutie Overwint*, p. 12 & documentary *11 Maart 1982*.
14 See documentary *11 Maart 1982*.
15 See documentary *11 Maart 1982*, *De Revolutie Overwint*, p. 12 and Dubois, *11 Maart 1982*, p. 17.

16 See documentary *11 Maart 1982* and *Rambocus had Suriname in handen, maar wilde geen bloedvergieten*, De Telegraaf, 15 Januari 1983.
17 The names mentioned were Ramon Abrahams, Arty Gorré, Paul Bhagwandas as well as police chief De Vrij and Inspector Monsels (Pinas, *Dagen*, p. 3).
18 Of the approximately 500 soldiers present, only two left. Dew, *Trouble*, p. 76.
19 See Pinas, *Dagen*, p. 4.
20 Correspondence and interview with Sergeant A. Panchu in July 2021, January 2022 and September 2022.
21 See documentary *11 Maart 1982*.
22 The defence of the fort was divided in three sections. The northern section under Abrahams covered the area between the Palmentuin and the Torarica hotel, the centre section under Gorré and Bhagwandas covered the area between the Palmentuin and the last section covered the Suriname River. Bouterse had set himself up within the confines of the fort. See documentary *11 Maart 1982*.
23 See documentary *11 Maart 1982* and ANP, foreign news bulletins 14 & 20, 11 March 1982.
24 Correspondence and interview with Sergeant A. Panchu in July 2021, January 2022 and September 2022.
25 ANP, foreign news bulletin 14, 11 March 1982.
26 Pinas, *Dagen*, p. 4.
27 Declassified coded messages (11 March 1982, Hoekman 146 & 147) from Dutch Ambassador to Dutch Ministry of Foreign Affairs.
28 ANP, *foreign news bulletin 26*, 11 March 1982 & Dubois, *11 Maart 1982*, p. 102.
29 ANP, *foreign news bulletin 26*, 11 March 1982.
30 *De Revolutie Overwint*, p. 13 & Pinas, *Dagen*, p. 4 & Jul M. Dubois, *11 Maart 1982*, p. 85.
31 For more information on the Mahes case, see *Terreur op Uitkijk by Bram Behr*.
32 See documentary *11 Maart 1982* & *De Revolutie Overwint*, p. 13 & Pinas, *Dagen*, p. 4 & Jul M. Dubois, *11 Maart 1982*, p. 85. According to Interview with Panchu on 21 July 2021, Bhagwandas – not Gorré – convinced Lachman to defect.
33 Main source for YP facts is the website *YP-408 Forgotten Hero?*, <https://www.dafyp408.nl>, accessed 17 July. 2020.
34 See documentary *11 Maart 1982* & ANP, *foreign news bulletin 26*, 11 March 1982 & *De Revolutie Overwint*, p. 12 & Pinas, *Dagen*, p. 5 & declassified coded message (11 March 1982, Hoekman 148) from Dutch Ambassador to Dutch Ministry of Foreign Affairs.
35 De Vries, *Mediastrijd*, p. 104.
36 ANP, *foreign news bulletins 31 & 37*, 11 March 1982, declassified coded message (11 March 1982, Hoekman 149) from Dutch Ambassador to Dutch Ministry of Foreign Affairs.
37 See documentary *11 Maart 1982* & ANP, *foreign news bulletin 45*, 11 March 1982 & Pinas, *Dagen*, pp. 5–7.
38 ANP, *foreign news bulletin 40*, 11 March 1982.
39 ANP, *foreign news bulletin 01*, 12 March 1982.
40 Pinas, *Dagen*, p. 7.
41 ANP, *foreign news bulletin 10*, 12 March 1982.
42 Declassified coded message (30 March 1982, Heldring 216) from Dutch embassy to Dutch Ministry of Foreign Affairs.
43 See documentary *11 Maart 1982*.
44 See documentary *11 Maart 1982* & *De Revolutie Overwint*, p. 14 & Pinas, *Dagen*, p. 7 & Jul M. Dubois, *11 Maart 1982*, p. 102.
45 See documentary *11 Maart 1982* & Pinas, *Dagen*, pp. 14–15.
46 Pinas, *Dagen*, pp. 7 & 79 & Jul M. Dubois, *11 Maart 1982*, p. 104 & ANP, *foreign news bulletin 14 & 16*, 12 March 1982 & ddeclassified coded message (12 March 1982, Hoekman 151) from Dutch embassy to Dutch Ministry of Foreign Affairs.
47 Pinas, *Dagen*, p. 7 & Jul M. Dubois, *11 Maart 1982*, p. 102.
48 Pinas, *Dagen*, p. 43.
49 During the second attack, many rebelling soldiers surrendered but a group that refused to do so threatened to kill the officers held in the stockade if they were attacked again. *Kamp rebellen veroverd – Macht Bouterse weer hersteld*, De Volkskrant, 13 Maart 1982.
50 See documentary *11 Maart 1982* & *De Revolutie Overwint*, p. 14 & Pinas, *Dagen*, p. 85 & Jul M. Dubois, *11 Maart 1982*, p. 77 & ANP, *foreign news bulletins 27 & 34*, 12 March 1982.
51 ANP, *foreign news bulletin 30*, 12 March 1982.
52 ANP, *foreign news bulletin 35 & 36*, 12 March 1982.
53 Pinas, *Dagen*, pp. 82–83.
54 The group that pressed on included S. Rambocus, Ramsandjal, R. Kasi, Bharos, Doerga and K. Mahabir. Sheombar, Dijksteel and Maharadjien decided to return to the capital. Anon.,*Gevangen van Desi Bouterse – vluchtelingen vertellen hun ervaringen* (Rotterdam: Uitgave Makmur – Stichting van Surinaamse Vluchtelingen/Landbouwers Rotterdam, 1984), p. 12–13.
55 See documentary *11 Maart 1982*.
56 *Gevangenen van Desi Bouterse*, p. 13.
57 Pinas, *Dagen*, p. 25.
58 *Gevangenen van Desi Bouterse*, p. 14–15.
59 For this section reference is made to Pinas, *Dagen*, p. 13–15.
60 The members of parliament who were accused of participating in the coup, were Baal Oemrawsingh (VHP), Paul Somohardjo (Pendawa Lima), Sahidi Rasam (Pendawa Lima) and Mahadewsingh (VHP) of whom all except Oemrawsingh, had been arrested. Other people arrested were industrialist Bharos, medical student Kasi, announcer Henry Sohansingh, ex-soldier Dijksteel and sergeant Sheombar. In the coming weeks, more people would be arrested with eventually 60 people arrested for their (alleged) participation in the Rambocus Coup.
61 See *De Revolutie Overwint*, pp. 8–9, Jul M. Dubois, *11 Maart 1982*, p. 83. & Pinas, *Dagen*, p. 18.
62 *De Revolutie Overwint*, pp. 22–24 and the documentary *11 Maart 1982* for more details on the alleged assassination attempts. Sergeant Panchu denies that there ever any assassination attempt on the NMR or the members of the *Militair Gezag*.
63 For references and accusations of foreign (Dutch and/or US) involvement see *De Revolutie Overwint* & *De Woelige Dagen van Maart 1982* as well as the documentary *11 Maart 1982*. According to Sgt Panchu, the coup had no foreigners in their midst and was a home-grown conspiracy, grown out of dissatisfaction with the *Militair Gezag*.
64 Jul M. Dubois, *11 Maart 1982*, p. 137. & Pinas, *Dagen*, pp. 94–95.
65 Leeuwarder Courant, *Nederland dreigt Suriname met stoppen ontwikkelingshulp*, 22 Maart 1982.
66 Declassified coded message (30 March 1982, Heldring 216) from Dutch embassy to Dutch Ministry of Foreign Affairs.
67 *Neijhorst lijkt nieuwe Premier van Suriname*, NRC Handelsblad, 26 Maart 1982.
68 *Suriname heeft een nieuw Regering*, Het Parool, 31 Maart 1981.
69 *Leger heeft in Suriname Macht via Beleidscentrum*, NRC Handelsblad, 1 April 1982.
70 *Ontslag Prade kwam niet bij Verrassing*, Het Parool, 15 April 1982.
71 <https://web.archive.org/web/20210226211241/https://cityofparamaribo.com/read/Fort_Zeelandia>, accessed on 29 Nov. 2022.
72 For more information on the mistreatment of prisoners at the hands of the *Militair Gezag*, please refer to the book *Gevangen van Desi Bouterse* (*Prisoners of Desi Bouterse*), where refugees and the conspirators of March 1982 recount their experiences.
73 The backstory to the loss of SAF100 comes from an interview with Jules Vasilda, veteran of the Surinamese armed services, held on 21 January 2021.
74 Hoogbergen, *Sergeanten*, p. 65.
75 *In Suriname opleiding voor Volksmilitie*, NRC Handelsblad, 15 July 1982.
76 Trouw, *De Volksmilitie: oren en ogen van het leger*, 24 July 2002.
77 *Machtsbehoud is eerste prioriteit*, NRC Handelsblad, 14 August 1982.
78 CIA Library document CIA-RDP84B00049R001604010011-3 – Suriname-Cuba: Expansion of Relations (dated 12 July 1982, declassified 29 June 2007). These weapons were most likely small arms for forces loyal to the *Gezag*, as many weapons went missing during the Rambocus coup.
79 CIA Library document CIA-RDP84B00049R001604010011-3 – Suriname-Cuba: Expansion of Relations (dated 12 July 1982, declassified 29 June 2007).
80 Verhey, *Legergroene Suriname*, pp. 49–59.
81 Parool, *Protest tegen arrestaties in Suriname*, 7 August 1982.
82 *Machtsbehoud is eerste prioriteit*, NRC Handelsblad, 14 Aug 1982.
83 Amigoe, *Leger Suriname laat boerenleiders vrij*, 19 August 1982 and Trouw, *Suriname krijgt genoeg van Leger*, 2 September 1982.
84 Amigoe, *Leger Suriname vermoed coup*, 20 August 1982.
85 *Krijgsraad in Suriname veroordeeld twee Officieren*, NRC Handelsblad, 23 August 1982.
86 *Vijftien jaar cel geëist tegen Rambocus*, De Volkskrant, 19 November 1982.
87 Please refer to Haakmat, *Revolutie*, pp. 167–178 for Bishop's visit to Suriname in October 1982.
88 Hoogbergen, *Sergeanten*, p. 68.
89 Haakmat, *Revolutie*, p. 177. The first of the four steps (the formation of a new parliament) was to be in place by the end of 1982 and the last step by May 1983.
90 Haakmat, *Revolutie*, Haakmat, pp. 159–167.

91 See Verhey, *Legergroene Suriname*, pp. 63–74 for the complete back story on Horb's visit to the US in September 1982 and its after-effects.
92 Although it is unknown whether the CIA spoke directly with Horb, he did speak with members of the State Department. It is alleged that during this meeting, Horb was asked if they could get him something. He requested two horses, which arrived in Suriname on 11 December 1982 and would be proof of Horb's association with the CIA. Verhey, *Legergroene Suriname*, p. 72.
93 Parool, *Staking Suriname voorlopig voorbij*, 3 November 1982.
94 *Bouterse: Maart 1983 plan voor democratie*, NRC Handelsblad, 17 November 1983.
95 *Vakbonden verwijten Bouterse woordbreuk*, NRC Handelsblad, 18 November 1982.
96 These include groups such as the CCK but also the association of the Surinamese business community, the bar association, the association of doctors, the national women's council, the press association and the centre of agricultural unions. *Bond voor democratie opgericht* in Suriname, NRC Handelsblad, 25 November 1982.
97 *Publiek protest tijdens vonnis over Rambocus* NRC Handelsblad, 4 December 1982.
98 *Suriname sluit militair verdrag met Venezuela*, NRC Handelsblad, 3 December 1982.
99 Dew, *Trouble*, p. 82.
100 Believed to have been 22. See *De Decembermoorden in Suriname – Verslag van een ooggetuige* (Het Wereldvenster (Unieboek Bv), Bussum, 1983), p. 33
101 Reports speak of the army using bazookas on the buildings. As the army had no bazookas, it must be assumed that recoilless rifles were used. There are rumours that weapons recently supplied from Venezuela were used in the attacks.
102 This was confirmed by an amateur ham radio operator who, by listing to the police frequencies, taped the conversation between the police headquarters and the fire department. *De Decembermoorden*, p. 35.
103 These included Johnny Kamperveen (announcer at Radio ABC), Cyrill Karg (newspaper editor), Wilfred Lionarons (editor of newspaper, *Vrije Stem*) and Paul Somohardjo (who had joined up with NBR forces during the *Rambocuscoup*). The latter was on leave from house arrest to attend a funeral in Commewijne. He had missed the last ferry at Meerzorg and was not in Paramaribo when the military went around the city to arrest the dissidents. He went into hiding and managed to escape to French Guiana and travel to the Netherlands.
104 Hoogbergen, *Sergeanten*, pp. 73–74.
105 In addition to specific references, this section refers to the documentaries *De Zonen van Suriname, Het Drama van Fort Zeelandia* and the report from the Nederlandse Juristen Comité voor de Mensenrechten, *De Gebeurtenissen in Paramaribo 8 – 13 December 1982: de geweldadige dood van 14 Surinamers en 1 Nederlander*, 14 February 1983.
106 See documentary *De Zonen van Suriname*.
107 See documentary *De Zonen van Suriname* and Buddingh', *Suriname*, p. 340.
108 See documentary *De Zonen van Suriname*, Haakmat, *Revolutie*, p. 198–199.
109 As reported in *De Ware Tijd* of 9 Dec 1982. The military had also held live fire exercises during one of the days that Rambocus' trail started. (*Militairen zorgen voor paniek in Paramaribo*, Trouw, 12 Oct 1982).
110 See *Wijlen Fred Derby over de Decembermoorden*, Waterkant.net, <https://www.waterkant.net/suriname/2006/12/08/wijlen-fred-derby-over-de-decembermoorden/>, accessed 21 September 2022.
111 *De Decembermoorden*, pp. 10–13, Hoogbergen, *Sergeanten*, p. 77.
112 *De Decembermoorden*, pp. 42–50.
113 Fred Derby would later say in an interview that by the time he left, only Hoost, Riedewald and Wijngaarde were still alive in their cells. He stated that he saw the bodies of several people on the platform of Bastion Veere before he left the fort. Thus, the facts as stated in the book *De Decembermoorden in Suriname* cannot be taken as the gospel truth. See *Wijlen Fred Derby over de Decembermoorden*, Waterkant.net, <https://www.waterkant.net/suriname/2006/12/08/wijlen-fred-derby-over-de-decembermoorden/>, accessed 21 September 2022.
114 See verdicts released by the Surinamese courts regarding the trial of the suspects of the December murders. These refer to the autopsy performed on the victims: 22 bullets found in the bodies of nine of the 15 victims were of 9mm (Uzi and Browning) and 7.62mm (Kalashnikov) calibres. In addition, the bullet holes in the walls of the Bastion Veere were examined and matched these calibres. See the verdict regarding Steven Dendoe (case 3979, verdict 51) as issued *bij de Krijgsraad* on 29 November 2019, <https://rechtspraak.sr/wp-content/uploads/2020/05/KRG-2019-51.pdf>, accessed 25 September 2022.
115 Hoogbergen, *Sergeanten*, pp. 79–81. Bouterse supposedly told Neede that he was away when the murders happened.
116 Hoogbergen, *Sergeanten*, p. 81.
117 See Documentary *Bewijs voor coup of bewijs voor moord?*
118 Algemeen Dagblad, *Angstig Suriname weer aan het werk*, 14 December 1982.
119 Trouw, *Suriname betoogt onderdanks verbod*, 16 December 1982.
120 *Washington reageert op executies Suriname met opschorting hulp*, NRC Handelsblad, 18 December 1982.

Appendix I

1 *Centraal Bureau voor de Statistiek* (Netherlands)

ABOUT THE AUTHOR

Sander Peeters

Born in Dubai, UAE in 1978, Sander spent most of his youth travelling around the world with his parents, where he became passionate about world history and aviation. Living in Suriname from 1987 to 1991, he returned to his native Netherlands to start high school.

After earning his master's degree in chemical engineering, he followed in his parents' footsteps and worked all over the globe in various industries, being employed in the Middle East, Southeast Asia, Europe and North America.

He is currently employed as a construction manager in the oil & gas industry in western Canada.